Jesus and the Ossuaries

Jesus and the Ossuaries

Craig A. Evans

A Markham Press Fund Publication

B

Baylor University Press
Waco, Texas USA

This volume is the forty-fourth published by the Markham Press Fund of Baylor University Press, established in memory of Dr. L. N. and Princess Finch Markham of Longview, Texas, by their daughters, Mrs. R. Matt Dawson of Waco, Texas, and Mrs. B. Reid Clanton of Longview, Texas.

All Biblical translations come from the Revised Standard Version unless otherwise stated.

The photo of the James Ossuary on the cover was supplied by Corbis.

Cover Design: Joan Osth

Library of Congress Cataloging-in-Publication Data

Evans, Craig A.
Jesus and the ossuaries / Craig A. Evans.
p. cm.
Includes bibliographical references and index.
ISBN 0-918954-88-6
1. Ossuaries—Palestine. 2. Funeral rites and ceremonies, Jewish—Palestine. 3. Excavations (Archaeology)—Palestine. 4. Palestine—Antiquities. 5. Inscriptions—Palestine. 6. Bible. N.T. Gospels—Criticism, interpretation, etc. 7. Jews—History—168 B.C.-135 A.D. I. Title.

DS111.9.E93 2003
933'.05—dc22

2003016223

Printed in the United States of America on acid free paper

For Carrie and Garth,
on the happy occasion of their marriage

Contents

Preface

One year ago the public was stunned by the announcement that an ossuary (or bone box) that had been in private hands for a number of years was discovered to bear the inscription: "James, son of Joseph, brother of Jesus." Excitement over this remarkable discovery (whose authenticity is briefly discussed in the introduction below) was tempered to a great extent by realization that much of what this ossuary could have told us is lost to us because no one knows or can remember where it was found. We simply have an empty box with an interesting inscription. In what crypt or burial cave it lay, what other ossuaries and inscriptions might have been with it, and what the ossuary itself may have contained (besides bones) will never be known.

For these reasons we have heard many archaeologists and scholars lament the loss of context. And this is true; the loss is quite significant and it is lamentable. But there is another context that is not lost. It is the wider context of Jewish burial practices and, more specifically, other ossuaries. If nothing else, the James bone box has awakened interest in the realia of the biblical world, the remains of the material culture, with which archaeologists are concerned. Perhaps this is the time to review what else has been discovered in this interesting field and to assess in what ways it sheds light on the world of Jesus and his earliest followers. As we shall see, ossuaries and burial inscriptions actually tell us a lot, some of it quite specific, related to events and teachings in the life, death, and burial of Jesus of Nazareth.

The book is titled *Jesus and the Ossuaries*, in order to underscore this broader context, of which the James ossuary is now a part. The book is introductory in nature at one level, for it contains little that veteran archaeologists do not already know (and indeed, I am heavily indebted to these veterans of the digs). But it also contains much that seasoned scholars do not know or do not know very well and often overlook in their research and writing. I have in mind this group, but I also have in mind the general reader who does not know much about burial practices in late antiquity but would like to learn more. My challenge has been to write this book in a way that both the scholar and the general reader will find interesting and helpful. This means that I supply full referencing (to satisfy the scholar), but without footnotes (to avoid tiring the general reader), and text in the original languages (to satisfy the scholar), but always with English translation (to avoid losing the general reader).

Most of the Jewish material is Palestinian, and most of it is from the time of the Herodian temple (*ca.* 20 B.C.E. to 70 C.E.). Of course, it is more complicated than that. Some Jews buried in Israel lived most of their lives outside the land; others lived most of their lives in Israel but died and were buried outside the land. Some of the Jewish material that will be considered reaches back to earlier periods; some to later periods. The non-Jewish materials considered are more diverse geographically and chronologically. The point here is to provide general comparison of similarities and differences, and not to offer any definitive assessment of Greco-Roman burial practices and beliefs. The basic point is to show that most of what the Jews did was not unique in the world of late antiquity.

It gives me pleasure to thank the faculty and staff of several schools that gave me the opportunity to present some of this material in classrooms and in public settings. These schools include Acadia Divinity College, Baylor University, Dallas Theological Seminary, and Fuller Theological Seminary. I might add that it was in preparation for a public presentation in Toronto, Ontario, sponsored by the Biblical Archaeology Society and in conjunction with the display of the James Ossuary at the Royal Ontario Museum, that the present book got under way. I thank too the good people at Vaughan Memorial Library here at Acadia University for their speed and efficiency in procuring a host of books and articles, many not readily accessible. And finally, I close with a word of appreciation for my Teaching Assistant Mr. Adam MacGregor, who with diligence and cheerfulness assisted me with gathering the needed sources and putting together the indexes.

Craig A. Evans
Acadia Divinity College

Introduction

The Find and the Controversy

Last year an ossuary (or bone box, used for reburial) bearing the inscription, "James, son of Joseph, brother of Jesus," was made public and touched off an uproar among academics and created a fair amount of excitement among general readers as well. For academics the controversy centered on the fact that the ossuary had not been excavated by qualified archaeologists. For the general public the controversy centered on the significance of the ossuary and its inscription for understanding an important figure in early Christianity and his relationship to Jesus of Nazareth.

Apparently the ossuary had been purchased on the antiquities market, sometime in the 1980s or 1970s. It has remained in the care of its owner since its purchase, coming to the attention of a European scholar in April of 2002. Not until October did its existence become public. An article appeared the following month in a popular archaeology magazine (Lemaire 2002). The ossuary itself was put on display in the Royal Ontario Museum in Toronto, Ontario, Canada, during the months of November through January, 2002–2003. The timing of the display coincided with the annual meeting of the American Academy of Religion and the Society of Biblical Literature (and other affiliated learned societies), which took place in Toronto. The present writer, along with thousands of others, had the opportunity to view the ossuary and its remarkable inscription.

The ossuary became the focus of an intense debate—a debate not limited simply to the ossuary itself, but to the larger issue of what to do with artifacts looted or otherwise not properly unearthed and handled. No consensus emerged at the meeting. Rather, arguments continued to be heard in favor of boycotting artifacts inappropriately obtained, or in favor of studying artifacts, however they may have come to light. The fact that I have written this book indicates that I am not opposed to discussing artifacts that have been inappropriately obtained. I think scholars have no choice but to take into account everything that is available. (We cannot ignore the Rosetta Stone, for example, simply because in antiquity it was looted from its original site, later used as a stone in a wall, where it was found by the French during the time of Napoleon, and then was seized by the British Navy and taken to London, where it is now on display in the British Museum.) Nevertheless, I do agree with those who urge that steps be taken to safeguard antiquities.

Whichever side one takes, it is a fact that archaeologists and scholars routinely discuss artifacts that were looted. Prior to the twentieth century almost everything was either outright looted, or unearthed and handled in ways that today are regarded as quite unprofessional. Some of the ossuaries that will be considered in the present study appeared on the antiquities market in Israel just as mysteriously and unprovenanced as did the James ossuary (see Ilan 2001 for discussion of an inscribed ossuary in private hands). Nevertheless, scholars study and discuss these artifacts (as they should).

Because the James ossuary was not discovered by archaeologists in a properly controlled excavation and because of its astonishing inscription, it is not surprising that many scholars initially reacted with skepticism. Subsequent study of the ossuary and inscription by geologists, epigraphers, paleographers, and linguists has provided substantial support in favor of authenticity—of the ossuary itself as a first-century artifact, and of the inscription as reflecting genuine first-century Aramaic. However, a report issued by the Israel Antiquities Authority in June 2003 concluded, on the basis of the study of the geologist Yuval Goren, that the patina on the surface of the inscription was of modern origin and that therefore the inscription (not the ossuary itself) was a forgery. Other geologists (two on the staff of the Israel Geological Survey and two associated with the Royal Ontario Museum in Toronto) who examined the box and inscription in the summer and fall of 2002 dispute this finding. Thus, at the time of writing this Introduction, the geologists are divided over the question of the authenticity of the inscription. Hershel Shanks, who has very ably summarized the pertinent issues in the first six chapters of the recently published *The Brother of Jesus* (HarperCollins, 2003), and others are calling for further testing. Apart from the question of the language of the inscription, which will be treated in a later chapter, matters touching authenticity will not be assessed.

The Purpose of the Present Study

The purpose of the present study is not to argue for the authenticity of the James ossuary but to place the ossuary *in context*. This is stated quite deliberately in the face of the many expressions of regret over the lost context of this ossuary. Now it is quite true that much valuable information very probably was lost when the ossuary was looted (and when it was looted—in antiquity or in modern times—we do not know). Apart from a few small bone chips and dust, the ossuary was found empty. Even more important is the fact that we do not know in what burial vault the ossuary lay. Was the burial vault part of a burial complex? Which one? Presumably it rested in a family vault, but whose? Were there other ossuaries in the vault? Were there other inscriptions? Who were the other people buried in the vault? Had the ossuary been found *in situ* (i.e., in its original setting), questions such as these may have been answered. Indeed, the question of authenticity likely would never have been raised, and even the question of identity—the most intriguing question of all—may also have been answered decisively.

Had the ossuary been found in its original context we probably would have learned much more about the person whose skeletal remains were placed in it. We may have learned about his relatives (beyond what is stated in the inscription itself), perhaps even something about his beliefs and associations. Analysis of the skeleton itself may have been revealing, providing data about the person's age and health at the time of death. After all, legend has it that James was thrown from a precipice and beaten with a club. Such trauma would have been plainly evident in the skeletal remains. But these things we shall never know. This part of the context is indeed lost.

But the James ossuary has a context, nevertheless. The ossuary is an important part of Jewish burial practices in late antiquity. Who is buried and how, what is inscribed on the ossuary or burial chamber, the quality of the ossuary itself, what artwork may be present, the inscription's names—all of these are important questions and addressing them may provide important clues that can in fact provide some meaningful context. Learning more about Jewish burial practices will put us in a position to assess more accurately several issues that relate to Jesus and his world (on this subject, see especially McCane 2003). For example, fuller understanding of Jewish burial conventions and sensitivities almost certainly rules out the controversial hypothesis advanced nearly a decade ago that Jesus was perhaps not buried at all, but was left hanging on the cross to be mauled and eaten by animals. (This hypothesis will be criticized in chapter 5.) Other ossuary inscriptions actually shed light on various teachings of Jesus and various persons and officials with whom Jesus probably came into contact. All considered, there is in fact much context to explore.

The discovery of the James ossuary and the interest it has aroused provide an opportunity (now that scholars, as well as the general public, are paying attention) to survey the most important artifacts for the study of Jesus and his earliest followers (for overview, see Meyers and Strange 1981; Meyers 1988; Strange 1992; Boadt 1993; Feldman and Roth 2002). Jewish sepulture is but one aspect of archaeology. We have important inscriptions, usually incised in stone, though sometimes in metal or pottery, and we have important things written in ink (e.g., on potsherds or *ostraca*) or even in charcoal (e.g., on the walls of burial vaults). Sometimes interesting things are found in ossuaries and burial vaults, such as coins and pottery, which help us with dates and sometimes surprise us with unexpected customs.

The focus of the present study is deliberately quite narrow. Ossuaries and burial inscriptions are the primary focus, but other important inscriptions will also be taken into account. Other aspects of archaeology are not the focus of the present study. Much here could be said about recent archaeology in Galilee—the ongoing work at Sepphoris, some of the new work under way at Nazareth (superseding the older reports in Bagatti 1967), the promising finds recently made at Capernaum, and so forth. Continuing work in and around Jerusalem is of immense importance, whether in reference to the Temple Mount, the ruins of the priestly mansion, and the many other building foundations and ruins from the Herodian period excavated since the Six Day War (June 1967). The impact that this work has had for better understanding of Jewish Palestine in the first century can hardly be overestimated.

One interesting and highly significant feature may be mentioned briefly. It is a feature that helps find the broader context for all that follows. Archaeology of Galilee in the last two decades or so has exposed the extent to which the Jews of Galilee prior to 70 C.E. adhered to their faith. It was not long ago that it was fashionable among New Testament scholars to think of Galilee as a Greek-speaking cosmopolitan world, where the Jewish people readily compromised in matters of tradition and religion, adopting Greco-Roman beliefs and practices. But commerce in earthenware (where the evidence suggests that Jews bought only from Jews, whereas non-Jews bought from Jews and non-Jews), the presence of stone water pots (which are not susceptible to impurity) and *mikvaot* (Jewish "baptistries," for ritual cleansing), the absence of pagan buildings (such as nymphaea and temples in honor of various Greco-Roman deities) strongly attest to the Torah-observant nature of the Jewish people. Pockets of non-Jews may well have been present in Galilee (and they were, especially in the cities of the Decapolis), but they did not dominate the province, nor did the Jewish people capitulate in matters of religion (Meyers 1992a).

The relevance of these findings cannot be more dramatically illustrated than in the case of Sepphoris (e.g., Meyers, Netzer, Meyers 1986; Miller 1992; Meyers 1993), a city just four miles from Nazareth. The discovery of a theatre, which may have been built in the early first century C.E. (Batey 1984), a paved, colonnaded street, and several buildings, which at points reflect Greco-Roman architecture, led some scholars to think that Jesus grew up in the shadow of a Greco-Roman city, a city perhaps not too Jewish in ambience. Add to this picture a hypothetical Cynic or two and perhaps one can conjure up a Cynic Jesus (Crossan 1991, among others).

But ongoing excavations at Sepphoris have dashed to pieces this fanciful picture. The city dump has been found, and stratigraphical analysis reveals that whereas one third of the faunal remains (i.e., animal bones) *after* 70 C.E. are pig, none of the faunal remains prior to 70 C.E. are pig. A non-Jewish population in Sepphoris *prior* to 70 C.E., that is, in the time of Jesus, either did not exist at all, or, if it did, did not eat as non-Jews usually do. It seems that the inhabitants of Sepphoris were rather strongly Jewish after all. But there is more. Several *mikvaot* have been uncovered, no pagan structures have been found, fragments of stone water pots have been found, no pagan images have been found, and Jewish symbols have been found (such as depictions of the menorah). The impression thus far gained is that Sepphoris was a thoroughly Jewish city (Chancey and Meyers 2001; Chancey 2002). The hypothesis of the presence of a Cynic philosopher or two, recruiting and making disciples of young Jewish men from nearby villages like Nazareth, seems most improbable. What we have learned is that although there were urban centers in Galilee of the first century, where Greek was in fact spoken, and that aspects of Jesus' teaching and activity reflect this reality (cf. Strange 1992), the Jewish population was committed to its historic, biblical faith. It is in this context that Jesus' teaching and activities should be understood.

The investigation of Jewish burial practices that follows is one aspect of the study of material culture, that is, the physical remains of culture (as opposed to culture inferred from written sources). The literary evidence will be consulted, to be sure, but the primary focus will be upon the artifacts that have been found, particularly those bearing inscriptions, artwork, and designs. What we shall find is that the newly discovered James ossuary is part of Jewish life in late antiquity, richly attested by the remains of material culture, that tells us a great deal about the world of James and his brother Jesus.

Scholarly Sources

The present study has been made possible by several important catalogues and studies. Foremost among these is Levi Yizhaq Rahmani's *A Catalogue of Jewish Ossuaries* (1994a), which catalogues some 895 ossuaries, providing descriptions, photographic plates (of most), and facsimiles of inscriptions (which appear on about one quarter of the ossuaries). This tool is indispensable. However, it is not complete. There are other Jewish ossuaries discussed in the literature that do not appear in this catalogue. The older work by Erwin Ramsdell Goodenough, *Jewish Symbols in the Greco-Roman Period*, though dated, is still useful. The first three volumes of this thirteen-volume work are the most pertinent, with volume 1 (1953a) discussing archaeological evidence, including ossuaries and tombs, from Palestine, volume 2 (1953b) discussing archaeological evidence, including ossuaries, from the Diaspora (i.e., places where Jews lived outside the land of Israel), and volume 3 (1953c) exhibiting photographic plates of the artifacts discussed in volumes 1 and 2. Pau Figueras's *Decorated Jewish Ossuaries* (1983) updates Goodenough's classic at important points. For synthesis and interpretation Eric Meyers's *Jewish Ossuaries* (1971) is the critical point of departure for the subject at hand.

Other scholars in the field of Jewish ossuaries, tombs, and burial practices, who have made important and helpful contributions, include Nahman Avigad, Zvi Greenhut, Rachel Hachlili, Amos Kloner, and Ronny Reich. Frequent reference will be made to the excavation and study of the Beth She'arim necropolis in Galilee. Volume 1, edited by Benjamin Mazar (1973), publishes the findings from catacombs 1–4, which includes some Hebrew and Aramaic inscriptions. Volume 2, edited by Moshe Schwabe and Baruch Lifshitz (1974), publishes the Greek inscriptions, and volume 3, edited by Nahman Avigad (1976), completes and summarizes the findings of all of the catacombs and tombs excavated. The finds at Dominus Flevit, at the Mount of Olives, Jerusalem, are also very important and are referred to many times (Bagatti and Milik 1958). The early collections of Jewish Palestinian inscriptions, collected and edited by Samuel Klein (1920) and Jean-Baptiste Frey (= *CIJ*), and Eleazar Lippa Sukenik's pioneering works in archaeology, involving tombs, ossuaries, and ancient synagogues, are quite valuable. I might also mention that the finds and seminal studies by the great French archaeologist of the late nineteenth century, Charles Clermont-Ganneau, though dated, are still worth consulting (see Clermont-Ganneau 1873; 1878; 1899; as well as the pioneering studies of others, such as Hornstein 1900; Vincent 1902; Macalister 1908; Lidzbarski 1913; Gray 1914; Spoer 1914; Sukenik 1928; 1929; 1931a; 1932a; 1934b; Savignac 1929; and Maisler 1931).

There are other important collections of primary texts that should be mentioned. The collection of Aramaic texts (literary and inscriptional) assembled by Joseph Fitzmyer and Daniel Harrington is invaluable (1978). The Jewish inscriptions of Greco-Roman Egypt catalogued by William Horbury and David Noy (1992), of Rome catalogued by Harry Leon (1995), and of the Diaspora in general catalogued by Pieter van der Horst (1991) were of great help. The published ostraca from Masada (= Mas), by Yigael Yadin and his many successors, were also of great help. And finally, Tal Ilan's *Lexicon of Jewish Names in Late Antiquity* (2002) was enormously helpful.

Terminology

At the close of this introduction it will be useful to review the terminology involved in Jewish burial practices. This terminology will at points have a bearing on some of the issues. The focus here is primarily on the terminology. Burial practices will be further discussed in chapter 1.

In the Hebrew Bible the words used most often for tomb (or grave) and burial are the verb קבר (*qabar*, "to bury") and its nominal cognates קבר (*qeber*) and קבור (*qeburah*), both meaning "grave." The Greek version of Scripture (i.e., either LXX or OG) usually translates these words with the verb θάπτειν (*thaptein*) and the cognate noun τάφος (*taphos*) or the nouns μνημεῖον (*mnemeion*) and μνῆμα (*mnema*; the root meaning of these last two is "memorial," not burial). Accordingly, Abraham buys a cave for Sarah, his deceased wife, as a "burying place" (so the

RSV), or tomb (Gen 23:4, with קֶבֶר, *qeber*, in the Hebrew, and τάφος in the Greek). Similarly, Rachel is buried near Bethlehem (Gen 35:19, with קבר in the Hebrew, and θάπτειν in the Greek) and her husband Jacob (Gen 35:20) places a pillar or monument (in Hebrew מַצֵּבָה, *mazebah*; in Greek στήλη, *stele*) over her grave (in Hebrew קְבוּר, *qeburah*; in Greek μνημεῖον). King Asa is buried in a "tomb [in Hebrew קֶבֶר, *qeber*; in Greek μνῆμα] which he had hewn out for himself in the city of David" (2 Chr 16:14). While engaged in his campaign of religious reform, King Josiah "asked, 'What is yonder monument [in Hebrew צִיּוּן, *ziyyun*; in Greek σκόπελον, *skopelon*] that I see?' And the men of the city told him, 'It is the tomb [in Hebrew קֶבֶר, *qeber*; no equivalent in Greek] of the man of God . . .'" (2 Kgs 23:17). Sometimes "house" (in Hebrew בַּיִת, *bayit*; in Greek οἶκος, *oikos*) is used euphemistically in reference to a tomb (e.g., Isa 14:18).

The biblical terminology appears in later Jewish epitaphs: ". . . with my bridal garments, I, untimely, have received this hateful tomb [τάφος] as my bridal chamber . . ." (*CIJ* no. 1508; Horbury and Noy 1992, no. 31); "But you, passer-by, beholding the grave [τάφος] of a good man, depart with these favorable words . . ." (*CPJ* no. 1530a; Horbury and Noy 1992, no. 39); "I am Theon, son of Paos, who, best in counsel, lie here dead in this tomb [μνημῆον, *mnemeon* = *mnemeion*]" (*CIJ* no. 1489; Horbury and Noy 1992, no. 114); "Tomb [μνῆμα] of Eusebius the Alexandrian and of Theodora his wife" (*CIJ* no. 696; Horbury and Noy 1992, no. 144); "Tomb [μνῆμα] of Cyril and Alexander, Alexandrians" (*CIJ* no. 934; Horbury and Noy 1992, no. 150); "The gravestone [στάλα, *stala* = *stele*] bears witness: 'Who are you that lie in the dark tomb [τύμβος, *tumbos*]?'" (*CIJ* no. 1530; Horbury and Noy 1992, no. 38); and "Look on my gravestone [στήλη], passer-by, and having considered it, weep" (*CIJ* no. 1512; Horbury and Noy 1992, no. 35).

Specific words that mean "ossuary" do not appear in the Bible, but words in the Bible that mean coffin, chest, or the like, were later used in reference to ossuaries. One of these words is גָּדִישׁ (*gadish*), which occurs four times in the Hebrew Bible, one of which refers to a coffin: "When he is borne to the grave, watch is kept over his coffin [גָּדִישׁ]" (Job 21:32). In the OG *gadish* is translated with σορός (*soros*). Another word is אֲרוֹן (*aron*), which can mean ark, box, or coffin, as in the interment of Joseph: "So Joseph died, being a hundred and ten years old; and they embalmed him, and he was put in a coffin [אֲרוֹן] in Egypt" (Gen

50:26). Again in the OG σορός is used in the translation. This Greek word appears in an inscription on an ossuary found in Jericho: "Ossuary [σορός] of Theodotos, freedman of Queen Agrippina" (Rahmani 1994a, no. 789; Hachlili 1979, 55). When σορός appears in Luke 7:14, it clearly refers to a coffin, in which a corpse not yet decomposed has been laid.

Various spellings of the Hebrew word *aron* appear in at least seven burial inscriptions found at Beth She'arim. Most, if not all of them, are in reference to coffins or sarcophagi. However, two of them may have been in reference to ossuaries, in which the bones of two or more persons were placed, e.g., "This is the *aron* of the three sons of Rabbi Judan" (Avigad 1976, no. 22), and perhaps "Miriam, the daughter of Rabbi Jonathan, with her two daughters" (Avigad 1976, no. 21). The first inscription seems to imply that the remains of the three sons of Rabbi Judan were together in the same *aron*. Since *bodies* as such were not placed in the same coffin or sarcophagus, it seems best to conclude, as does Meyers (1971, 52), that it was the *bones* of the three sons, which were placed in the single *aron*, not their corpses, prior to decomposition. Thus, the *aron* mentioned in the inscription is an ossuary. The second inscription that refers to Miriam "with her two daughters" does not mention an *aron*. But the statement that the mother is *with* her daughters seems to imply that we have yet another instance of the use of an ossuary at Beth She'arim (probably dating to the third or fourth century C.E.). The other five inscriptions where *aron* is used are all in reference to single individuals, but whether the word is in reference to a full body-sized coffin or to an ossuary, in which the bones of the deceased were later placed, is not certain.

In late antiquity the coffin was often called a *sarcophagus*, from the Greek word σαρκοφάγος, which literally means "flesh eater" (i.e., the genitive σαρκός, "of flesh," plus φάγος, "eater"; accordingly, "eater of flesh"). Many sarcophagi were made of stone, though they could be made of wood or even of clay (which are attested at Beth She'arim). The Greek word does not occur in the Bible, but its nominal cognate σαρκοφαγία ("eating flesh" or "meat") does (4 Macc 5:8, 14), as well as the verbal cognate σαρκοφαγεῖν (4 Macc 5:26). The related term σοματοθήκη, meaning "place of body," is attested in Jewish epitaphs (*CIJ* nos. 785, 792, 793; Meyers 1971, 50). The concept of "flesh eater" is seen in rabbinic literature: "At first they would bury them in ditches, and when the flesh decayed they would gather the bones and bury them in ossuaries" (*y. Sanh.* 6.12; translation by Meyers 1971, 59). What is translated "when the flesh decayed" is literally "when the flesh was eaten" (נתאכל הבשר, *nitekol habasar*).

The similar word *ostophagus*, from the Greek word ὀστοφάγος, which literally means "bone eater" (on analogy with sarcophagus), is our earliest term for ossuary attested in Palestine (Conder 1876; Meyers 1971, 49–50; Hachlili 1979, 55–56). An ossuary was discovered in the Kidron Valley, Jerusalem, on which only the word ὀστοφάγος, written twice, appears (cf. Sukenik 1937, 130 + plates 5–6; Rahmani 1994a, no. 85). Meyers (1971, 49) rightly comments (*pace* Sukenik 1937, 13) that ostophagus was not understood to mean "bone eater," since the receptacle was meant to *preserve*, not *consume*, the bones of the deceased. He is probably correct. Nevertheless, the word ὀστοφάγος literally does mean "bone eater," just as surely as σαρκοφάγος literally means "flesh eater." But in what sense are these receptacles—coffins, ossuaries, or whatever—"eaters" of anything? The answer may lie in the observation of ancient bone receptacles fashioned to resemble a head and face, with mouths opened wide. These receptacles "ate" (or perhaps, better, "swallowed") whatever was placed in them, whether a corpse that still possessed flesh, or a satchel of bones, whose flesh had long ago disappeared. In other words, the receptacle itself does not consume, or "eat," either the flesh or the bones, it merely swallows what is placed in it. The receptacle becomes an "eater" of something, merely by virtue of having something placed in it.

Meyers (1971, 49–50) draws our attention to several other related Greek terms that refer to ossuaries, or bone boxes. These include ὀστοθήκης, ὀστοθήκιον, and ὀστοθηκάριον, all of which basically mean "bone chest" (from ὀστέον, "bone," and θήκη, *theke*, "chest," i.e., a place where things, in this case bones, are *placed*, from the verb τίθεναι). Apparently ὀστόν, "bone," by itself, can mean "bone box" or ossuary, as we see in an inscription from Beth She'arim: "This is the very grave, the one from the lowermost of the ossuaries [ὀστῶν]" (Schwabe and Lifshitz 1974, no. 131; cf. Meyers 1971, 51). The Greek word ὀστόν may well underlie the textually uncertain reading in an important passage in the rabbinic tractate *Mourning*: "Whoever finds bones in a tomb [*qeber*] should place them in an arcosolium, so Rabbi Aqiba. The Sages say, 'One should not remove them from their place. If one found them in a niche or ossuary, he should not move them from their place'" (*Semahot* 13.6; Zlotnick 1966, 84; Meyers 1971, 61). The Hebrew underlying the word translated here "ossuary" is, in most manuscripts, איסטרון (*isteron*). But Meyers (1971, 62) plausibly suggests that the original reading was

איסטדון (*istedon*), on the assumption that the *dalet* (i.e., the letter d) became confused with *resh* (i.e., the letter r). If איסטדון (*istedon*) is the correct reading, then we probably have a loanword from the Greek ὀστόν, "bone." Accordingly, איסטדון may well mean "bone box" or "ossuary," as was translated.

The most common word for ossuary is the Greek word γλωσσόκομον, which is transliterated into Hebrew and Aramaic as גלוסקמא and דלוסקמא (cf. Jastrow 247; Krauss 2:175–75), meaning "chest," "box," "coffin," or "coffer" (originally, *apud* LSJ, "a case for the mouthpiece of a pipe"; cf. Meyers 1971, 53). The Greek form of this word occurs in only one passage in the OG, where it appears in reference to a money box placed by the Jewish temple, into which people could drop money (cf. 2 Chr 24:8-11). In the New Testament the word appears twice in the Gospel of John, with essentially the same meaning, both times in reference to the money box kept by Judas Iscariot (cf. John 12:6; 13:29). The word appears in one of the Greek inscriptions from Beth She'arim, though spelled irregularly: "Magna rests in the ossuary [γλοσοκόμῳ]" (Schwabe and Lifshitz 1974, no. 78; cf. Meyers 1971, 54; Hachlili 1979, 55).

The Hebrew and Aramaic forms of the word are common in rabbinic and targumic literature. We see this at Genesis 50:26 (as pointed out my Meyers 1971, 53): "So Joseph died, being a hundred and ten years old; and they embalmed him, and he was put in a coffin in Egypt" (RSV). In the Hebrew "coffin" is ארון (*aron*), in Greek it is σορός (*soros*), and in the Targum, that is, the Aramaic paraphrase of the Hebrew Bible, it is (*apud* Ps.-Jonathan, Fragment, and Neofiti in a marginal note) גלוסקמא (*glosqoma*). We also see it in the oft-cited passage in the rabbinic tractate on *Mourning*: "My son, bury me at first in a fosse. In the course of time, collect my bones and put them in an ossuary [גלוסקמא]; but do not gather them with your own hands" (*Semahot* 12.9, following the translation by Zlotnick 1966, 82; cf. *Semahot* 3.2).

Aramaic and Hebrew, however, had their own terms for ossuary. The above mentioned ארון (*aron*) is one. Another is חלה (*halah*), or חלת / חלתה / חלתא (*halat* / *haltah* / *halta'*) in the construct, which appears in several ossuary inscriptions: "Ossuary [חלת] of Salome, daughter of Saul, who failed to give birth" (Rahmani 1994a, no. 226; Fitzmyer and Harrington 1978, 172–73 no. 88); "Ossuary [חלת] of Balzama" (Rahmani 1994a, no. 461); "Everything that a man will find to his profit in this ossuary [חלתה] . . ." (Milik 1956–1957: 235 + figs. 2 and 3; Fitzmyer 1959; Fitzmyer and Harrington 1978, 168–69 no. 69); and

"Ossuary [חלתא] of Maryam, daughter of Simeon" (Rahmani 1994a, no. 502).

Finally, a few words need to be said about the general design and function of the Jewish tomb. Many tombs consist of a central chamber, with two or more niches branching out from it. Some tombs are honeycombed with niches (cf. Oren and Rappaport 1984). In Hebrew the niche is called a כוך (*kokh*); in Latin *loculus*. Some tombs also contained *arcosolia*. An arcosolium is a ledge beneath an arch, on which a body or a sarcophagus could be placed. Bodies were placed in these arcosolia and niches. The family mourned for seven days (cf. Josephus, *Ant.* 17.8.4 §200). Usually about one year later (as inferred from *b. Qiddushin* 31b; cf. Figueras 1984–1985, 45) the bones of the deceased were gathered and placed in an ossuary. The ossuaries themselves were then placed in a room, often stacked. They were sometimes placed in the niches themselves or in the central chamber. (In a tomb at Jericho four ossuaries were found in a single niche; cf. Hachlili 1979, 56–57.) There are burial inscriptions in which the word *kokh* appears: "This *kokh* [כוכה] was made for the bones of our fathers. Length two cubits. Not to be opened!" (*CIJ* no. 1300; Fitzmyer and Harrington 1978, 168–69; Meyers 1971, 66). *Kokh* can also be spelled קוק (*qoq*), as in this poorly preserved inscription: "This is the *kokh* [קוקא] of . . . Alas! And his daughter" (*CIJ* no. 1222; Fitzmyer and Harrington 1978, 182–83). Sometimes the niches were sealed with stone blocks or doors. The tombs themselves were sealed with large stones, which were usually square blocks; but the wheel-shaped stones that rolled in front of the opening were also used (as in the popular Garden Tomb in Jerusalem).

Relevance of Topic for New Testament Study

Acquaintance with Jewish burial customs will shed light on many passages in the New Testament Gospels. Here are a few examples; others will be treated in context of specific finds that will be reviewed in chapters that follow.

The presence of tombs and monuments is presupposed in the Gospels. One immediately thinks of Jesus' angry denunciation of religious leaders: "Woe to you, scribes and Pharisees, hypocrites! for you are like whitewashed tombs [τάφοι], which outwardly appear beautiful, but within they are full of dead men's bones [ὀστέων νεκρῶν] and all uncleanness" (Matt 23:27); and "Woe to you, scribes and Pharisees, hypocrites! for you build the tombs [τάφοι] of the prophets and adorn monuments [μνημεῖα] of the righteous" (Matt 23:29; cf. Luke 11:47–48).

Secondary burial may well be presupposed in Jesus' startling retort to the would-be follower: "Leave the dead to bury their own dead!" (Matt 8:22 = Luke 9:60). According to rabbinic tradition, secondary burial of one's family members was one of the three most important religious ceremonies (cf. *Semahot* 12.5; Figueras 1983, 9). In at least one tradition, a father specifically commands his son regarding the former's eventual reburial (*Semahot* 12.9). Accordingly, when the would-be follower of Jesus says to Jesus, "Lord, let me first go and bury my father" (Matt 8:21 = Luke 9:59), he is not talking about waiting for the death of an aging or ailing father, but anticipation of the approaching time when he must gather his father's bones and place them in an ossuary, at which time the mourning and rites for his father are finally completed. Jesus' reply, moreover, probably should be taken as referring to the literal dead, not metaphorical or spiritual dead. "Leave the dead to bury their own dead!" means let the dead who are in the family tomb with the corpse of the would-be follower's father see to the burial (McCane 1990, 40–41). The surviving and living son should get on with the urgent work of proclaiming the kingdom of God.

Josephus and the Gospels narrate the arrest and execution of John the Baptist (cf. Josephus, *Ant.* 18.5.2 §116–19; Mark 6:14-29 and parallels). According to the Gospels, to keep an oath made before dinner guests Herod Antipas has John beheaded and then delivers his head on a platter to his step-daughter (Mark 6:27-28). John's disciples collect the body (but not his head, we should assume) and they place it in a tomb (v. 29). The head went to the girl's mother, the new wife of Herod (v. 28). What is interesting is that some time later, when Herod hears of Jesus' ministry, he comes to believe that Jesus is John, declaring "John, whom I beheaded, has been raised" (v. 16). To readers familiar with Jewish burial customs and beliefs, this would be truly astounding. The raising of John would be amazing in itself. But for him to be raised without his head would only add to the hyperbole of the comparison with Jesus. The skull was the most important bone of the skeleton. In fact, some secondary burial only involved the skull (cf. Meyers 1970, 19, who draws our attention to the basket of skulls found in the Bar Kokhba cave at Nahal Hever; see also Bennett 1965, 525 + fig. 266; Meyers 1971, 9). The absence of the skull, which in the possession of Herod's angry and vengeful wife would surely not have been properly buried and therefore would never have been rejoined to the rest of John's body, would make resurrection all the more doubtful, at least a resurrection before the time of the general resurrection and judgment. Herod's declaration that Jesus must be John, whom he beheaded, attests to the despot's fearful respect of the power he sensed was at work in Jesus, a power that not only must be from beyond the confines of the mortal realm, but a power not limited by the conventions of death, burial, and resurrection.

Familiarity with Jewish burial practices fills in details in the story of the death, burial, and resuscitation of Lazarus, brother of Mary and Martha (John 11). Lazarus dies and is buried in a μνημεῖον, or tomb (vv. 17, 31), which later we are told is a σπήλαιον, or cave (v. 38). Many of the tombs in Israel, including in and around Jerusalem itself, are natural caves, which have been shaped and dressed to some extent (and recall, too, that Abraham purchased a cave [OG: σπήλαιον] for the burial of Sarah, and then was later himself buried in it; Gen 23:9, 19; 25:9-10). Although obviously dead and interred, Lazarus is said, euphemistically, to be "asleep" (cf. the verb κοιμᾶν in v. 11; the noun κοίμησις in v. 13). We find this euphemism in early Jewish Christian literature (e.g., 1 Cor 15:20; 1 Thess 4:13; 2 Pet 3:4) and in Jewish burial inscriptions: ". . . I too, who loved my brothers and was a friend to all the citizens, fell asleep [κοιμᾶν] . . ." (*CIJ* no. 1489; Horbury and Noy 1992, no. 114); "May your portion be a good one, Aristeas; may the sleep [κοίμησις] of the pious Aristeas be in peace" (from Beth She'arim; cf. Schwabe and Lifshitz 1974, no. 173); and "May your sleep be in peace" (see *CIJ* no. 1535; Horbury and Noy 1992, no. 120; for the same formula, but in Latin, see *CIJ* no. 644; Horbury and Noy 1992, no. 142); as well as in Christian epitaphs, "Father Menas has fallen asleep in Christ" (Lifshitz 1963b, 265).

There is another detail in this story that is clarified by Jewish burial traditions. Twice it is stated that Lazarus had been dead for four days (vv. 17, 39). We probably have an allusion to the popular belief that the soul, having lingered near the body for three days, has now finally departed: "For three days (after death) the soul hovers over the body, intending to re-enter it, but as soon as it sees its appearance change, it departs" (*Lev. Rab.* 18.1 [on Lev 15:1-2]). This tradition presupposes the idea that after three days, the corpse bursts and is no longer recognizable: "The full intensity of mourning lasts up to the third day because the appearance of the face is still recognizable" (*Qoh. Rab.* 12:6 §1). Thus, when Jesus arrives at the tomb of Lazarus, despair has reached its lowest point. There is now, even with the arrival of Jesus, absolutely no hope of recovery: the body is dead (and has begun to stink; cf. v. 39) and the soul has departed. Hence, the sister of Lazarus says, "Lord, if you had been here, my brother would not have died" (v. 21). The only hope left is resurrection some day in the future (v. 24). Seen in the light of these popular assumptions, Jesus' ability to raise Lazarus, dead for four days, would have been viewed as astounding.

Jesus' command to "Remove the stone" (v. 39), in order to enter the tomb of Lazarus, parallels the story of his own burial and the subsequent discovery of the empty tomb. In this story too a stone is rolled against the opening of the tomb (cut from rock; not a natural cave; Mark 15:46). The stone is large, for although it is round (as implied by the question, "Who will roll away the stone for us from the door of the tomb?" in Mark 16:3; and "it was rolled back" in 16:4), it is too heavy for the women (Mark 16:4: "it was very large"). Again, what the Gospels depict is consistent with what is known from archaeology and from literary and epigraphical sources.

Finally, we may wonder if Jewish burial practices, particularly the custom of gathering bones and placing them in ossuaries, can clarify the exceedingly odd story found in Matt 27:51-53, where at the moment of Jesus' death an earthquake occurs:

> And behold, the curtain of the temple was torn in two, from top to bottom; and the earth shook, and the rocks were split; the tombs also were opened, and many bodies of the saints [*hagioi*] who had fallen asleep were raised, and coming out of the tombs after his resurrection they went into the holy city and appeared to many.

This story is unparalleled; there is no counterpart in Mark, Matthew's principal narrative source. Nor does the story appear in Luke, which also follows Mark. The story does remind us somewhat of John 5:28-29: ". . . the hour is coming when all who are in the tombs will hear his voice and come forth . . . to the resurrection . . ." (cf. Dan 12:2: ". . . many of those who sleep in the dust of the earth shall awake . . ." ; Zech 14:4-5: ". . . the Mount of Olives shall be split in two . . . earthquake . . . the LORD your God will come, and all the saints with him"; and Ezek 37:12-13: "I shall open your tombs"). If Daniel and Zechariah in part lie behind this strange story, then we are perhaps to imagine the prophecy in Daniel 7:22, 27, in which the saints (OG: *hagioi*) are given the kingdom, have their tombs opened by God (Ezek 37:12-13), are raised up

(Dan 12:2), and, in Zechariah 14:4-5, after the earthquake, come as saints (OG: *hagioi*).

The absence of the story in Mark, the parallel with the saying in John, and the grammatical and temporal awkwardness of the story in its Matthean context lead one to suspect that this story is a later interpolation, perhaps inspired by John 5. The greatest difficulty is the temporal problem. According to our amazing story, the saints "who had fallen asleep," that is, died, were raised when their tombs were unsealed during the earthquake, which occurred at the moment of Jesus' death. But because Jesus is the "first fruits" of them that sleep (cf. 1 Cor 15:20, 23), these raised saints can hardly emerge from their tombs before Jesus himself does a couple days later. Consequently, they must linger in their tombs until Sunday morning. Then they may emerge and show themselves alive. The clumsiness of the chronology argues for viewing this strange story as an insertion into the Matthean narrative, an insertion perhaps dating to the second century (though some think it may be older, traditional material, dating to the first century).

Whatever the editorial history of the story, the practice of gathering bones and placing them in ossuaries is very probably presupposed. These dead saints are resurrected, as foretold in Daniel 12, and come with the Lord, as foretold in Zechariah 14. As such, they foreshadow the fulfillment of Ezekiel's vision of the bones that are reassembled and restored to life (Ezek 37). In Ezekiel 37:12-13 God promised to open the tombs of his people; in the death and resurrection of Jesus God fulfilled this promise.

In the chapters that follow several other Gospel passages will be examined in light of burial practices and inscriptions. It is hoped that readers will find this admittedly macabre topic enlightening and interesting. I am reminded, of course, that in the opinion of some rabbinic authorities long ago the reading of epitaphs impedes learning (cf. *b. Hor.* 13b). Let us hope in this instance their warning does not apply!

Chapter 1

Jewish Burial Practices in Late Antiquity

In what must be one of the eeriest stories narrated in the New Testament Gospels, we are told that when Jesus crossed the Sea of Galilee (or Kinneret Lake) and entered the country of the Gerasenes, "there met him out of the tombs a man with an unclean spirit, who lived among the tombs," a man no one was able to subdue, a man who "night and day among the tombs" was "crying out, and bruising himself with stones" (Mark 5:1-5). The tombs, among which this tormented man lived, formed in all probability a necropolis (Greek: νεκρόπολις), or a "city of the dead." According to Jewish beliefs, a necropolis was the favorite haunt, not just for the spirits of the departed, but for the far more dangerous spirits, the evil spirits that could, it was believed, take possession of people (cf. *Jub.* 22:17; LXX Isa 65:3-4; *b. Ber.* 18b). The man described in this story was such a man.

Readers and hearers of this story in late antiquity would readily imagine a necropolis, which oftentimes resembled a miniature city. Tombs, monuments, and mausolea were designed to resemble small houses and temples, complete with windows, doors, pillars, and gabled or vaulted roofs (for survey, see Kurtz and Boardman 1971; Fedak 1990). Sometimes grave robbers broke into these buildings. It is easy to imagine the tormented man living among, and perhaps even inside, these tombs and monuments, his only companions restless spirits.

Notable Tombs in Israel in Late Antiquity

The sepulture in the story narrated in Mark 5 is not described; it is merely an assumed part of the backdrop of the story. But the remains of many tombs and monuments are visible today, some in remarkably good condition (Avigad 1950–1951; Rahmani 1961). It is estimated that the necropolis surrounding Jerusalem (north, east, and south of the city) is made up of some 800 tombs. Several impressive tombs and mausolea line the Kidron Valley (Yamauchi 1985), at the base of the Mount of Olives, opposite the eastern side of the Temple Mount (The Mount of Olives has yielded a rich harvest of ossuaries; see Allegretti 1982; Puech 1982). As one walks down the valley one can view the so-called Tomb (or Pillar) of Absalom, an unusual mausoleum that dates to the first century C.E. and stands some twenty meters, eclectically ornamented with Ionic columns, a Doric frieze, and an Egyptian cornice. The structure is crowned with a concave conical roof, its most distinctive feature. It gains the name "Pillar of Absalom" from 2 Samuel 18:18: "Now Absalom in his lifetime had taken and set up for himself the pillar, which is in the King's Valley, for he said, 'I have no son to keep my name in remembrance'; he called the pillar after his own name, and it is called 'Absalom's pillar' to this day." Next, one encounters the Tomb of the Sons of Hezir, a priestly family, whose entrance is adorned with two Doric columns and which dates to the first century B.C.E. After that comes the so-called Tomb of Zechariah, with its Ionic pilasters and pyramid roof. The tomb is covered with small, neatly incised Hebrew inscriptions, and probably dates to the first century B.C.E. And finally, one comes to the Cave of Jehoshaphat, a tomb with eight chambers and whose entrance is supported by two square pillars. These tombs and others were whitewashed annually, usually just prior to major holidays, such as Passover.

Elsewhere in Jerusalem we find the tomb of Queen Helene (or Helena) of Adiabene, daughter of Izates the proselyte (Josephus, *J.W.* 5.4.2 §147). (The tomb is also called, mistakenly, the Tombs of the Kings.) It is by far the largest and most impressive tomb in Jerusalem. A staircase leads down through an arch and into an expansive garden area. The broad opening included a facade twenty-seven meters wide, supported by two large pillars. The queen and two members of her family were interred in this tomb some time after 50 C.E. When excavated the tomb contained several decorated sarcophagi. On one of them were inscribed the words צדן מלכתה ("Queen Saddan"). According to Josephus (*Ant.* 20.3.5 §95), her tomb was adorned with three pyramids (though the location of these pyramids and their relation to Helene's tomb are disputed), possibly one for herself and one for each of her two sons. Supposedly F. de Saulcy in 1865 entered the tomb and found an inscription in Aramaic or Palmyrene that included the title and name "Helene the Queen." There is no trace of this inscription today (Rahmani 1994d).

The Tomb of Nicanor was discovered on Mount Scopus in 1902. This large tomb, dating to the first century C.E. and possessing four branches of burial chambers, contained several decorated ossuaries, including an important inscription (see discussion in chapter 5). The Cave of Umm el-'Amed (named after the wadi in which it is located) was decorated with a facade and possessed two chambers with burial niches. The so-called Sanhedrin Tombs boast a beautiful gabled facade, large central hall, several burial chambers, with staircases leading to various levels (Jotham-Rothschild 1952). Not far from this complex is the so-called Tomb of the Grapes, which derives its name from the sculpted grape clusters that adorn the space above the entrance. There is also the Tomb of Herod's Family, discovered in 1892 not far from the modern King David Hotel. The tomb is beautifully decorated and contained several decorated sarcophagi. Its distinctive feature is the large wheel-shaped stone that served as the door to the vault. The Tomb of Jason was discovered in 1956 in Rehavia (or Rehov), Jerusalem, and is supported by a single pillar, instead of the traditional two pillars. Along with a Greek inscription and several Aramaic inscriptions, charcoal drawings of ships were found scrawled on the walls of the crypt. Coins and pottery found in the crypt date the earliest use of the tomb to the beginning of the first century B.C.E., continuing to the beginning of the first century C.E. In the French Hill district of Jerusalem a number of tombs and ossuaries have been found (Geraty 1975; Strange 1975; Kloner 1980).

Perhaps the most interesting narratives concerning tombs in the writings of Josephus involve the tomb of David. The Hasmonean ruler, John Hyrcanus (ruled 134–104 B.C.E.), when besieged by Antiochus VII (ruled *ca.* 139–129 B.C.E.), looted David's tomb, removing some 3000 talents (of silver?) to pay off the Syrian despot and lift the siege (see *Ant.* 7.15.3 §393; cf. *J.W.* 1.2.5 §61; *Ant.* 13.8.4 §249, where we are told that David "excelled all other kings in riches"). About one century later, Herod the Great, having heard the story of how Hyrcanus had looted David's tomb, decided to enter the tomb himself (*Ant.* 16.7.1 §179–82). Josephus tells us that Herod opened the tomb at night, and entered it, taking precautions that none in the city would know of it. He did not find money, but he did find many valuables, which he removed. He decided to penetrate further into the tomb and even open the sarcophagi of David and Solomon. However, as he and his associates entered the vault, they were met with flame that killed two of Herod's guards. The king fled in terror, later erecting an impressive memorial of white marble at the entrance of the tomb. Josephus goes on to say that it was believed that Herod's domestic troubles and health problems commenced not long after and because of his violation of David's tomb (*Ant.* 16.7.2 §188). David's tomb is specifically mentioned in the New Testament (cf. Acts 2:29, where Peter tells the crowd: "Brethren, I may say to you confidently of the patriarch David that he both died and was buried, and his tomb is with us to this day").

Josephus also accuses Cleopatra (born in 69 B.C.E., died in 30 B.C.E., and ruled Egypt, more or less, 48–31 B.C.E.), lover and ally of Marc Antony, of grave robbery: "If there were any hopes of getting money, she (Cleopatra) would violate both temples and tombs. Nor was there any holy place that was esteemed the most inviolable, from which she would not fetch the ornaments it had in it; nor any place so profane, but was to suffer the most flagitious treatment possible from him, if it could but contribute somewhat to the covetous humor of this wicked creature" (*Ant.* 15.4.1 §90). This accusation, however, may have arisen from Roman vilification of the wily politician and seductress.

These accounts of violation of royal sepulture provides important contextual insight to a burial plaque, on which is inscribed in Aramaic the name of Uzziah the king. The plaque was discovered in 1931 by Eleazar Sukenik (1931b; 1932b) in the Russian Convent on the Mount of Olives. The stone measures 25 cm x 34 cm and apparently was engraved to commemorate the reburial of the remains of Judah's king from the first temple period (cf. 2 Chr 26:1-23). The epitaph, now housed in the Israel National Museum, reads:

לכה התית
טמי עוזיה
מלך יהודה
ולא לפתוח

Hence were brought
the bones of Uzziah
king of Judah;
and do not open! (*NEAEHL* 2:753)

William F. Albright (1932, 10) speculates plausibly that the bones of Uzziah, originally buried "in the city of David" (2 Kgs 15:7), had to be relocated outside the city, "because he was a leper" (2 Chr 26:23). Eric Meyers (1971, 84) dates the plaque to *ca.* 50 C.E. and speculates that the bones of Uzziah, the "leper" king (cf. 2 Chr 26:19-23), were moved to the new location, either because his bones were at a later time thought eligible to be included in the "sepulchres of the kings," or because his tomb had been disturbed by recent renovations, such as those ascribed to Agrippa I during 41–44 C.E. (cf. Josephus, *J.W.* 2.11.6 §218). Agrippa's extension of the city wall may have required the relocation of the king's remains. The warning not to open the vault is commonplace in late antiquity.

Albright further remarks that it "is a most interesting illustration of the growing reverence paid to the graves and relics of great men of the past" (1932, 10). One thinks of Jesus' criticism directed against the scribes and Pharisees, "You build the tombs of the prophets and adorn the monuments of the righteous" (Matt 23:29; cf. Luke 11:47-48).

Josephus often mentions tombs and burials in his narratives. He tells us that the monument and tomb of Eleazar the high priest, son of Aaron and colleague of Joshua, are in the city of Gabatha (*Ant.* 5.1.29 §119, probably a corruption of the Hebrew "in Gibeah"; cf. Josh 24:33: "And Eleazar the son of Aaron died; and they buried him at Gibeah, the town of Phinehas his son"; Jeremias 1958, 48–49). Josephus also says that Asahel, one of David's soldiers, was buried by his brothers in "the tomb of their fathers" in Bethlehem (*Ant.* 7.1.3 §19; cf. 2 Sam 2:32). He mentions the burial of several of ancient Israel's monarchs (e.g., Rehoboam in *Ant.* 8.10.4 §264: "He was buried in Jerusalem in the tombs of the kings"; Abijah in *Ant.* 8.11.3 §285: "buried in Jerusalem in the tomb of his forefathers"; Josiah in *Ant.* 10.5.1 §77–78: "buried magnificently in the tombs of his fathers . . . great was the mourning for him observed by all the people, who bewailed him and grieved for him for many days") and later rulers, such as Hasmoneans (e.g., Aristobulus in *J.W.* 1.9.1 §184; *Ant.* 14.7.4 §124: "His dead body also lay, for a good while, embalmed in honey, until Antony afterwards sent it to Judea, and caused him to be buried in the royal tombs") and Herodians (e.g., Herod's son Aristobulus, whom Herod arranged to have murdered, in *Ant.* 15.3.4 §61: "he made all the more display of lavishness in the burial rites, providing a very fine tomb and a great quantity of perfumes"; Herod the Great in *Ant.* 17.8.3 §196–99: "Herod was borne upon a golden bier studded with precious stones . . . followed by five hundred servants carrying spices"; Herod Philip in *Ant.* 18.4.6 §108: "when he was carried to that monument which he had already erected for himself beforehand, he was buried with great pomp"). He mentions also the burial of Jehoiada (or Jodas, according to Josephus) the high priest. Scripture says, "they buried him in the city of David among the kings, because he had done well in Israel and to God and his house" (2 Chr 24:16); but Josephus describes the priest as "an upright man and good in all ways," who "was buried in the royal tombs at Jerusalem because he had restored the kingdom to the line of David" (*Ant.* 9.8.3 §166). According to a variety of sources, including and especially the pseudepigraphal first-century work *Lives of the Prophets*, there were many tombs and monuments in Israel associated with prophets and other Old Testament worthies (for a study of the subject, see Jeremias 1958).

In 1 Maccabees we are told that the Hasmonean Simon (ruled 142–134 B.C.E.), son of Mattathias and brother of Judas Maccabeus,

> built a monument over the tomb of his father and his brothers; he made it high that it might be seen, with polished stone at the front and back. He also erected seven pyramids, opposite one another, for his father and mother and four brothers. And for the pyramids he devised an elaborate setting, erecting about them great columns, and upon the columns he put suits of armor for a permanent memorial, and beside the suits of armor carved ships, so that they could be seen by all who sail the sea. This is the tomb which he built in Modein; it remains to this day. (1 Macc 13:27-30; cf. Josephus, *Ant.* 13.6.6 §211; Jeremias 1958, 49–50)

It was mentioned above that apparently three pyramids adorned the tomb of Queen Helene. Pyramids, of course, are associated with Egypt, but these structures were also built in other parts of the Mediterranean world (e.g., the well-known Pyramid of Cestius, in Rome, dating to the first century B.C.E.; cf. Gordon 1983, 101–2). Roman architecture also influenced building in Israel in late antiquity, and Roman mausolea have been discovered (e.g., at Neapolis, at the foot of Mount Gerizim, not far from Shechem; cf. Dajani 1966; Damati 1972; *NEAEHL* 4:1358–59), complete with ornamentation and imagery that conservative, Torah-observant Jews would have found offensive.

Some burial vaults have special importance. In describing Roman siege works, encircling Jerusalem, Josephus states the wall ascended from Siloam "over against the tomb of the high priest Ananus" (*J.W.* 5.12.2 §506). This tomb may well have been discovered among the tombs and monuments found in Akeldama (cf. Avni 1993; Ritmeyer and Ritmeyer 1994; Avni, Greenhut, Ilan 1994; Avni and Greenhut

1996). It is palatial in size, design, and ornamentation, and at one time was adorned with an impressive superstructure. The quality of this tomb complex and its location (remnants of the siege wall mentioned by Josephus are nearby) support the identification. Indeed, the very resting place of the former high priest (known in the New Testament as Annas) may also have been discovered.

What is so interesting are the forensic findings with respect to the human remains. Joe Zias (1996) finds evidence of high infant mortality and widespread illness, such as caused from parasites. The skeletal evidence indicates that nearly one half of those interred in this tomb (i.e., forty-eight percent) did not reach adulthood and that several that did suffered from various infirmities, including those caused by parasites, such as tapeworm (as indicated by the calcified cysts that were left behind). Zias (1996, 118; cf. 1992, 79) remarks that "the relative wealth of the families buried here, manifested by tomb architecture and the ossuaries, did not confer any significant health advantages" (see also Goldstein, Arensburg, and Nathan 1981; Zias 1990, where dietary deficiencies are mentioned). It might be mentioned that the forensic evidence from the so-called Caiaphas tomb is similar. This tomb contained the remains of approximately sixty-three persons (looting makes an exact body count impossible). Only one third of these persons reached adulthood and some skeletons exhibited signs of degenerative disease (Zias 1992). The evidence from these two tombs, though admittedly as a sample quite limited in time and place, nevertheless does assist us in better appreciating the healing dimension in Jesus' ministry. If the wealthy, who have access to the best physicians and medicines, were no better off than the inmates of the Akeldama tombs, it is not hard to see why Jesus, who enjoyed the reputation of a healer, drew large crowds, which at times actually interfered with his activities (e.g., Mark 1:28, 32-34, 36-37, 45; 2:1-4; 3:7-12; 4:1). Even the wealthy would likely have sought aid from Jesus, as perhaps in the case of the synagogue official (Mark 5:21-24), or the woman of means who had spent much on doctors (Mark 5:25-26).

The Tomb of Jason, already mentioned above—a large, ornate complex—offers many features of interest (Avigad 1967; Benoit 1967; Puech 1983; Rahmani 1967). Again, forensic evidence is suggestive. Of the twenty-five individuals interred in this tomb, only three lived beyond the age of 25 (ten died by the age of 12). One of the curious features of this tomb is the graffiti. We have pictures of warships, a stag (which is so well drawn that it has been identified as a red deer, which to this day inhabits Turkey), a palm branch, a menorah with its traditional seven branches, a chalice, and what could be a bearded man wearing a helmet. Glass bowls, stone bowls, cooking pots, jugs, lamps, spindle-shaped bottles, and various utensils (such as a mirror and a knife) were found in the tomb complex. A few small fragments of textiles were found. Several coins were found, ranging from Alexander Jannaeus (103–176 B.C.E.) to Herod the Great (37–34 B.C.E.) and to the time of Emperor Tiberius (*ca.* 31 C.E.). The tomb was violated, perhaps toward the beginning of the reign of Herod. Moreover, the tomb was damaged by the earthquake of 31 B.C.E. The tomb gains its name from the Aramaic inscription in which the tomb builder's name, Jason (יסון), appears (see discussion of the epithet "elder" pp. 55–56 below). A badly preserved Greek inscription has also been found in this tomb. The first line reads: "Rejoice, you who live," while the second line seems to read: "as for what remains, drink and eat" (Benoit 1967, 112–13; restored somewhat differently in Puech 1983, 492–93). The point here does not seem to have anything to do with gluttony or drunkenness (as we probably have in the Latin example cited on p. 60 below). It may be no more than an exhortation to cease mourning for the deceased. Accordingly, we probably have not encountered, as Benoit thinks (1967, 113), an exhortation surprisingly materialistic for a Jewish inscription.

Shortly before the outbreak of the Six Day War (June 1967) a tomb-cave was discovered on the Mount Scopus campus of Hebrew University, some 140 meters from the well-known Tomb of Nicanor. The newly discovered tomb was excavated by Nahman Avigad (1971). Though a cave, stone masons dressed the interior at a very high standard, especially seen in the door posts and lintels and facades. The interior walls are lined with stone masonry and as such is without parallel in Jerusalem. The tomb contained decorated ossuaries and sarcophagi. What is special about this tomb are the inscriptions that mention the "Nazirite." On ossuary no. 7 we read "Hananiah, son of Jonathan the Nazirite [הנזר]" (Avigad 1971, 196); and on ossuary no. 2, with "Nazirite" spelled fully: "Salome, wife of Hananiah, son of the Nazirite [הנזיר]" (Avigad 1971, 197). Here we have archaeological attestation of the practice of taking Nazirite vows (cf. Num 6:1-8) in the first century, which fills in helpfully part of the backdrop to Paul's vow in Acts 18:18 ("At Cenchreae he cut his hair, for he had a vow") and the more sinister vow of the men who volunteered to assassinate the apostle (cf. Acts 21:23).

Shortly before the outbreak of the Yom Kippur War in 1973 a rock-cut tomb on Mount Scopus was discovered near the Botanical Gardens of Hebrew University. The tomb, which had been violated in antiquity, consists of one chamber and seven niches (or *kokhim*), three of which were found sealed and undisturbed (Rahmani 1980). The interesting feature of this tomb is seen in the fact that no fewer than five skeletons (in niches 2, 4, 5, 6, and 7) were still lying in the original burial position; they had not been gathered and placed in ossuaries (and six ossuaries were present in niche 1, one in niche 6, and two more in the central chamber). One ossuary bears the name "Eleazar, son of Zechariah." The pottery ranges in date from late Hasmonean (i.e., first century B.C.E.) to the Herodian period (first century C.E.). The presence of skeletons not placed in ossuaries suggests that use of this tomb came to an abrupt and unexpected end. Rahmani plausibly suggests that this "seems to be evidence of the final use of this tomb, at the time either immediately preceding the First War against the Romans or some decades earlier" (Rahmani 1980, 54). In my view it is very unlikely that reburial of several decedents would have been neglected during peace time. It is therefore probable that Rahmani's first alternative explains the condition of this tomb.

Important crypts, with impressive, ornate sarcophagi (usually two meters long), have been found in several locations in Samaria. Whether these sarcophagi are necessarily Samaritan is debated and what they may tell us about ossilegium is unclear (Barkay 1983; Magen 1993; see also Smith 1973).

Finally, the burial vault of the Goliath family of Jericho may be mentioned. Sometime in the mid-1970s looters discovered a burial vault in Jericho. The sale of ossuaries and other artifacts taken from this tomb alerted authorities, who then located the tomb and began proper excavation and study (Hachlili 1979; Hachlili and Smith 1979; Hachlili and Killebrew 1983c). Because the patriarch, Yoezer, is called "Goliath" (Γολίαθος), the tomb has become known as the Goliath Family Tomb. This tomb is one of 120 tombs that have been discovered in and around Jericho (for descriptions of other tombs, see Hachlili 1978; 1980; 1997; Hachlili and Killebrew 1983b). The Goliath family tomb is the largest and certainly one of the richest tombs, with a large central chamber and several niches. Besides many decorated ossuaries, the tomb boasts remarkable artwork. On the right hand wall, over two of the niches, as one enters the central chamber, one sees tendrils of a grapevine with red and brown leaves and bunches of grapes, painted on the plaster wall (cf. Hachlili and Killebrew 1983c, 46; for photo and description). But the tomb also boasts another interesting inscription: "Ossuary of Theodotos, freedman of Queen Agrippina" (Hachlili 1979, 33 inscription no. 3 + figs. 40–43). Theodotos has a Hebrew name (Nathanael, "given of God"; cf. ossuary no. 15). Queen Agrippina is probably Agrippina the Younger (15–59 C.E.), who in 49 C.E. married Emperor Claudius, her uncle (cf. Tacitus, *Annals* 12.1–8). She was on good terms with the Jewish king Agrippa II and his family. When Theodotos was manumitted and how old he was at the time cannot be determined. On the question of whether this Theodotos is related to the man of the same name in the Theodotos synagogue inscription from Jerusalem, see discussion at pp. 38–43 below.

Burial Practices and Beliefs

In the Greco-Roman world cremation was commonly practiced, a practice not only attested by the artifactual remains, but sometimes by the burial inscriptions themselves (e.g., *CIL* 1.2.1222: *et ossa cinis* ["her bones but ash"]; cf. Shore 1997: 34; *CIL* 4.2965: the deceased *in ignem inlatus est* ["was cremated"]; cf. Gordon 1983, 96; Keppie 1991, 98; and *CIL* 6.889 = *ILS* 181: "Gaius Caesar, son of Germanicus Caesar, was here cremated [*hic crematus est*]"; cf. Gordon 1983, 107–8). One thinks of the remarkable discovery in northern Greece of the royal tomb of Philip II of Macedon, the father of Alexander the Great. The charred bones of the late despot were preserved by the fire of his cremation (and are now on display at the museum in Thessaloniki, a.k.a. Salonica).

In contrast to this custom, the Jewish people buried their dead (as did also many Greeks and Romans), later gathering the bones and placing them in containers or a vault set aside for this purpose. The practice of gathering the bones [*liqut 'azamot*] of the deceased is called *ossilegium*, or "secondary burial" (cf. *y. Moe'ed Qatan* 1.5, 80c: "At first they would bury them in ditches, and when the flesh had decayed, they would gather the bones [*meliqtin et 'azamot*] and bury them in ossuaries"; (Rahmani 1994b, 193–94; for introductory discussion, see Gafni 1981; Silberman 1991; McCane 2000). How far back this practice may be traced and where the practice originated are major questions that lie at the heart of the debate surrounding the significance of the numerous ossuaries found in and around Jerusalem, dating to the Herodian period (see Graetz 1881; Calloway 1963).

It has often been assumed and sometimes has been asserted that the Jewish ossuaries of the Herodian period represent an innovation, perhaps due to a change in religious thinking and perhaps due to foreign influence. Although one cannot conclusively rule out the possibilities of changes in religious beliefs or foreign influence, the evidence suggests that Jewish ossilegium in the Herodian period is not nearly as innovative as many think. In fact, the great quantity of ossuaries from this period, with their almost standardized ornamentation, may have a far more pedestrian explanation.

Eric Meyers (1970; 1971, 3–11) has reviewed the practices of secondary burial in the middle east, from the Neolithic period (sixth millennium B.C.E.) to the Greco-Roman period and beyond. There is ample evidence over this period of time of the practice of gathering the bones of the deceased (and sometimes only the skulls) and placing them in tombs or containers. The use of ossuaries, or small caskets meant to hold only bones and not the undecomposed corpse itself, is ancient and finds a close parallel in the use of *astodans* (or "ossuaries") by the ancient Persians (Yamauchi 1990, 61–63). The evidence for secondary burial in Chalcolithic and Bronze Age Palestine is considerable.

More significantly, there is important evidence for secondary burial in the Bible itself. Meyers (1970, 11) calls our attention to the story of David's reburial of Saul and his sons: "and he brought up from there the bones of Saul and the bones of his son Jonathan; and they gathered the bones of those who were hanged. And they buried the bones of Saul and his son Jonathan in the land of Benjamin in Zela, in the tomb of Kish his father . . ." (2 Sam 21:13-14). The verb "gather" (אסף) is frequently used in reference to interment, e.g., "Abraham breathed his last and died in a good old age, an old man and full of years, and was gathered to his people" (Gen 25:8); "These are the years of the life of Ishmael, a hundred and thirty-seven years; he breathed his last and died, and was gathered to his kindred" (Gen 25:17); "I will gather you to your fathers, and you shall be gathered to your grave in peace" (2 Kgs 22:20). See also Genesis 49:29-33 (where Jacob is "gathered to his people"); Judges 2:10; 1 Kings 13:22 (where the disobedient prophet is told that his body will not go to the tomb of his fathers); 2 Kings 9:28 (where Ahaziah king of Judah is slain and buried "in his tomb with his fathers in the city of David"). This way of speaking is attested in the late Hasmonean and early Heriodian periods, as seen in CD 20:13–14, which refers to the day that the Beloved Teacher (i.e., the Teacher of Righteousness at Qumran) "was gathered," that is, died (on the possibility that the bones of this mysterious person have been found near Qumran, see Broshi and Eshel 2003). For other examples in Jewish late antiquity, see *Jub.* 23:1, 23; *T. Levi* 19:4; 4 Ezra 7:95 ("they understand the rest which they now, being gathered in their chambers, enjoy in profound quietness guarded by angels, and the glory which awaits them at their latter end").

Meyers (1970, 12–13) acknowledges that concepts of the ossuary in Palestine may well have been influenced by designs and artwork from the Aegean world that were introduced to the Philistines. But this influence, if any, is quite ancient and in any case coincided with practices to which the inhabitants of Palestine were well accustomed.

One of the interesting features of ossilegium is that it likely reflects the belief that the dead are still with the living and, perhaps, still able to be of some influence. In other words, the dead are not completely dead, but are diminished and weakened (Tromp 1969, 186: "reduced existence"; Meyers 1970, 16–17). They mutter as shades (Isa 8:19; 29:4) and feel worms gnawing at them (Job 14:22; Isa 66:24). Indeed, mere contact with the bones of Elisha, who was a powerful "man of God," restores life to a dead man (2 Kgs 13:21). The idea that some life still lingers in the bones of the deceased may help us understand better Ezekiel's vision of the dry bones (Ezek 37), bones that are still capable of returning to a full life.

The tombs of the Hellenistic and Roman periods, well before the Herodian period itself, provide evidence of ossilegium, involving either a common bone pit or charnel house or the placement of bones in ossuaries. The evidence compels us to disagree with those who have said, for example that "this burial-custom . . . is alien to the Jewish tradition" (Kahane 1952, 127 n. 2; cf. Meyers 1970, 17, who disagrees with Kahane). The evidence that Meyers and others have adduced suggests that secondary burial, including secondary burial involving ossuaries, was a Jewish practice long before the Herodian period and was continued after the fall of Jerusalem in 70 C.E. It is simply not true that ossuaries appeared of a sudden around 40 B.C.E. (e.g., Hachlili 1980, 239: "their sudden appearance") and then were discontinued after 70 C.E. Rabbinic tradition (e.g., *Semahot* 12–13; *m. Sanh.* 6:6) and archaeological finds attest the continuing practice of ossilegium and the use of ossuaries. Moreover, it is simply wrong to claim that ossuaries were a phenomenon confined to Israel, particularly in and around Jerusalem. Jewish ossuaries have been found in Alexandria, Egypt (Goodenough

1953a, 115; 1953b, 63 + fig. 113), and elsewhere, including Carthage, North Africa, and Spain (Meyers 1970, 24 n. 35).

The most plausible explanation for the dramatic increase in the number of ossuaries put into use in the Herodian period is that it had to do with Herod's extensive building projects in and around Jerusalem, especially those concerned with the Temple Mount and the new Sanctuary. According to Josephus, Herod "prepared a thousand wagons to carry the stones" for the temple and employed "ten thousand of the most skilled workmen," training "some as masons, others as carpenters" (*Ant.* 15.11.2 §390). The Temple Mount was enormous (and still is) and included a series of buildings and colonnades, with the Sanctuary itself the most impressive of all of the structures. Josephus makes a point to emphasize the size and beauty of the stones (e.g., *Ant.* 15.11.3 §399; cf. Mark 13:1: "Look, Teacher, what wonderful stones and what wonderful buildings!"). Although the Sanctuary itself and other key structures were completed in Herod's lifetime, work on the Temple Mount continued until 64 C.E. Accordingly, the meaning of the remark in John 2:20 implies ongoing construction and not completion. It should read: "For forty-six years this sanctuary has been under construction" (with "sanctuary" referring to the whole complex, not to the Sanctuary proper). When work on the Temple Mount was finally completed, 18,000 workers were laid off (*apud* Josephus, *Ant.* 20.9.7 §219). This massive layoff contributed to the growing social and political instability that just two years later exploded into open rebellion. Some of the laid-off stone-cutters would later employ their tools and skills in building secret passageways for the rebels (*J.W.* 7.2.2 §26–27).

It is in this chronological coincidence between Herod's massive building program, which employed thousands of stone-cutters and which ran from his reign, beginning in the 30s B.C.E., and extended to 64 C.E., and the appearance of thousands of ossuaries, carved from the same stone (limestone) from which almost all of the Temple Mount buildings were fashioned, that we find the answer to our question. The number of ossuaries, made of limestone, increased dramatically during the one century of temple-related building in Jerusalem, not because of a shift in theology, or foreign influence, but because of the great number of stone-cutters, quarries, and rejected blocks of limestone. The increase of the city's population and its urban and suburban sprawl also encouraged greater density in burial sites. Simply put, more dead relatives can be interred in the family vault if they are placed in ossuaries than if they are left lying in niches or in full-sized sarcophagi. Although these factors came into play primarily in Jerusalem, their influence may account for the appearance of ossuaries in Jericho during this period of time (on the evidence at Jericho, see Hachlili 1980).

Meyers has been criticized by Rahmani (1958, 105; 1994b, 193–95), who has suggested that Jewish use of ossuaries in the Herodian period was prompted by resurrection hopes and desire to expiate sin through decay of the flesh. At points he has been followed by Hachlili and others (e.g., Hachlili and Killebrew 1983b, 128). But these arguments are questionable. We have no reason to think that the bones of Sadducees who did not believe in resurrection were not placed into ossuaries. Many, if not most, of the ruling priests in the Herodian period were Sadducean in sympathies, and we have ossuaries of ruling priests and members of their immediate families (e.g., Rahmani 1994a, no. 871; possibly the tomb of Annas and family, which contained ossuaries; and the ossuary of Caiaphas, if this inscription has been properly identified). Moreover, it is not clear that ossuaries per se had anything to do with expiation. It is the decay of the flesh in primary burial (not secondary) that atones for sin, as seen, for example, in *m. Sanh.* 6:6: "When the flesh had wasted away they gathered together the bones and buried them in their own place." Resurrection hope may have been involved in ossilegium (and perhaps the menorah and other ornamentation were part of this), but this hope did not give rise to the practice (for discussion of ossuary art work and Jewish belief in the afterlife, see Sellers 1945; Birkeland 1949; Wirgin 1964; Rahmani 1968; 1994c; Braude 1969; Meyers 1971–1972; Meyers and Meyers 1981; Bivian 1991; Kloner 1994; Grossberg 1996; Fine 2000; Kraemer 2000; Regev 2001). In my opinion, the arguments of Meyers remain compelling.

Chapter 2

Inscriptions—Non-Burial

Before we begin a review of burial and ossuary inscriptions it will be helpful to consider seven important non-ossuary inscriptions. As it so happens, one of them directly relates to the conventions and laws of sepulture. In various ways these inscriptions illuminate details found in or presupposed by the New Testament Gospels. Indeed, two of the inscriptions directly concern persons mentioned in the Gospels.

Unlike ossuary inscriptions, which were hidden from public view and were intended for families in the privacy of the family burial crypt, the inscriptions that we shall consider next were public; they were meant to be seen and—more importantly—to be heeded. We shall survey these inscriptions in the order of their discovery.

The Jewish Temple Warning Inscription – 1871

In 1871 Charles Clermont-Ganneau found a limestone block (about 85 cm long, about 57 cm high, and about 37 cm thick), on which was inscribed a warning to Gentiles to stay out of the perimeter surrounding the sanctuary (the find was first announced in *PEFQ* 1871, 132; for critical discussion, see Clermont-Ganneau 1872; Derenbourg 1872; Deissmann 1927, 79–81 + fig. 9; Bickerman 1946–1947; Zeitlin 1947–1948; Schürer 1973–1987, 2:284–87, esp. 285 n. 57; Baumgarten 1982; Segal 1989). The inscription reads as follows (cf. *OGIS* no. 598; *CIJ* no. 1400; *SEG* VIII no. 169):

ΜΗΘΕΝΑΑΛΛΟΓΕΝΗΕΙΣΠΟΡΕΥΕΣΘΑΙ
ΕΝΤΟΣΤΟΥΠΕΡΙΤΟΙΕΡΟΝΤΡΥ
ΦΑΚΤΟΥΚΑΙΠΕΡΙΒΟΛΟΥΟΣΔΑΝ
ΛΗΦΘΗΑΥΤΩΙΑΙΤΙΟΣΕΣΤΑΙ

ΔΙΑΤΟΕΞΑΚΟΛΟΥΘΕΙΝ
ΘΑΝΑΤΟΝ

Or, with spacing, punctuation, and diacritical marks: μηθένα ἀλλογενὴ εἰσπορεύεσθαι ἐντὸς τοῦ περὶ τὸ ἱερὸν τρυφάκτου καὶ περιβόλου· ὃς δ' ἂν ληφθῇ αὐτῷ αἴτιος ἔσται διὰ τὸ ἐξακολουθεῖν θάνατον. It may be translated as follows:

Let no Gentile enter
within the partition and barrier
surrounding the temple; whosoever
is caught shall be responsible
for his subsequent
death.

A fragment of a second inscription was found in 1935 outside the wall around Jerusalem's Old City (Iliffe 1936; cf. Finegan 1969, 119–20). The second fragment is 50 cm high, 31 cm thick, and about 25 cm wide (the width varies due to the jagged right-hand edge). The inscribed letters were originally painted red, making them stand out against the off-white limestone. The extant text of the fragmentary inscription matches closely the wording and layout of the fully preserved inscription. The fragment, which corresponds to the left third of the full inscription, reads:

ΘΕΝΑΛΛ
ΟϹΤΟΥ
ΤΟΥΚΑΙ
ΗΦΘΗΑΥ
ΙΑΤΟΕΞ
ΑΝΑΤ

. . . no Gen[tile] . . . within the . . . [par]tition and . . . caught . . . sub[sequent d]ea[th.]

What is translated "Gentile" in the first line is literally "other-race" (ἀλλογενής), that is, a non-Jewish person (cf. LXX Exod 12:43; Lev 22:25; Ezek 44:9). See also Josephus (*Ant.* 12.3.4 §145), where ἀλλόφύλος is used: "It is unlawful for any foreigner to enter the enclosure of the temple that is forbidden to the Jews, except to those of them who are accustomed to enter after purifying themselves in accordance with the law of the country." Concerning the "partition" (τρύφακτος = סורג;

cf. *m. Midd.* 2:3) and "barrier (surrounding)" (περίβολος) mentioned in line 3, the former "was a stone barrier which stretched across the outer court to protect the flights of stairs leading up to the inner court," while the latter "was the wall which encompassed the holy terrace within the outer court" of the temple (Bickerman 1946–1947, 389). On the meaning of "responsible for his (death)" (αὐτῷ αἴτιος), see Bickerman (1946–1947, 395–96; and Segal 1989).

This inscription is almost certainly one of the inscribed warnings mentioned by Josephus. For example, he states: "Upon [the partition wall of the temple court] stood pillars, at equal distances from one another, declaring the law of purity, some in Greek, and some in Roman letters, that 'no foreigner should go within that holy place [μηδένα ἀλλόφυλον ἐντὸς τοῦ ἁγίου]' . . ." (*J.W.* 5.5.2 §193–94; cf. 6.2.4 §124–28; *Ant.* 15.2.5 §417; *Ag. Ap.* 2.8 §103). Philo refers to the same law and penalty, though without mention of the inscribed warnings: "Still more abounding and peculiar is the zeal of them all for the temple, and the strongest proof of this is that death [θάνατος] without appeal is the sentence against those of other races who penetrate into its inner [ἐντός] confines" (*Legatio ad Gaium* 31 §212). Allusions to the death penalty for temple violations are found also in the later rabbinic literature (e.g., *Sifre Num.* §116 [on Num 18:1-32]: "Rabbi Joshua ben Hananiah sought to help Rabbi Yohanan ben Gudegedah [at the gates of the temple. But] he said to him, 'Go back, for you already have risked your life, since I belong to the gatekeepers, but you are a singer'").

The scriptural backdrop for these posted warnings includes 1 Kings 8:41-43, which recounts Solomon's prayer of dedication, in which it is anticipated that Gentiles will visit the temple, Numbers 1:51, which warns, "If any one else comes near [the tabernacle], he shall be put to death" (RSV; cf. Num 3:38; 19:13; Lev 10:2; 15:31; 22:9), and Leviticus 16:2, where Moses is warned by God, "Tell Aaron your brother not to come at all times into the holy place within the veil, before the mercy seat which is upon the ark, lest he die . . . " (RSV). Thus there was the expectation, on the one hand, that Gentiles may approach the temple, but there were restrictions, with deadly consequences, on the other. Subsequent interpretation, custom, and tradition established the guidelines that were observed late in the second temple period. Partitions and warnings against trespass by non-members or the uninitiated were common in late antiquity, and were observed by non-Jews, as well as Jews (see examples cited in Bickerman 1946–1947, 389–90; e.g., "From here only the covenanters"; "The uninitiated may not enter";

"Approach the sacred precincts in condition of purity and with pious mind").

The inscription discovered by Clermont-Ganneau corroborates, to be sure, an important second-temple detail recounted in Philo and Josephus. But from a Christian perspective the primary value of this inscription is its contribution to a better understanding of the setting and context of Jesus' action in the temple precincts (cf. Mark 11:15-18 and parallels) and of the riot that overtook Paul in the same precincts some years later (cf. Acts 21:27-36, esp. v. 28, where the accusation is leveled against Paul that "he also brought Greeks into the temple, and he has defiled this holy place [εἰς τὸ ἱερὸν καὶ κεκοίνωκεν τὸν ἅγιον τόπον τοῦτον]"). It is in the light of this highly sensitive appreciation of the temple precincts, especially that of the carefully protected sanctuary within them, that Jesus' remarks should be understood: "Is it not written, 'My house shall be called a house of prayer for all the nations'? But you have made it a 'den of robbers'" (Mark 11:17; with Jesus quoting or alluding to Isa 56:7 and Jer 7:11).

That Jesus' critical comment provoked a malevolent reaction on the part of the ruling priests (cf. Mark 11:18, 27-33; 12:12; 14:1-2, 43, 53, 58; 15:1-3, 11, 31-32) should hardly occasion surprise. However, his allusion to Isa 56:7, which is part of an oracle (i.e., Isa 56:3-8) that envisioned the day when the "foreigner" (בן־הנכר / ἀλλογενής) will be welcomed into the house of God and receive "within the walls" a monument and name (Isa 56:3, 5), may have been particularly offensive. Indeed, Jesus' teaching may have been understood as directly opposed to the polity presupposed by the public warnings that "no foreigner enter within" the restricted area of the temple.

Moreover, the Pauline (or post-Pauline) assertion in Ephesians 2:14-15 that Jesus "has broken down the dividing wall of hostility, by abolishing in his flesh the law of commandments and ordinances," may well represent a development of Jesus' teaching. This teaching and its later development in Pauline communities would have been highly controversial in some Jewish circles. Not only does it stand in tension with the polity presupposed by the posted warning inscriptions, it is sharply out of step with the eschatological vision expressed at Qumran:

> ["I appointed judges] over My people Israel" (2 Sam 7:10-11a). This "place" is the house that [they shall build for Him] in the Last Days, as it is written in the book of Moses: ["A temple of] the Lord are you to prepare with your hands; the Lord will reign forever and ever" (Exod 15:17). This passage describes the temple that no [man with

> a] permanent [fleshly defect] shall enter, nor Ammonite, Moabite, bastard, foreigner or alien [ובן נכר וגר], forevermore. Surely His holiness shall be rev[eal]ed there; eternal glory shall ever be apparent there. Strangers shall not again defile it, as they formerly defiled the Temp[le of I]srael through their sins. To that end He has commanded that they build Him a Temple of Adam, and that in it they sacrifice to Him proper sacrifices. (4Q174 1–2 i 2-7; adaptation of Wise, Abegg, Cook 1996, 227; for further discussion of the possible linkage between the warning inscriptions, Isa 56:7, and 4Q174; see Baumgarten 1982)

It is not an exaggeration to say that the temple warning inscription constitutes an important artifact that bears witness to a sensitive and controversial issue. Evidently this was an issue that seems to have played a part in Jesus' teaching in the sacred precincts and in the deadly opposition he encountered at the hands of the ruling priests.

Caesar's Edict against Grave Robbery Inscription – 1878

In 1878 a marble slab, 61 cm high, 38 cm wide, and 8 cm thick, came to light, on which was inscribed an imperial edict forbidding robbing and vandalizing graves. It is believed that the stone came from Nazareth (though the provenance of this discovery has never been confirmed; it may well have come from one of the cities of the Decapolis). In 1925 it was sent to the Paris Bibliothèque Nationale and was published in 1930 by Franz Cumont (1930; 1933; Brown 1931; Cook 1932). It has been discussed subsequently in several studies (see esp. de Zulueta 1932; Metzger 1980; van der Horst 1991, 159–60; Boffo 1994, 319–33 [for additional bibliography, see pp. 319–20]; Brown 1994, 2:1293–94). The date of the inscription is unknown, but most epigraphers think it is from the first century, though possibly from just before the turn of the era (Cumont 1930, 265). The unqualified use of "Caesar" favors identification with Augustus (de Zulueta 1932, 186–87).

The inscription reads (*SEG* VIII no. 13):

1 ΔΙΑΤΑΓΜΑΚΑΙϹΑΡΟϹ
2 ΑΡΕϹΚΕΙΜΟΙΤΑΦΟΥϹΤΥΝΒΟΥϹ
3 ΤΕΟΙΤΙΝΕϹΕΙϹΘΡΗϹΚΕΙΑΝΠΡΟΓΟΝΩΝ
4 ΕΠΟΙΗϹΑΝΗΤΕΚΝΩΝΗΟΙΚΕΙΩΝ
5 ΤΟΥΤΟΥϹΜΕΝΕΙΝΑΜΕΤΑΚΕΙΝΗΤΟΥϹ
6 ΤΟΝΑΙΩΝΑΕΑΝΔΕΤΙϹΕΠΙΔΙΞΗ̣ΤΙ
7 ΝΑΗΚΑΤΑΛΕΛΥΚΟΤΑΗΑΛΛΩΤΙΝΙ

8 ΤΡΟΠΩΤΟΥϹΚΕΚΗΔΕΥΜΕΝΟΥϹ
9 ΕΞΕΡΡΙΦΦΟΤΑΗΕΙϹΕΤΕΡΟΥϹ
10 ΤΟΠΟΥϹΔΩΛΩΠΟΝΗΡΩΜΕ
11 ΤΑΤΕΘΕΙΚΟΤΑΕΠΑΔΙΚΙΑΤΗΤΩΝ
12 ΚΕΚΗΔΕΥΜΕΝΩΝΗΚΑΤΟΧΟΥϹΗΛΙ
13 ΘΟΥϹΜΕΤΑΤΕΘΕΙΚΟΤΑΚΑΤΑΤΟΥ
14 ΤΟΙΟΥΤΟΥΚΡΙΤΗΡΙΟΝΕΓΩΚΕΛΕΥΩ
15 ΓΕΝΕϹΘΑΙΚΑΘΑΠΕΡΠΕΡΙΘΕΩΝ
16 ΕϹΤΑϹΤΩΝΑΝΘΡΩΠΩΝΘΡΗϹ
17 ΚΙΑϹΠΟΛΥΓΑΡΜΑΛΛΟΝΔΕΗϹΕΙ
18 ΤΟΥϹΚΕΚΗΔΕΥΜΕΝΟΥϹΤΕΙΜΑΝ
19 ΚΑΘΟΛΟΥΜΗΔΕΝΙΕΞΕϹΤΩΜΕΤΑ
20 ΚΕΙΝΗϹΑΙΕΙΔΕΜΗΤΟΥΤΟΝΕΓΩΚΕ
21 ΦΑΛΗϹΚΑΤΑΚΡΙΤΟΝΟΝΟΜΑΤΙ
22 ΤΥΜΒΩΡΥΧΙΑϹΘΕΛΩΓΕΝΕϹΘΑΙ

Or, with spacing, punctuation, and diacritical marks (and line numbers moved to the left when word-breaks are joined): [1]Διάταγμα Καίσαρος· [2]Ἀρέσκει μοι τάφους τύνβους [3]τε, οἵτινες εἰς θρησκείαν προγόνων [4]ἐποίησαν ἢ τέκνων ἢ οἰκείων, [5]τούτους μένειν ἀμετακεινήτους [6]τὸν αἰῶνα. ἐὰν δέ τις ἐπιδίξῃ [7]τινὰ ἢ καταλελυκότα ἢ ἄλλῳ τινὶ [8]τρόπῳ τοὺς κεκηδευμένους [9]ἐξερριφφότα ἢ εἰς ἑτέρους [10]τόπους δώλῳ πονηρῷ [11]μετατεθεικότα ἐπ' ἀδικίᾳ τῇ τῶν [12]κεκηδευμένων ἢ κατόχους ἢ [13]λίθους μετατεθεικότα, κατὰ τοῦ [14]τοιούτου κριτήριον ἐγὼ κελεύω [15]γενέσθαι καθάπερ περὶ θεῶν [16]ἐς τὰς τῶν ἀνθρώπων [17]θρησκίας. πολὺ γὰρ μᾶλλον δεήσει [18]τοὺς κεκηδευμένους τειμᾶν. [19]καθόλου μηδενὶ ἐξέστω [20]μετακεινῆσαι· εἰ δὲ μή, τοῦτον ἐγὼ [21]κεφαλῆς κατάκριτον ὀνόματι [22]τυμβωρυχίας θέλω γενέσθαι.

Cumont (1930, 243), de Zulueta (1932, 188–89), and van der Horst (1991, 160), have concluded that the Greek inscription is a translation of a Latin *Vorlage* (and Cumont, on the reference and page just cited, is able to retrovert the Greek into Latin). Following Metzger (1980, 77) the inscription may be translated as follows:

> [1]Ordinance of Caesar: [2]It is my pleasure that graves and tombs—[3]whoever has made them as a pious service for ancestors [4]or children or members of their house—[5]that these remain unmolested [6]in perpetuity. But if any person lay information that [7]another either has destroyed them, or has in any other [8]way cast out the bodies [9]which have been buried there, or [10]with malicious deception has [11]trans-

> ferred them to other places, to the dishonor of those [12]buried there, or has removed the headstones or other [13]stones, in such a case [14]I command that a trial [15]be instituted, just as if they were concerned with the gods [16]for the pious services of mortals. [17]For beyond all else it shall be obligatory [18]to honor those who have been buried. [19]Let no one remove them for any reason. [20]If not, however (i.e. if anyone does so), [21]capital punishment on the charge of [22]tomb robbery I will to take place.

The imperial ordinance testifies to the sanctity with which tombs were regarded in late antiquity, especially in Israel. De Zulueta (1932, 195) thinks the edict was addressed either to the legate of Syria or to the procurator (or prefect) of Judea. Most interesting is the warning in lines 10 and 11 not to transfer bodies from one grave to another. This part of the ordinance is especially relevant to the Gospels' stories about the visit of the women to the tomb and, especially, the story in Matthew about Pilate sealing the tomb and the claim that the disciples stole the body of Jesus (Matt 27:62-66; 28:11-15; see also Brown 1994, 2:1294). It has been suggested that the edict was issued by Tiberius, to Pilate, in the aftermath of the priestly charge that the disciples had stolen the body of Jesus. This is quite speculative. Equally speculative is the suggestion that the edict is in response to the Samaritan desecration of the Jewish temple (*ca.* 8 C.E.), in scattering human bones in the precincts (cf. Josephus, *Ant.* 18.2.2 §30). The difficulty with these suggestions is that the inscription gives no indication that a specific incident is in view (cf. de Zulueta 1932, 195–97).

Even if the Matthean story is discounted as later apologetic, the laws pertaining to graves, such as what we find in the Nazareth inscription, contribute to the general backdrop of the Easter story and how readers and hearers of this story would have understood it (see McCane 1999). Metzger remarks: "If in fact the ordinance was published in Palestine some time prior to the death of Jesus, then . . . at the time of the resurrection there was in force a severe law against tampering with buried bodies, the consequences of infringing which the panic-stricken disciples are very unlikely to have braved" (Metzger 1980, 91; quoted by van der Horst 1991, 160; Metzger is paraphrasing de Zulueta 1932, 197). Interpreters have discussed what the threatened "capital punishment" (κεφαλῆς κατάκριτον) entailed. De Zulueta (1932, 195) thinks heavy fines were in mind.

Theodotos Synagogue Inscription – 1913

During excavations in and around Mount Ophel, or the "City of David," in 1913 Raimund Weill (1919, pl. XXVa; 1920a, 30–34) discovered a stone slab (75 cm x 41 cm), which probably had served as a foundation stone, bearing what is now usually called the Theodotos Inscription. The stone is now housed in the Rockefeller Museum. This Greek inscription may provide evidence of the existence of buildings prior to 70 C.E. specifically designated as "synagogues." The inscription reads (cf. *CIJ* no. 1404; Lifshitz 1967, 70–71; Deismann 1927, 440 + fig. 80; Kloppenborg Verbin 2000, 244–45 + plate):

1 ΘΕΟΔΟΤΟϹΟΥΕΤΤΗΝΟΥΙΕΡΕΥϹΚΑΙ
2 Α[ ]ΧΙϹΥΝΑΓΩΓΟϹΥΙΟϹΑΡΧΙϹΥΝ[ ]
3 Γ[ ]ΥΥΙΩΝΟϹΑΡΧΙϹΥΝ[ ]ΓΩΓΟΥΩΚΟ
4 ΔΟΜΗϹΕΤΗΝϹΥΝΑΓΩΓΗΝΕΙϹΑΝ[ ]Ω
5 Ϲ[ ]ΝΟΜΟΥΚΑΙΕΙϹ[ ]ΙΔΑΧ[ ]ΝΕΝΤΟΛΩΝΚΑΙ
6 Τ[ ]ΝΞΕΝΩΝΑΚΑ[ ]ΔΩΜΑΤΑΚΑΙΤΑΧΡΗ
7 Ϲ[ ]ΗΡΙΑΤΩΝΥΔΑΤΩΝΕΙϹΚΑΤΑΛΥΜΑΤΟΙ
8 Ϲ[ ]ΡΗΖΟΥϹΙΝΑΠΟΤΗϹΞΕ[ ]ΗϹΗΝΕΘΕΜΕ
9 Λ[ ]ϹΑΝΟΙΠΑΤΕΡΕϹ[ ]ΥΤΟΥΚΑΙΟΙΠΡΕ
10 Ϲ[ ]ΥΤΕΡΟΙΚΑΙϹΙΜΩΝ[ ]ΔΗϹ

Or, with spacing, punctuation, restorations, and diacritical marks (and line numbers moved to the left when word-breaks are joined): [1]Θεόδοτος Οὐεττήνου, ἱερεὺς καὶ [2]ἀ[ρ]χισυνάγωγος, υἱὸς [3]ἀρχισυν[αγώ]γ[ο]υ, υἱωνὸς ἀρχισυν[α]γώγου, [4]ᾠκοδόμησε τὴν συναγωγὴν εἰς [5]ἀν[άγν]ωσ[ιν] νόμου καὶ εἰς [δ]ιδαχ[ὴ]ν ἐντολῶν, καὶ [6]τ[ὸ]ν ξενῶνα κα[ὶ τὰ] δώματα καὶ τὰ [7]χρησ[τ]ήρια τῶν ὑδάτων εἰς κατάλυμα [8]τοῖς [χ]ρῄζουσιν ἀπὸ τῆς ξέ[ν]ης, ἣν [9]ἐθεμελ[ίω]σαν οἱ πατέρες [α]ὐτοῦ καὶ οἱ [10]πρεσ[β]ύτεροι καὶ Σιμων[ί]δης.

It may be translated: "Theodotos, (son) of Vettenus, priest and synagogue ruler, son of a synagogue ruler, (and) grandson of a synagogue ruler, built the synagogue for the reading of the law and the teaching of the commandments, and the guest room, and the chambers, and the water fixtures, as an inn for those in need from foreign parts, (the synagogue) which his fathers and the elders and Simonides founded" (for discussion of text, see Riesner 1995, 192–200).

Initially most archaeologists and epigraphers dated the inscription to the Herodian or early Roman period (i.e., before 70 C.E.; cf. Clermont-Ganneau 1920, 193; Boffo 1994, 275; Dalman 1922, 30; Deissmann 1927, 441; Lietzmann 1921, 172–73; Foakes Jackson and

Lake 1932, 4:67–78; Lifshitz 1967, 71; Llewelyn and Kearsley 1994; Meyers 1992b; Reinach 1920, 53; Sukenik 1934a, 69; Vincent 1921 [after initial doubts]; Weill 1920c, 30–34). Almost none demurred (for one example, see Bees 1921).

Objections to the pre-70 C.E. dating of the Theodotos inscription have been set forth recently by Howard Kee. In a series of articles Kee (1990; 1994; 1995) has argued that there is no evidence for synagogue buildings prior to 70 C.E. and that references to synagogues as buildings in the New Testament (especially in Luke–Acts) are anachronistic. The Greek word συναγωγή, Kee contends, refers to the gathering of people, not to the building in which the people gathered. People gathered in private homes. After 70 C.E., that is, after the destruction of the Temple, public buildings were constructed for the specific purpose of worship, prayer, and study. Accordingly, Kee concludes that the Theodotos inscription probably dates to the second century C.E.

Kee's injunctions to caution are welcome (for sometimes συναγωγή is taken to refer to a building, when it may only refer to the gathering of people), but his principal conclusion, viz. that there were no synagogue buildings prior to 70 C.E., stumbles over compelling literary and inscriptional evidence. This evidence is conveniently summarized by Richard Oster (1993; cf. Levine 1996) and John Kloppenborg Verbin (2000; see also Chilton and Yamauchi 2000).

In at least three places Josephus refers to "synagogues," which can only be understood as buildings, and not simply as gatherings of people:

> The Jews in Caesarea had a synagogue [συναγωγή] adjoining a plot of ground owned by a Greek of that city; this site they had frequently endeavored to purchase offering a price far exceeding its true value . . . On the following day, which was a sabbath, when the Jews assembled at the synagogue [συναγωγή]. . . . (*J.W.* 2.14.4–5 §285–89)

> Although Antiochus surnamed Epiphanes [175–164 B.C.E.] sacked Jerusalem and plundered the temple, his successors on the throne restored to the Jews of Antioch all such votive offerings as were made of brass, to be laid up in their synagogue [συναγωγή] . . . (*J.W.* 7.3.3 §44)

> "Inasmuch as certain of you have had such mad audacity . . . not to obey this edict . . . in that you have prevented the Jews from having a synagogue [συναγωγή] by transferring to it an image of Caesar, you have thereby sinned not only against the law of the Jews, but also

> against the emperor, whose image was better placed in his own shrine than in that of another, especially in the synagogue [συναγωγή]; for by natural law each must be lord over his own place, in accordance with Caesar's decree." (*Ant.* 19.6.3 §305)

The first passage, which describes one of the incidents that instigated the first major war with Rome, took place in 66 C.E. The second describes events from the Hasmonean period (presumably the second century B.C.E.), while the third summarizes the words of Publius Petronius, governor of Syria, who in 41 C.E. rebuked the people of Dora for placing an image of Caesar in a synagogue. In all three passages it is quite clear that συναγωγή refers to the building in which the Jewish people meet.

Kee responds to this evidence by suggesting that Josephus is speaking anachronistically (much as does the Lukan evangelist, he supposes), retrojecting post-70 C.E. Jewish realities, which in the aftermath of the destruction of the Temple of Jerusalem now included the building of synagogues as places of worship (Kee 1994, 282). This objection, however, is little more than special pleading. Would Josephus, to whom synagogue buildings were an innovation (assuming Kee's hypothesis), retroject them into earlier periods in Israel's history? It seems unlikely.

And in any case, Kee's hypothesis does not account for usage of συναγωγή in Philo, who long before the Temple was destroyed had this to say about the Essenes:

> In these they are instructed at all other times, but particularly on the seventh days. For that day has been set apart to be kept holy and on it they abstain from all other work and proceed to sacred places [εἰς ἱεροὺς . . . τόπους], which they call synagogues [συναγωγαί]. There, arranged in rows according to their ages, the younger below the older, they sit decorously as befits the occasion with attentive ears. Then one takes the books and reads aloud and another of especial proficiency comes forward and expounds what is not understood. (*Prob.* 12 §81–82)

In this passage "synagogues" (συναγωγαί) cannot simply mean "gatherings" of people, but must mean actual places, or buildings, which were regarded by Essenes as "sacred places." What is described here is essentially what all religiously observant Jews did, including seating conventions. In fact, in broad outline Philo's description of the proceedings of the Essene synagogue matches the description seen in Luke 4:16-30, where Scripture is read and then expounded (v. 16: "And he came to

Nazareth, where he had been brought up; and he went to the synagogue, as his custom was, on the sabbath day. And he stood up to read"; cf. vv. 20, 28).

Perhaps most devastating of all for Kee's argument is the inscription from the North African city Berenike (in Cyrenaica). This inscription is especially helpful, for it is readily dated (*SEG* XVII 823 = *CJZC* no. 72; Oster 1993: 187; Strange 1995, 73–74; Kloppenborg Verbin 2000, 247–48):

> In the second year of the emperor Nero Claudius Caesar Drusus Germanicus, on the 16th of Chorach. It was resolved by the congregation [συναγωγή] of the Jews in Berenike that (the names of) those who donated to the repairs of the synagogue [συναγωγή] be inscribed on a stele of Parian marble.

In this inscription we see the word συναγωγή used in both senses of congregation and building. The reference to the second year of Nero dates the inscription to 56 C.E. In view of this evidence (and Oster and Kloppenborg Verbin provide additional evidence) it seems clear that buildings referred to as "synagogues" existed prior to 70 C.E. Moreover, the evidence of Jewish connections between Cyrenaica and Judea (see Kloppenborg Verbin 2000, 248 n. 16; Yamauchi 1992) increases the probability that the pre-70 C.E. existence of Jewish synagogues in North Africa corroborates the existence of the same in Judea. Thus, a pre-70 C.E. inscription, found in Jerusalem, in which reference to a synagogue appears, makes sense.

Finally, paleographical and archaeological evidence also supports the pre-70 C.E. date of the Theodotos inscription, for the orthography matches the Herodian style (as seen, for example, in comparison with the orthography of the temple warning inscription considered above or the temple donation inscription [*SEG* XXXIII no. 1277]), not the post-70 C.E. style, and the stratigraphy of the find itself also supports a pre-70 C.E. date (i.e., in that nothing was built on the site after 70). Moreover, the ruins of the large public rooms at Gamla and Jericho in all probability were synagogues, as indicated by various architectural features, as well as a nearby *miqveh*, and almost certainly predate 70 C.E. In the case of the Jericho synagogue (excavated in 1998 by Ehud Netzer) there is evidence that the building was damaged by the earthquake of 31 B.C.E. The ad hoc secondary modifications of rooms in the Herodium and at Masada, which also predate 70 C.E., reflect an architectural and seating pattern that by the time of the Jewish revolt had become established. (For further arguments in favor of the early date of the Theodotos inscription, see Kloppenborg Verbin 2000; Strathmann 1967, 267. Kloppenborg Verbin's critique of Kee's views is devastating.)

Some identify the synagogue mentioned in Acts 6:9, "some of those who belonged to the synagogue of the Freedmen (as it was called), and of the Cyrenians" (τινες τῶν ἐκ τῆς συναγωγῆς τῆς λεγομένης Λιβερτίνων καὶ Κυρηναίων) with the synagogue mentioned in the Theodotos inscription (e.g., Clermont-Ganneau 1920, 191; Reinach 1920; Vincent 1921; Sevenster 1968, 132; Sukenik 1934a, 70: the identification is plausible, but not proven; see also Hengel 1989, 13). Although not impossible, the identification is speculative and is rejected by many (e.g., Lietzmann 1921; Deissmann 1927, 441; Grabbe 1988).

The importance of the Theodotos inscription, securely dated to the first half of the first century, is in its corroboration of the existence of synagogue buildings. One immediately thinks of the many references to Jesus teaching in the synagogue (συναγωγή), especially the synagogue in Capernaum (Mark 1:21, 39). The original foundation of this synagogue may well be the older basalt foundation that now can be seen beneath the newer limestone synagogue that was erected in the third century C.E. (Strange and Shanks 1982; 1983). The very site in which Jesus taught has probably been identified.

The Theodotos inscription also attests the title of "synagogue ruler" (ἀρχισυνάγωγος) in the period before 70 C.E. Here again one immediately thinks of the desperation of Jairus, one of the "rulers of the synagogue," who sought from Jesus help for his dying daughter (Mark 5:21-24, 35-43), or the unnamed ruler of the synagogue who criticized Jesus for healing on the Sabbath (Luke 13:10-17).

In the book of Acts synagogues (6:9; 9:2, 10; 13:5; passim) and synagogue rulers (13:15; 18:8, 17) continue to be mentioned. We also encounter those whom the Lukan evangelist calls "God-fearers" (σέβεσθαι τὸν θεόν) or "devout persons" (σεβόμενοι). For examples, see Acts 16:14: "a woman named Lydia . . . a worshiper of God"; and 17:17: "he argued in the synagogue with the Jews and the devout persons." In this connection, brief mention might also be made of an inscription from the theatre of Miletus (discovered by Theodor Wiegand in 1906), which reads (*CIJ* no. 748):

ΤΟΠΟϹΕΙΟΥΔΕΩΝΤΩΝΚΑΙΘΕΟϹΕΒΙΟΝ

Or, with spacing, punctuation, and diacritical marks: τόπος Εἰουδέων τῶν καὶ Θεοσεβίον ("Place of the Jews, who are also called 'God-fearers'"). The inscription refers to reserved seating. From time to time the author of Acts refers to "God-fearing" proselytes or gentiles (13:43, 50; 16:14; 17:4, 17; 18:7, 13). In one passage he refers to one Τιτίου Ἰούστου σεβομένου τὸν θεόν (cf. Acts 18:7: "And he left there and went to the house of a man named Titius Justus, a worshiper of God; his house was next door to the synagogue"). One of the cities that Paul visited was Miletus (cf. Acts 20:15, 17). For further discussion of this discovery, see Adolf Deissmann (1927, 451–52 + plate).

The Seat of Moses Inscription – 1926

In the 1920s excavations at Hammath-Tiberias uncovered the ruins of an ancient synagogue. Among other things, what may well have been a "seat of Moses" was also uncovered. In 1926 a seat of Moses was discovered in the ruins of the synagogue of Chorazin (for reports, see Ory 1927; Marmorstein 1927), on which was inscribed the following Aramaic dedication:

דכיר לטב יודן בר ישמעל
דעבד הדן סטוה
ודרגוה בפעלה יהי
לה חולק עם צדיקים

Remembered for good be Judan ben Ishmael,
who made this στοά
and its staircase. As his reward may
he have a share with the righteous.

The seat is made of black basalt stone. The first line of the inscription runs along the top edge of the seat. On the top surface of the seat there are arm rests, while there is a rosette design etched into the back of the seat. The seat measures 73 cm wide, 56 cm high, and 55 cm or so thick (from the front edge to the back edge). The artifact is on display in the Israel National Museum in Jerusalem. It has been suggested (Marmorstein 1927, 101–2) that the inscription's Judan ben Ishmael, the donor of the synagogue's stoa (or colonnade) and its staircase, is the rabbinic authority Judah ben Ishmael (e.g., *b. Hullin* 118b). The evidence, however, is insufficient to prove or disprove this identification (Sukenik 1934, 60–61 n. 1).

Archaeologists have remarked that this stone seat is probably an example of the "seat of Moses," to which Jesus and later rabbinic literature make reference. Commenting on 1 Kings 10:19 (ASV: "and the top of the throne was round behind"), Rabbi Aha states that the throne of Solomon was "like the seat (or cathedra) of Moses [כהדא קתדרא דמשה]" (*Pesiq. Rab Kah.* 1.7). The word קתדרא ("seat") is a loanword (as also is סטוה = στοά), from the Greek καθέδρα, the very word that appears in Matthew 23:2, where Jesus says, "The scribes and the Pharisees sit on Moses' seat" (ἐπὶ τῆς Μωϋσέως καθέδρας ἐκάθισαν οἱ γραμματεῖς καὶ οἱ Φαρισαῖοι). The stone seats found at Hammath-Tiberias and Chorazin provide archaeological proof that the "seat of Moses" to which Jesus and, years later, Rabbi Aha referred was not a metaphor or symbol, but an actual piece of furniture (which no doubt had great symbolic meaning for the faithful) found in synagogues. (This is not to claim, however, that the seats of Moses archaeologists have uncovered necessarily date to the time of Jesus.)

The discovery of literal stone seats of Moses coheres at additional points with Jesus' criticism of the scribes and Pharisees in Matthew 23, in which reference is made to their preaching (cf. v. 3), binding "heavy burdens" and laying them on "people's shoulders" (v. 4), desiring the "best seats in the synagogues" (v. 6), and being called "rabbi" (v. 7). The very best seat in the synagogue, of course, would be the "seat of Moses." The "heavy burdens," to which Jesus makes reference, are the legal (*halakic*) rulings and requirements that the scribes and Pharisees enjoin upon the faithful. Saying that these legal rulings are laid on "people's shoulders" probably presupposes the image of the student who "takes upon himself the yoke of Torah." For example, Rabbi Nehunya ben Haqqaneh is remembered to have said, "From him who accepts upon himself the yoke of Torah do they remove the yoke of the state and the yoke of hard labor. And upon him who removes from himself the yoke of the Torah do they lay the yoke of the state and the yoke of hard labor" (*m. 'Abot* 3:5; cf. *m. Ber.* 2:2, where there is reference to the "yoke of the kingdom of heaven"). Finally, Jesus' critical reference to those who like being called "rabbi," a term of honor not ordination in pre-70 C.E. Israel, coheres with a synagogue setting.

The seats of Moses discovered at Hammath-Tiberias and Chorazin may also clarify a detail in the Lukan narrative of Jesus' preaching in the synagogue at Nazareth, where we are told that he "stood up to read" from Scripture and then "sat down" to begin his teaching (Luke 4:16, 20). In all probability it was on the "seat of Moses" in the synagogue in his hometown that Jesus sat as he proclaimed his understanding of God's rule (for further discussion, see Finegan 1969, 58; Sukenik 1934a, 57–61; and Renov 1955–56, who argues against the hypothesis that the "Seat of Moses" was only a reading stand).

The Pilate Inscription – 1961

In 1960, Roman scholar A. H. M. Jones published an essay, in which he argued that the rank of Pontius Pilate, governor of Judea, was praefectus, not procurator (Jones 1960). Jones's conclusion stands in tension with Tacitus, who writing in the early second century C.E. explained: "Christus . . . suffered the death penalty during the reign of Tiberius, by sentence of the procurator [*per procuratorem*] Pontius Pilate" (*Annals* 15.44). The following year the Pilate inscription of Caesarea Maritima was unearthed and published by Antonio Frova (1961, 424 + fig. 3). Jones was vindicated; the rank of Pilate was indeed that of a prefect. It is rare thing that a scholarly hypothesis receives such speedy and incontrovertible confirmation.

The left hand side of the inscription has been chipped away, probably to make the stone fit better in its secondary usage to repair a landing for a set of steps leading into the theatre at Caesarea Maritima. Fortunately, the inscription side of the stone was placed face down, thus protecting what remained of the inscription. It reads:

[ ]S TIBERIÉVM
[ ]TIVS PILATVS
[ ]ECTVS IVDA[EA]E
[ ]É[ ]

Restoration of the partially preserved words in the second and third lines was not difficult:

[PON]TIVS PILATVS
[PRAEF]ECTVS IVDA[EA]E

Restoration of the first and fourth lines has been far more difficult. Frova (1961) suggested DÉDIT ("has given") for the fourth line and CAESARIENS (an abbreviation for CAESARIENIBUS—"to the [people] of Caesarea"). Accordingly, the inscription may have originally read: "To the people of Caesarea Pontius Pilate, Prefect of Judea, has given the Tiberieum." Jack Finegan (1969, 80) understands the Tiberieum as a temple dedicated to emperor Tiberius (ruled 14–37 C.E.). Finegan (1969, 77, 80) points to the example of the Hadrianeion inscription, also found at Caesarea Maritima, which apparently dedicated a temple in honor of the emperor Hadrian (rule 117–138 C.E.).

Several other restorations of the first line have been offered (Betz 1982; Boffo 1994, 217–33; Brusa Gerra 1966, 217–20; Gatti 1981; Lémonon 1981, 23–32; Lifshitz 1963a; Prandi 1981; Rinaldi 1962; Ringel 1975, 98–99; Solin 1970, 108–10; di Stefano Manzella 1997; Vardaman 1962; Volkmann 1968; Weber 1971). Géza Alföldy (1999) has recently suggested REFÉCIT ("has restored") in the fourth line and NAUTIS ("the seamen's") in the first line (for archaeological reports concerning the harbor of Caesarea Maritima, see Raban and Linder 1978; Hohlfelder 1982, 1983; Vann 1983; the harbor is described in Josephus, *J.W.* 1.21.5–7 §408–14; *Ant.* 15.9.6 §331–41). Given Pilate's participation in the refurbishing of the harbor of Caesarea Maritima, Alföldy plausibly speculates that the Tiberieum was a building related in some way to the harbor, perhaps a lighthouse. Thus, it is the Seamen's Tiberieum that Pontius Pilate, Prefect of Judea, has restored. Ongoing archaeological work at Caesarea Maritima may further clarify the governor's involvement in the updating and expansion of the harbor that took place during his administration (Evans 2000b).

The greater appreciation of Pilate's building activities in Caesarea may shed light on his relationship to the Jewish powerbrokers in Jerusalem. The New Testament Gospels' portrait of a governor who arrives in Jerusalem for the Passover feast and acquiesces to requests of the ruling priests (viz. that Jesus of Nazareth be executed and Bar Abbas the rebel be released) is consistent with the possible implications of the Maritima inscription (viz. that the Roman prefect was occupied with other, far more important matters). Consistent too with this portrait is the fact that Pilate served alongside Caiaphas the high priest for the entire tenure of his office (a tenure that probably began in 19 C.E., not 25 or 26, as is commonly supposed; cf. Schwartz 1992, 395–401). Pilate assumed office about one year after Caiaphas was appointed high priest. The two held office until both were removed in early 37, in the aftermath of the Samaritan incident in late 36 (cf. Josephus, *Ant.* 18.4.1 §85–87). Unlike his predecessor Valerius Gratus, who appointed a new high priest every year (according to Josephus, *Ant.* 18.2.2 §33–35), Pilate appears to have been content with Jewish leadership. It has been pointed out that in none of the incidents, in which Pilate clashed with the Jewish people, was the governor at odds with the ruling priests. This important point has been underscored by Richard Horsley and John Hanson (1988, 38–39).

Brian McGing (1991) finds the Gospels' portrait of a cautious, opportunistic Pilate wholly credible. This both explains his lengthy tenure, the lack of conflict with the Jewish leaders, the fact that Pilate did not appoint a single high priest, and finally was removed from office, in all probability for acting uncritically and incautiously according to the wishes of Caiaphas in the Samaritan affair. It seems clear that the Roman governors of Judea and Samaria were guided by the counsel of the ruling priests, who would have explained the significance of the actions of men like Theudas and the anonymous Jew from Egypt. This would explain why the governors reacted the way they did. In all probability Caiaphas urged Pilate to quash Samaritan hopes to rebuild the temple at Mount Gerizim, not because such a program would have fomented sedition (with which Rome would have been very concerned), but because the Jewish high priest was not about to allow a rival temple to be rebuilt and a rival priesthood to be reestablished. Thus, Caiaphas' professional jealousies may have clouded his better political judgment.

The Priestly Courses Inscription – 1962

Excavations at Caesarea Maritima uncovered in the vicinity of the ruins of a synagogue (third century C.E.?) three fragments of a dark marble slab inscribed with Hebrew. Comparison with 1 Chronicles 24:7-19, which lists the twenty-four priestly courses, aids in restoring this formulaic and repetitive text. Fragment A, measuring 15 cm x 12 cm (and 2.4 cm thick), has gained special attention owing to the probable appearance of the name of the town Nazareth (נצרת) in line 2. In line 4 of this fragment we are also able to restore [מ]גדל, perhaps referring to Magdal.

The three fragments may be joined and the entire inscription restored (as in Avi-Yonah 1962, 138 fig. 1). The four lines of fragment A, which are partially supported by the other two fragments, read as follows (Avi-Yonah 1962, 139):

[מש]מר שב[ע עשרה חזיר מ]מליח
מ[שמר שמונה עשרה הפצץ]נצרת
מש[מר תשע עשרה פתחיה]אכלה [ערב
מש[מר עשרים יחזקאל מ]גדל[נוניא

The seventeenth course (is) Hezir of Mamliah
The eighteenth course (is) Happizzez of Nazareth
The nineteenth course (is) Pethahiah Akhlah of Arab
The twentieth course (is) Jehezkel of Migdal Nunaiya

One may compare 1 Chronicles 24:15-16: ". . . the seventeenth to Hezir, the eighteenth to Happizzez, the nineteenth to Pethahiah, the twentieth to Jehezkel . . ." (see also 4Q325 frag. 2).

It is surmised that after the destruction of Jerusalem in 70 C.E. the priestly courses were identified not only by name but also by locale. The priestly course Happizzez evidently took up residence in Nazareth, while the priestly course Jehezkel (so the RSV; but the name may also be vocalized as Ezekiel) took up residence in Migdal (or Magdala). This could be the city, on the western-most shore of the Sea of Galilee, from which Mary Magdalene (i.e., "Mary the Magdalene [person]") came (as Vardaman 1964 thinks could be the case; cf. Mark 15:40: Μαρία ἡ Μαγδαληνή). What is interesting is that the reference to Nazareth in this inscription is the earliest non-Christian example that has come to light (for further discussion, see Avi-Yonah 1962, 1964).

In the New Testament Nazareth is spelled variously Ναζαρέτ, Ναζαρά, and Ναζαρέθ, with all three forms attested in the Matthean Gospel (2:23; 4:13; 21:11). The first and third forms represent the closest approximations of the pronunciation of נצרת, with the first more exactly matching the spelling and the third more exactly matching the pronunciation.

King Herod Ostraca from Masada – 1963–1965

In 42/41 B.C.E. Mark Antony appointed Herod and his brother Phasael as tetrarchs (τετράρχαι) of Judea (Josephus, *J.W.* 1.12.5 §244; cf. 1.14.4 §282). Recognizing Herod's skill and loyalty, Antony persuaded the Roman Senate to make Herod "king of the Jews" (βασιλέα καθιστᾶν Ἰουδαίων; cf. *J.W.* 1.14.4 §283; *Ant.* 14.1.3 §9; 15.10.5 §373; 15.11.4 §409; 16.9.3 §291; 16.10.2 §311). The title was confirmed by Augustus, after Antony's defeat at Actium (cf. *J.W.* 1.20.2 §391–92). Following Herod's death, whom Josephus three times calls "Herod the Great" (Ἡρώδης ὁ μέγαλος; cf. *Ant.* 18.5.4 §130, §133, §136), his three surviving sons failed in their respective bids to succeed their father as king. Archelaus was appointed "ethnarch" (ἐθνάρχης) over one half of Herod's kingdom, that is, Judea and Samaria (cf. Josephus, *J.W.* 2.6.3 §93; *Ant.* 17.11.4 §317). Antipas was appointed tetrarch over Galilee and Berea (*J.W.* 2.6.3 §94–95; *Ant.* 17.8.1 §188), while Philip was appointed tetrarch over Trachonitis and Gaulanitis (*J.W.* 2.6.3 §94–95; 1.33.8 §668; *Ant.* 18.4.6 §106).

Josephus refers to some of Herod's predecessors as "king of the Jews." These include David (cf. *Ant.* 7.4.1 §72: ὁ τῶν Ἰουδαίων βασιλεύς; *J.W.* 6.10.1 §439: ὁ τῶν Ἰουδαίων βασιλεὺς Δαυίδης), Jeconiah (cf. *J.W.* 6.2.1 §103: βασιλεύς Ἰουδαίων Ἰεχονίας), and Hasmoneans Alexander Jannaeus (*J.W.* 7.6.2 §171: βασιλεύς Ἰουδαίων Ἀλέξανδρος; *Ant.* 14.3.1 §36: Ἀλέξανδρος τοῦ τῶν Ἰουδαίων βασιλέως) and Antigonus (*Ant.* 17.5.2 §92: Ἀντιγόνῳ . . . Ἰουδαίων βεβασιλευκότι). It is probable that this language reflects later Roman terminology, which Josephus has applied to various Jewish kings that preceded Herod the Great.

In the Infancy Narratives Herod the Great is called "Herod the king" (ὁ βασιλεὺς Ἡρῴδης; cf. Matt 2:1, 3, 9; Luke 1:5: ἐν ταῖς ἡμέραις Ἡρῴδου βασιλέως τῆς Ἰουδαίας). The Gospel of Mark also suggests, however, that sometimes Herod's sons were referred to as "king," or at least Antipas (cf. Mark 6:14, 22, 25-27), and probably only informally. The official Roman title, "king of the Jews," appears once in the New Testament Gospels, but not in reference to Herod himself (cf. Matt 2:2: "Where is he who has been born king of the Jews [βασιλεὺς τῶν Ἰουδαίων]?").

Greco-Roman writers refer to Herod the king: "Later a certain Herod, a descendant of his and a native of the country, who slinked into the priesthood [sic!], was so superior to his predecessors, particularly in his intercourse with the Romans and in his administration of affairs of state, that he received the title of king [βασιλεύς], being given that authority first by Antony and later by Augustus Caesar" (Strabo of Amaseia, *Geographica* 16.2.46); and to the division of his kingdom among his sons: "Antony gave the kingdom [*regnum*] to Herod, and Augustus, after his victory, increased his territory. After Herod's death, a certain Simon assumed the name of king [*regium*] without waiting for Caesar's decision. He, however, was put to death by Quintillius Varus, governor of Syria; the Jews were repressed; and the kingdom was divided into three parts [*tripertito rexere*] and given to Herod's sons" (Tacitus, *Historiae* 5.9.2). Similarly, Eusebius the Church historian says: "Antipater was assassinated from envy of his great good fortune, and succeeded by a son Herod, who later was appointed by Antony and by decree of the august Senate to be king of the Jews [τῶν Ἰουδαίων ἐκρίθη βασιλεύειν]" (*Eccl. Hist.* 1.7.12).

Not only does King Herod's name appear in Greco-Roman literature, his name appears inscribed on stone. In Athens an inscription in honor of Herod has been found: βασιλέα Ἡρώδην Φιλορώμαιον (*OGIS* no. 414 = *IG* no. 3440): "King Herod, friend of Rome." And on a weight found in Palestine we find inscribed: ε[(τους) λβ βασ(ιλέως) Ἡρ(ώδου) εὐ(σεβοῦ) φιλοκ(αισάρου) (cf. *DTBMT* no. 228): "year 32 of pious King Herod, friend of Caesar."

Elsewhere in Palestine coins minted by Herod have been found, bearing legends that read ΗΡΩΔΟΥ ΒΑΣΙΛΕΩΣ ("of King Herod") and ΗΡΩΔΗΣ ΒΑΣΙΛΕΥΣ ("King Herod") exhibiting various emblems, some unmistakably Roman (such as an eagle; cf. Meyshan 1959; Meshorer 1967, 64–68; for reference to Herod's mounting a Roman eagle over the temple gate, see Josephus, *Ant.* 17.6.2 §149–54; *J.W.* 1.33.2 §648–50).

During the excavation of Masada (1963–1965) Yigael Yadin's team uncovered hundreds of ostraca (mostly fragments of jars), on which had been inked or inscribed numerous Jewish names, including some thirteen wine-amphorae bearing the Latin name and title *Regi Herodi Iudaico* ("for Herod, king of the Jews") (cf. Mas nos. 804–10, 812–13, and 815–16), which have been dated to 19 B.C.E., and were imported from Italy (cf. Josephus, *Ant.* 15.7.4 §233, where we are told that in Herod's employ was an οἰνοχόος, or "wine-steward"; for more on Herod's wine amphorae, see Cotton and Geiger 1989).

On the Latin form of Herod's name and title, one finds the more precise form *Herodes rex Iudaeorum* ("Herod, king of the Jews") in fifth-century Macrobius (cf. *Saturnalia* 2.4.11), well known for reporting the famous remark of Augustus, namely, "I would rather be Herod's pig than his son." (The remark was probably originally uttered in Greek, playing on the words ὗς ["pig"] and υἱός ["son"].)

The significance of this literary, as well as inscriptional, evidence is that it clarifies the meaning of the *titulus*, stating the *causa poenae* ("reason for punishment"), placed over or near Jesus' cross (Mark 15:26): καὶ ἦν ἡ ἐπιγραφὴ τῆς αἰτίας αὐτοῦ ἐπιγεγραμμένη· ὁ βασιλεὺς τῶν Ἰουδαίων ("and the inscription of the charge against him read, 'The King of the Jews'"). The epithet, "king of the Jews," is Roman and was only worn (at least legitimately in the eyes of the Roman Empire) by Herod the Great (even if Josephus later applies it to previous Jewish rulers). This epithet is not a piece of Christian confession, for Christians called Jesus "Messiah," "LORD," "Savior," and "Son of God." Nor is the epithet authentically Jewish; rather, the preferred

Jewish epithets are "Messiah" (as in Mark 8:29; John 1:41; 12:34; *2 Bar.* 29:3; and often in rabbinic literature and in some of the older targumic literature), "king of Israel" (as in Mark 15:32; *Pss. Sol.* 17:42) and "son of David" (as in Mark 10:47, 48; 12:35). In the later targumic literature the epithets "Messiah" and "king of Israel" are combined as "King Messiah" (e.g., in Targum Ps.-Jonathan and the Fragment Targum). Governor Pontius Pilate's form of the question, "Are you the king of the Jews?" (Mark 15:2), authentically reflects the official language of Rome.

Chapter 3

Burial Inscriptions—Themes

Burial inscriptions serve a variety of purposes. Their principal purpose is simply to identify the person whose remains lie within the tomb (or ossuary). Family relations are sometimes given, as in the most common formula "so-and-so, son of somebody." Sometimes the inscriptions are far more elaborate, identifying parents, brothers, sisters, children, and other relatives. The deceased is sometimes identified by referring to his vocation or title of office. Many times the age of the deceased is given.

Burial inscriptions often tell us much about social, political, and economic standing in society, as well as personal hopes and fears, and religious and philosophical beliefs. These features will be surveyed briefly.

Titles and Rank

In the New Testament Gospels we find references to priests (Mark 1:44: "Show yourself to the priest"), ruling priests (Mark 8:31; 11:18), rabbis (Matt 23:7-8; John 1:38), synagogue rulers (Mark 5:22; Luke 13:14), and elders (Mark 8:31; 11:27). All of these titles and identifications of rank are attested in Greek and Hebrew/Aramaic inscriptions, many of them on ossuaries. Most titles and occupations are in reference to men, though there are exceptions (Peleg 2002).

Priest (כהן / ἱερεύς) *and ruling priest* (כהן הגדול / ἀρχιερεύς)

In Jerusalem ossuaries have been found that identify priests (Hachlili 2000, 100). We have "Pinhas and 'Aqaviah the priests" (*CIJ* no. 1221), "Shelomzion, daughter of Simeon the priest" (*CIJ* no. 1317), "the son of Simeon the priest" (*CIJ* no. 1411), "Menahem of the sons of Yakim the priest" (Bagatti and Milik 1958, no. 83), "So'am, son of Menahem, priest" (Dalman 1914, 136), "Yehohanah, daughter of Yehohanan, son of Theophilus the high priest" (Barag and Flusser 1986, 39; Rahmani 1994a, no. 871), and "of Megiste the priestess" (Ilan 1991–1992, 157–58). On a jar found at Masada we have "A[nani]as the high priest, 'Aqaviah his son" (Mas no. 461), and at Beth She'arim, from a later period, we have "Yehudah the priest" (Schwabe and Lifshitz 1974, no. 181), "the priests" (Schwabe and Lifshitz 1974, no. 49), and, in Hebrew, "This place belongs to priests" (Mazar 1973, no. 67).

Rabbi (רבי / ῥαββί)

Shaye Cohen (1981–1982) has catalogued some fifty-eight inscriptions, in which the title or epithet "rabbi" and variants appear. Most of these inscriptions have been found in Israel, though a few are from the Diaspora. Cohen (1981–1982, 12, 16) agrees with Goodenough's conclusion (1953a, 90, 241) that the title "rabbi" in late antiquity referred to prominent individuals, not to ordained clerics. In fact, Cohen finds little that links the rabbis of the inscriptions to the synagogues (and we find no solid evidence in the New Testament Gospels for such a link). He further makes the interesting observation that almost no one—perhaps none—of the epigraphical rabbis can with confidence be identified with the rabbinic authorities who produced the rabbinic literature. The evidence argues strongly against those who have claimed that the use of "rabbi" (e.g., when people address Jesus) in the Gospels is anachronistic, because rabbinic ordination did not begin until some time after 70 C.E. The inscriptions, some of which predate 70 C.E., make it clear that prominent individuals were in fact addressed in this manner.

Synagogue ruler (ארכון or ראש הכנסת / ἀρχισυνάγωγος)

We have already reviewed the Greek Theodotos synagogue inscription (see pp. 37–43 above), where Theodotus, son of Vettenus, identifies himself as priest and synagogue ruler (*CIJ* no. 1404). There are other inscriptions of this kind, e.g., from the Greek island Aegina: "I, Theodorus, the synagogue ruler, who administrated four years, built this synagogue from its foundations . . ." (Sukenik 1934a, 44; cf. Luke 7:5 "he loves our nation, and he built us our synagogue"); from Italy: "Tomb of Joseph, a synagogue ruler, son of Joseph, a synagogue ruler" (*CIJ* no. 584; Kant 1987, 679); from Caesarea, but from a later period: "Beryllos, synagogue ruler and administrator, the son of Justus, made the mosaic work of the triclinium of his own means" (Lifshitz 1967, 51; Finegan 1969, 78); from fourth-century Beth She'arim of Galilee: "Here lies Eusebius the most illustrious, synagogue ruler of the people of Beirut" (Schwabe and Lifshitz 1974, no. 164), "Jacob from Caesarea, synagogue ruler of Pamphylia" (Schwabe and Lifshitz 1974, no. 203), and "Yose the synagogue ruler from Sidon" (Schwabe and Lifshitz 1974, no. 221); and others (e.g., *CIJ* nos. 722 and 803; cf. *TDNT* 7:846). These inscriptions are in Greek. The Hebrew ארכון is itself a Greek loanword (from ἄρχων).

Sage (חכם or משכיל / σόφος)

How early "sage" or "wise man" functioned as a title is difficult to determine. In the Mishnah (early third century C.E.) the "sages" are ubiquitous (e.g., *m. Ber.* 1:1 et passim). In the second century B.C.E. Sirach a man who is σόφος is simply "wise" and not a designation. But the titular function seems to have currency in the first century, as we see in Paul's rhetorical questions: "Where is the wise man [σόφος]? Where is the scribe? Where is the debater of this age? Has not God made foolish the wisdom of the world?" (1 Cor 1:20). Being linked with "scribe" and "debater" suggests that σόφος may mean "sage" and not simply a man who is wise. The title, at least in Jewish circles, may have gained in popularity thanks to the book of Daniel. For "sage" at Qumran, employing משכיל, see CD 12:21; 13:2; 1QS 3:13; 9:12; 1QSb 1:1; 3:22; 5:20). For examples employing חכם, see CD 6:3; 1QH 9:35; 4Q249 1 iii 6; 4Q432 2 2. Jesus may have alluded to the "wise" as a class (cf. Matt 23:34: "I send you prophets and wise men and scribes"; perhaps also Matt 11:25 = Luke 10:21: "I thank thee, Father, Lord of heaven and earth, that thou hast hidden these things from the wise and understanding and revealed them to babes").

Elder (סבא or הזקן / πρεσβύτερος)

Prominent, respected men were sometimes called "elder" (which carries over into the Christian Church; cf. Acts 11:30; 15:2; 1 Tim 5:17; Yamauchi 2000). An Aramaic inscription from the Tomb of Jason in Rehov, Jerusalem, reads: "Make a powerful lament for Jason . . . who has built for yourself a tomb, Elder [סבא], rest in peace!" (Avigad 1967, 102–5). We find inscribed on wall of a tomb in the Kidron Valley: "Simeon the elder [הזקן]" (Hachlili 2000, 105); and from Talpiot, Jerusalem: "Simeon, son of the elder [בר סבא]" (Sukenik 1947, 357;

Hachlili 2000, 104–5; see comment on Barsabbas in chapter 4 below). Also from Beth She'arim we have "The tomb of Aidesios, chief of the elders [γερουσιάρχου], from Antioch" (Schwabe and Lifshitz 1974, no. 141). Though not exactly titles, sectarian affiliations also serve to identify people. Josephus refers to "Menahem the Essene" (*Ant.* 15.10.5 §373–79; Menahem foretold that someday Herod would be "king of the Jews") and "Zadok the Pharisee" (*Ant.* 18.1.1 §4; Zadok was an ally of Judas of Gamala).

Professions and Trades

Several professions and trades are mentioned in ossuary inscriptions. Some, such as scribe and farmer, are mentioned in the New Testament. Again, the ossuaries shed light on living conditions in Jewish late antiquity.

Scribe (סופר / γραμματεύς)

On ossuaries we have "Yehudah the scribe" (*CIJ* no. 1308) and, from Jerusalem, "Yehudah, son of Eleazar the scribe" (Klein 1920, no. 10) and "Joseph, son of Hananya the scribe" (Sussman 1994, 228; Rahmani 1994a, no. 893). From Masada we have an ostracon that reads "Eleazar, son of the scribe" (Mas no. 667), but its authenticity is doubted. In the New Testament Gospels scribes are usually seen in conflict with Jesus. In one polemical context, Jesus' denunciation sheds some light on scribal activities, or at least on public perceptions of them: "Beware of the scribes, who like to go about in long robes, and to have salutations in the market places and the best seats in the synagogues and the places of honor at feasts, who devour widows' houses and for a pretense make long prayers" (Mark 12:38-40). Jesus sometimes encounters scribes in synagogue settings (e.g., Luke 6:6-11).

Builder, artisan, and other professions

Among the ossuaries we find the inscriptions "Simon, builder of the temple" and "Nicanor of Alexandria, who built the doors" (see below in chapter 5). From the Mount of Olives we have an ossuary inscription that reads "Yehoni the artisan (or smith)" (Bagatti and Milik 1958, no. 12). On ostraca from Masada we have "the butcher" (Mas no. 512), "the hunter" (Mas no. 440), and "Judah, son of the druggist" (Mas no. 471). On an ossuary from Giv'at ha-Mivtar, Jerusalem, we have

"Jonathan the potter" (Naveh 1970, 35). From Abu Tor, Jerusalem, we have a curious ossuary inscription that seems to read "the captive physician" (Rahmani 1994a, no. 80). And at Beth She'arim, Galilee, we find inscriptions in memory of a goldsmith, physician, banker, two perfumers, a dyer of cloth, a cloth merchant, and reference to morticians (Schwabe and Lifshitz 1974, nos. 61, 81, 92, 79 and 168, 188, 189, and 202 respectively).

Personal

Some ossuary inscriptions are quite personal, referring to physical defects and disabilities. Others may even convey insults. However, more frequently we find, as we would expect, expressions of honor and endearment.

Defects, disabilities, and insults

On an ossuary from Mount Scopus, Jerusalem, we read "Gaius the midget" (Rahmani 1994a, no. 421). The Hebrew גאיס ננים transliterates the Greek Γαῖος ὁ νᾶνος. From Beth She'arim we have, in Greek, "Rabbi Hanina the midget" (Schwabe and Lifshitz 1974, no. 175; see also *Semahot* 8.7, where there is mention of one "Simeon, son of the midget"; see discussion of James the Small in chapter 4 below). In contrast to these inscriptions, we have the so-called Goliath tomb from Jericho, where the sobriquet "Goliath" refers to the great stature of some of the members of this family (as confirmed by the skeletal remains; cf. Hachlili 1979, 53–55). Similarly, Josephus refers to one "Eleazar, who on account of his size was called 'the giant'" (*Ant.* 18.4.5 §103). Other defects and disabilities are mentioned below in chapter 5. Some inscriptions refer to one's faults. On an ossuary from Mount Scopus an inscription refers to the deceased as "the dour" or perhaps "the grump" (Rahmani 1994a, no. 44). The same epithet appears on an ostracon from Masada (Mas no. 432). On an ossuary of uncertain provenance, probably from Jerusalem, we read "Maryam, wife of the cow," probably in reference to her obese husband (Rahmani 1994a, no. 821). From Masada we have an ostracon on which is inked the words "son of Qarzela," probably meaning "son of the round one" (Mas no. 421 line 7), and another ostracon reading "son of Qasa," which may mean "son of the stick" (Mas no. 420 line 6). From Beth She'arim we have the epitaph "of Samuel, son of Germanus the poor" (Schwabe and Lifshitz 1974, no. 206).

Terms of endearment

Far more frequent are epithets that honor or express affection for the deceased. Persons are referred to as "the proselyte" (e.g., *CIJ* nos. 1385 and 1390; Bagatti and Milik 1958, nos. 13, 21, and 31; Ilan 1991–1992, 150–55), or the "Nazirite" (e.g., Avigad 1971, 196–98), or the "scholar" (Avigad 1967, 131), or the "wife of goodness" (Mas no. 400). On a child's ossuary from Jericho, from the Goliath family tomb mentioned above, we find "Yehoezer Aqabia the cinnamon" (Hachlili 1979, 55–57). On an ossuary, probably from Jerusalem, we read "ossuary of Balzama," probably meaning "ossuary of the fragrant one" (Rahmani 1994a, no. 461). Inscribed on the wall of one of the tombs of Beth She'arim we find "The pious ['Οσεία]" and "Here lies Sara, the pious Jewess ['Ιουδέα ὁσία]" (Schwabe and Lifshitz 1974, nos. 157 and 158; cf. nos. 34, 35, 38, 44, 163, and 173). And from the Mount of Olives an ossuary reads "Yehudah the beautiful" (Bagatti and Milik 1958, no. 2). On the attribute the "just," see chapter 5 below.

Philosophical and Religious Themes in non-Jewish Inscriptions

Burial inscriptions sometimes offer hope or advice, either in reference to the deceased, or in reference to the grieving passerby or to the stranger who passes by. Sometimes inscriptions offer warnings, even threats and curses, in order to discourage vandals and grave robbers. Samples of all of these themes are found in Jewish and non-Jewish inscriptions alike (Deissmann 1927; Sandys 1927, 60–81 [Latin only]; Lattimore 1942 [Greek and Latin]; Toynbee 1971; Gordon 1983; Cook 1987; Keppie 1991; Shore 1997).

Pagan Inscriptions

According to Hesychius (Lattimore 1942, 21 n. 1), death (θάνατος) is the "separation of the soul from the body" (χωρισμὸς τῆς ψυχῆς ἀπὸ τοῦ σώματος). Similarly, Iamblichus opines that the soul "goes forth from the body, and upon going forth is separated and scattered" (*apud* Stobaeus, *Eclogae* 1). Some likened the body to a house in which the soul is imprisoned (e.g., Plato, *Cratylus* 400c; *Phaedo* 81d; cf. Toynbee 1971, 33–39). In keeping with these ideas many people in late antiquity hoped for or assumed some sort of life beyond the grave, though in what form it may take there was much doubt. Here is a sample:

EG 21b (= Thucydides 1.63; cf. Lattimore 1942, 31):

Αἰθὴρ μὲν ψυχὰς ὑπεδέξατο, σώ[ματα δὲ χθών.

Air has taken their souls, but earth their bodies.

IG 9.2.641.6 (cf. Lattimore 1942, 32):

ψ]υχὴν αἰθέρι δοὺς σῶμα ἐκάλυψε [κόνει.

The soul given to the air, the body concealed in dust.

EG 288.2–3 (cf. Lattimore 1942, 32):

τὸ δὲ σῶμα καλύπτει
γαῖα, λαβοῦσα γέρας τοῦθ' ὃ δέδωκε πάλαι.

Earth hides your body,
taking back the gift that she gave long ago.

EG 90 (cf. Lattimore 1942, 33):

ὀστέα μὲν καὶ σάρκας ἔχει χθὼν παῖδα τὸν ἡδύν,
ψυχὴ δ' εὐσεβέων οἴχεται εἰς θάλαμον.

Earth keeps the bones and flesh of the dear child,
but his soul has gone to the house of the blessed.

IG 12.7123.5–6 (cf. Lattimore 1942, 35):

μήτηρ μή με δάκρυε· τίς ἡ χάρας; ἀλλὰ σεβάζου·
ἀστὴρ γὰρ γενόμην θεοῖς ἀκρεσπέριος.

Mother, do not weep for me. What is the use? Instead, revere me.
For I have become an evening star, among the gods.

EG 338.1–2 (cf. Lattimore 1942, 36):

Μίκκς οὔνομα μοῦνον ἔχει τάφος, εὐσεβέες δὲ
ψυχὴν καὶ πεδίων τέρμονες Ἠλυσίων.

The tomb keeps only the name of Micca; with the pious
is her soul, even among the Elysian fields.

EG 533 (cf. Shore 1997, 48):

Ὕπνος ἔχει σε, μάκαρ, πολυήρατε δῖε Σαβῖνε,
καὶ ζῇς ὡς ἥρως καὶ νέκυς οὐκ ἐγένου·

> εὕδεις δ' ὡς ἔτι ζῶν ὑπὸ δένδρεσι σοῖς ἐνὶ τύμβοις·
> ψυχαὶ γὰρ ζῶσιν τῶν ἄγαν εὐσεβέων.
>
> Sleep holds you fast, blessed and much loved, noble Sabinus.
> And you live on as a hero and have not become a corpse.
> You sleep as if yet living, beneath the trees among the tombs of your people.
> For the souls of the truly pious live.

CIL 3.293 (cf. Shore 1997, 50):

> T. CISSONIUS Q.F. SER. VET. LEG. V. GALL.
> DUM VIXI, BIBI LIBENTER: BIBITE VOS QUI VIVITIS.
>
> I was T(itus) Cissonius brother of Q(uintus?), veteran of the fifth Gallic Legion.
> While I lived I drank freely. You who still live, drink!

It is interesting to note that in a general sense these expressions—apart from the last one—are coherent with Genesis 2:7: "then the LORD God formed man of dust from the ground, and breathed into his nostrils the breath of life; and man became a living being." Many in the ancient world and the world of late antiquity understood human ontology in dichotomized terms, with the physical reality shed at death and the non-physical (the soul, spirit, ether, and the like) released. What was distinctive to the Jewish people, at least to some groups of the Jewish people, was belief in the resurrection of the body (as in Dan 12:2; Mark 12:18-27; John 5:29; 11:24; but flatly rejected by the Sadducees; cf. Mark 12:18; Josephus, *J.W.* 2.8.14 §165).

According to Josephus, the Essenes believed something similar to the Greek idea of the soul separating from the body and passing into the air, heavenward. His comments are occasioned by mention of the Essenes' courage in the face of death. When captured and tortured by the Romans during the great Jewish rebellion, Josephus says of the Essenes:

> Smiling in their agonies and mildly deriding their tormentors, they cheerfully resigned their souls, confident that they would receive them back again. For it is a fixed belief of theirs that the body is corruptible and its constituent matter impermanent, but that the soul is immortal and imperishable. Emanating from the finest ether, these

> souls become entangled, as it were, in the prison-house of the body, to which all are dragged down by a sort of natural spell; but when once they are released from the bonds of the flesh, then, as though liberated from a long servitude, they rejoice and are borne aloft. Sharing the belief of the sons of Greece, they maintain that for virtuous souls there is reserved an abode beyond the ocean . . . The Greeks, I imagine, had the same conception when they set apart the isles of the blessed for their brave men. . . . (*J.W.* 2.8.10–11 §153–56).

Some scholars think Josephus is either misinformed or being disingenuous. Although on the basis of what has survived of the Essene library it does not appear that the idea of the resurrection of the dead was emphasized, it is explicitly expressed in at least one writing from Qumran. When the Messiah appears, "whom heaven and earth will obey," the infirm will be healed and "the dead he will make alive" (4Q521 2+4 ii 12). In keeping with his apologetical interests, Josephus is probably presenting the beliefs of the Essenes in philosophical terms that his Roman readers will appreciate. Although their beliefs have been misrepresented to some extent, the circulation of a pseudepigraphal book like the *History of the Rechabites*, parts of which may have been originally Jewish, with its interest in the "isle of the Blessed Ones," cautions against the conclusion that Josephus' description is wholly misleading.

Unlike devout Jews who rarely depicted the human form (because of Exod 20:4: "You shall not make for yourself a graven image, or any likeness of anything that is in heaven above, or that is in the earth beneath, or that is in the water under the earth"), affluent Greeks and Romans sometimes commissioned sculpted reliefs portraying the deceased seated, bidding loved ones farewell, or busts below which the deceased's life and virtues are summarized, perhaps with a word of advice for the passerby. Here are a few:

> *CIG* 3256 (cf. Cook 1987, 26–27), a relief depicting the deceased seated:
>
> > The man (who was) wise in all things and eminent among the citizens, reaching the end of a long life, the black bosom of gloomy Hades welcomed (him) and laid (him) on the hallowed couch of the pious. His son, together with his wedded wife, set up this memorial of (one who) perished along a rough path.

Stranger, having bidden farewell to Democles, (son) of Democles, may you travel with safe footsteps.

IG 14.2131 (cf. Cook 1987, 26, 28), a relief depicting the deceased, with a somewhat skeletal, cadaverous appearance, lying on his back:

Who can say, having looked at a fleshless corpse, whether it was Hylas or Thersites, passerby?

SEG 12.561 (cf. Cook 1987, 26–27), a marble bust:

Recognize Rhoummas when you look at him in a portrait carved in marble, a man who performed great (deeds of) faith through prayer; dying he did not indeed die, for he came by a good repute.

CIL 6.37075 = *ILS* 8964; cf. Gordon 1983, 106–7):

POTITUS VALERIUS, MARCI FILIUS . . . MESSALLA . . . TRIB[UNUS] MILIT[UM], Q[UAESTOR], PR[AETOR] URB[ANUS], C[ONSUL], PROCO[NSUL] PROVINC[IAE] ASIAE BIS, LEG[ATUS] IMP[ERATORIS] CAESARIS AUGUSTI IN SYRIA.

Potitus Valerius Messalla, son of Marcus . . . military tribune, quaestor, urban praetor, consul, proconsul of the province of Asia twice, legate of the Emperor Augustus in Syria.

Christian Inscriptions

Christian epitaphs often refer to belief in the resurrection and/or faith in Christ. However, traces of pre-Christian conventions often remain. Here are a few examples:

CIG no. 9439 (cf. Lattimore 1942, 306):

τοὶς γλυκυτάτοις γονεῦσιν ἕως ἀναστάσεως

To my sweet parents, until their resurrection.

CIG no. 9687 (cf. Lattimore 1942, 302):

Discreet Maritima, you have not left the sweet light. For you have with you Christ [fish symbol, instead of actual name Christ] who is immortal through all things. For it is ever piety that leads you on.

IG 14.134 (cf. Lattimore 1942, 302):

ψυχὴ χαίρει ἀώνιος.

"The immortal soul rejoices."

EG 726.8–9 (cf. Lattimore 1942, 302):

He has died and lives and looks on the light, which is really imperishable; he lives for the living, and has died for those who are in truth dead.

SEG 6.295.5–6 (cf. Lattimore 1942, 302):

ψυχὴ δ' αὐτοῖο ἵν' ἀθάνατος Θεὸς ἔστιν·
'Αβραμίοις κόλποις ἀναπαύετε ὡς μακάρων τις.

His soul is where immortal God is.
He rests in Abraham's bosom, like one of the blessed ones.

RGM 489 (cf. Shore 1997, 24):

Here lies Artemia, a child bright and sweet, fair visage, and most charming in her speech. having lived four years, in her fifth year she departed to Christ, an innocent who passed over without warning into the heavenly kingdom [*ad caelestia regna transivit*].

In some Christian epitaphs the pagan themes are more clearly pronounced. This is especially seen in warnings:

CIG no. 9292 (cf. Lattimore 1942, 307);

And the angels of God, to whom on this day all souls are humbled to suppliance, that He may avenge this innocent blood, and that with all speed.

IG 7.583.4–5 (cf. Lattimore 1942, 308):

Lest the dreaded fiery judgment of Gehenna [πυρόεσσα κρίσις δεινήεσσα Γεέννης] overtake you, and great agony of the soul from cold Tartarus.

Lattimore 1942, 308:

May he find no pity in any god; may Satan [Σατανᾶς] come into their house and destroy them utterly.

Lattimore 1942, 308:

ἐχέτω τὴν μερίδα τοῦ Ἰούδα τοῦ προδότου.

May he share the lot of Judas the betrayer.

Lattimore 1942, 308:

He shall be answerable to God.

Philosophical and Religious Themes in Jewish Inscriptions

Consolation, praise, and warnings against violation of sepulture are the most common themes in Jewish burial inscriptions.

Warnings against theft and violation is somewhat milder in Jewish sepulture, though threats, even curses are sometimes found. We begin with a few warnings in Hebrew and Aramaic. On an ossuary from Jerusalem we read (on the side), "father Dostas," and (on the lid), "Dostas, our father, and not to be opened" (Sukenik 1928; Yellin 1929; Rahmani 1994a, no. 70). More ominous are the warnings found in the necropolis of Beth She'arim in Galilee: "Anyone who shall open this burial upon him who is inside it shall die of an evil end" (Avigad 1976, no. 1); "He who is buried here is Simeon, son of Yohanan; and on oath whoever shall open upon him shall died of an evil end" (Avigad 1976, no. 2; cf. no. 3, which is only partially preserved: "Anyone who shall open . . ."). Here are a few Greek examples: "Nobody shall open, in accordance with the divine and secular law" (Schwabe and Lifshitz 1974, no. 134); "Anyone who changes this lady's place, He who promised to make alive the dead [ζωποιῆσε τοὺς νεκρούς] will Himself judge (him)" (Schwabe and Lifshitz 1974, no. 162; ζωποιῆσε = ζωποιήσει); and "I, Hesychios, lie here with my wife. May anyone who dares to open (the grave) above us not have a portion in eternal life [μέρος εἰς τὸν [βίον] ἀόνιο[ν]" (Schwabe and Lifshitz 1974, no. 12). We should recall the Uzziah plaque mentioned above. Implicit in the "qorban" ossuary inscription (see pp. 96–98 below) is a warning not to open.

Outside of the land of Israel, Jewish warnings against violation of sepulture sometimes become more threatening (Strubbe 1994). Several epitaphs, all of them written in Greek, threaten fines and divine judgment: "he will have to reckon with the judgment (of God)"; "Whoever will do something against these (prescriptions) will undergo the judgment with God"; "But the man who will attempt to place another (corpse) in it (the tomb) will receive eternal scourging from the immortal God"; "if one is not deterred by these curses, may the sickle of curse enter into their houses and leave no one behind"; "if anyone will bury another corpse . . . he will receive the curses that are written in Deuteronomy"; the tomb robber "will be accursed and may as many curses as are written in Deuteronomy befall him and his children and his descendants and his whole family"; "whoever will disturb (the tomb), may an iron broom mangle his house and (the same) for the man who has given advice (to violate the tomb)"; and finally, "whoever breaks open (this tomb) and puts in another corpse, or purchases the tomb and defiles the inscription, the wrath of God will destroy his whole family" (Strubbe 1994, 106–25, with some adaptation).

Returning to the land of Israel, many inscriptions contain dolorous elements: ". . . having gone to Hades, I, Justus, lie here . . ." (Schwabe and Lifshitz 1974, no. 127), including the common exclamation of woe: "Woe [חבל]!" (Mazar 1973, nos. 67, 130, and 132; Schwabe and Lifshitz 1974, nos. 117 and 119). Consider also this one, reinterpreted by Frank Cross (1983) to read: "No man can go up from the grave."

The wish for "peace" (שלום) is quite common in Jewish epitaphs (usually written in Hebrew, even when the inscription itself is in Greek or Latin; e.g., Schwabe and Lifshitz 1974, no. 203): "Rabbi Joshua, son of Rabbi Hillel, son of Ation. (May his) resting place be in peace" (Avigad 1976, no. 16).

We find hope for resurrection, eternal life, or heaven expressed in some Jewish epitaphs: "This is the grave of dear father Yehudah known as Gurk. May his resting place be with the righteous, his resurrection [עמידתו] with the worthy" (Avigad 1976, no. 15); "May your portion be good, my lord father and my lady mother, and may your soul(s) be bound (in the bond) of immortal life [ἀθανάτου βίου]" (Schwabe and Lifshitz 1974, no. 130); "Good luck in your resurrection [εὐτυχῶς τῇ ὑμῶν ἀναστάσι]!" (Schwabe and Lifshitz 1974, no. 194); and "This tomb contains the dwindling remains of noble Karteria . . . (your daughter) erected this monument so that even after the end of life's term you may both enjoy again new indestructible riches" (Schwabe and Lifshitz 1974, no. 183). One is reminded of Jesus' advice to his followers: "Lay up for yourselves treasures in heaven, where neither moth nor rust consumes and where thieves do not break in and steal" (Matt 6:20).

Some expressions of hope seem fainter: "Be of good courage [θάρσι], lady Calliope from Byblos; no one is immortal [ἀθάνατος]" (Schwabe and Lifshitz 1974, no. 136; cf. nos. 59, 127, 187, and 193); "May your lot be good [εὐμοίρει], Aristeas!" (Schwabe and Lifshitz 1974, nos. 171 and 173; cf. nos. 52, 57, 69, and 124); "Lady Esther, Esther, have courage [θάρσι], Esther" (Schwabe and Lifshitz 1974, no. 39; cf. nos. 40, 41, 43, 87, 88, 89, and 102); "Farewell, Athan, son of Doron" (Schwabe and Lifshitz 1974, no. 90); "Lord, remember your servant" (Schwabe and Lifshitz 1974, no. 184); and "The tomb of Calliope the elder, the freed woman of Procopios, of blessed memory" (Schwabe and Lifshitz 1974, no. 200). For recent studies on afterlife ideas in late antiquity, see Bauckham (1998), Bolt (1998), and Yamauchi (1998). For older studies see Charles (1913), Sellers (1945), and Tromp (1969).

Chapter 4

Burial Inscriptions—Names

One of the great values of burial inscriptions is their contribution to our understanding of what names were current in a given place and time and how these names were understood. But it is not simply formal names that are of interest; nicknames and sobriquets are also of great interest, for they quite often tell us things about the life, health, vocation, and social or legal standing of the deceased.

Nicknames and Sobriquets

Rachel Hachlili and Tal Ilan have assembled many Jewish nicknames and sobriquets. In Ilan's *Lexicon of Jewish Names* we find the nickname "the bean" (האפון; cf. *y. Yoma* 6.3, 43c; Ilan 2002, 445), "the Galilean" (הגלילי; cf. *CIJ* no. 1285, inscribed on an ossuary lid from Bethphage; Ilan 2002, 445; and on Mur 52, a papyrus from Murabba'at; Hachlili 2000, 98; one thinks of the famous second-century rabbi Yose the Galilean), "the wool-dresser" (הגרדיאן; cf. Mas no. 420, on an ostracon from Masada; Ilan 2002, 445), "the robber" (החוטף; cf. *m. Kil.* 3:7; Ilan 2002, 445), "the fugitive" (הנדוד; cf. Mur 74, on an ostracon from Murabba'at; Ilan 2002, 445–56), "the baker" (הנחתם; cf. Mas no. 429, on an ostracon from Masada; Ilan 2002, 446), "the migrant" (הנסען; cf. Mur 74, on an ostracon from Murabba'at; Ilan 2002, 446), "the chief" (הסגן; cf. *m. Sheq*. 8:5; Ilan 2002, 446), "the cake" (cf. העגי; cf. *CIJ* no. 1285, on ossuary lid from Bethphage; Ilan 2002, 446), "the messenger" (הציר; cf. *CIJ* no. 1285, on ossuary lid from Bethphage; Ilan 2002, 447), "the butcher" (הקצב; cf. *m. Ketub.* 2:9; Ilan 2002, 447), "the horn" or "Cyrene" (הקרני; cf. Mas no. 424, on an ostracon from Masada; Ilan 2002, 447), "the murderer" (הרצחן; cf. *Sifre Deut*. §205 [on Deut 21:1]: "originally called 'son of Perisha,' he was then renamed 'son of the murderer'"), "the Shilonite" (השלני, i.e., the man from Shiloh, where the "house of God" once stood [1 Sam 1:24]; cf. Mur 24b, on a papyrus deed, from Murabba'at; Ilan 2002, 447–48), and "the whistler" or "painter" (השרק; cf. *CIJ* no. 1285, on an ossuary lid from Bethphage; Ilan 2002, 448; Hachlili 2000, 86, takes the sobriquet as "painter").

To this interesting list Hachlili adds "Judah the Proselyte" (יהודה הגיור; inscribed on an ossuary from Akeldama; cf. Hachlili 2002, 85), "Nehunia the trench-digger" (נחוניא חופר; *m. Sheq.* 5:1; *t. Sheq.* 2.14; cf. Naveh 1990, 109–11; Hachlili 2000, 86), "Salome the Gali[lean]" (שלומ הגלי[לית]; Mas no. 404, on an ostracon from Masada; cf. Hachlili 2000, 87), "Eleazar called the forceful [῎Αυαραν = עורן]" (as in 1 Macc 2:5; cf. Hachlili 2000, 97), "Jonathan called the digger [῞Απθους = חפש]" (as in 1 Macc 2:5; cf. Hachlili 2000, 97), and Alexander Jannaeus "the Thracian [Θρακίδας]" (as in Josephus, *Ant.* 13.14.2 §383; Thracians were known for their cruelty; cf. Hachlili 2000, 97). For more nicknames, see Goitein (1970).

Names

We cannot, of course, review all Jewish names from the time and place of Jesus, but it is instructive to review the names of his disciples. The number is not exactly twelve, for some of the disciples have the same names (i.e., Simon Peter and Simon the Cananaean; James, son of Zebedee, and James, son of Alphaeus; and perhaps two Judases: Judas Iscariot and Judas, son of James) and there seem to be more than twelve men who at one time or another during the ministry of Jesus were numbered among the "twelve," especially if we take into account the men named in the Gospel of John. Discussion of the name James (or Jacob) will be reserved for chapter 5, when the three names of the James Ossuary (James, Joseph, and Jesus) are considered. We shall also review briefly a few other names in the Gospels and Acts.

Formal apostolic rosters are found in Mark 3:14-19; Matt 10:1-4; Luke 6:13-16; and Acts 1:13. Here are the names of the apostles according to Mark's list:

> Simon whom he surnamed Peter; James the son of Zebedee and John the brother of James, whom he surnamed Boanerges, that is, sons of thunder; Andrew, and Philip, and Bartholomew, and Matthew, and Thomas, and James the son of Alphaeus, and Thaddaeus, and Simon the Cananaean, and Judas Iscariot, who betrayed him.

To this apostolic list we may add the name Nathaniel (John 1:45). We shall review the apostolic names in the order of the Markan list.

Simon whom he surnamed Peter (ἐπέθηκεν ὄνομα τῷ Σίμωνι Πέτρον)

Simon is biblical, deriving from שמעון (*shim'on*, though usually written Simeon; cf. Gen 29:33), the name of one of the patriarchs and a name popular in the Hasmonean period (on popularity of Hasmonean names, see Ilan 1987–1988). Ilan (2002, 218–35) identifies more than 250 Jewish men in late antiquity who bore this name (see also Hölscher 1925, 148–57; Fitzmyer 1963, 105–10). It is sometimes written שמון (*Shimon*) or סמון (*Simon*), probably under the influence of the shorter, simpler Greek transliteration Σίμων (*Simon*), which was also written Συμεών (*Symeon*). The Greek form Simon (Σίμων) occurs in several ossuaries (e.g., Rahmani 1994a, nos. 332 [where the spelling is Σίμον], 794, and 795; Bagatti and Milik 1958, no. 37d).

Greek examples from ossuaries include "Sarah, (daughter) of Simon of Ptolemais" (Rahmani 1994a, no. 99), "Mathia and Simon, brothers, sons of Ya'ir; masters of the tomb" (Rahmani 1994a, no. 560), "(Ossuary) of Simon, age 41" (Rahmani 1994a, no. 778), and "Alexa Mara, mother of Judas Simon, her son" (Rahmani 1994a, no. 868).

The Greek form Συμεών appears many times in the LXX, Josephus (e.g., *J.W.* 4.3.9 §159: "Symeon, son of Gamaliel"; cf. *Vita* 38 §190: "Simon, son of Gamaliel"), and the New Testament (e.g., Luke 2:25; 3:30; Acts 13:1; 15:14; 2 Pet 1:1; Rev 7:7). The shortened Hebrew forms סמון and שמון occur once each (Rahmani 1994a, nos. 200 and 651). The first one is interesting: "Simon, builder of the temple." The temple that Simon helped to build was, of course, the Herodian temple, a project not fully completed until 64 C.E.

The longer, conventional spelling שמעון (*Shim'on*) occurs many times: "Shim'on, son of Zechariah" (Dalman 1914, 135), "Our father, Shim'on the elder, Yehosef his son" (Rahmani 1994a, no. 12), "Yehosef, son of Shim'on" (Rahmani 1994a, no. 16), "Shim'on, son of Alexa" (Rahmani 1994a, no. 18), "Shlamzion, daughter of Shim'on" (Rahmani 1994a, no. 26), "Hoshea, son of Shimu'on" (Rahmani 1994a, no. 38, note the spelling variation), "Shim'on, son of Yannai" (Rahmani 1994a, no. 61), "Shim'on and his wife" (Rahmani 1994a, no. 150), "Eli, son of Shim'on, Yeho'ezer" (Rahmani 1994a, no. 151; Ilan 2002, 168), "Qyria Shim'on" (Rahmani 1994a, no. 428; the name Shim'on is crossed out), "Hanania, son of Shim'on" (Rahmani 1994a, no. 488), "—m, son of

Shim'on" (Rahmani 1994a, no. 501), "Ashuni, son of Shim'on, son of Ashuni" (Rahmani 1994a, no. 520; the deceased was named after his grandfather), and "Maris and Shim'on, sons of Sha'ul" (Rahmani 1994a, no. 820; Sha'ul is also Saul). For additional Hebrew examples, see Bagatti and Milik 1958, 76–77 no. 5. The Hebrew name occurs on several Masada ostraca (e.g., Mas nos. 415, 416, 421, 423, 693, 694) and jars (e.g., Mas nos. 462, 463, 464, 465, 466, 467, 478, 479, 514, 898, 899). The Greek form of the name is found on epitaphs in Rome (see Leon 1995, 289 nos. 163 and 165; 326 no. 403: "Here lies Simon. May his sleep be in peace") and on a Greek marble epitaph from Jaffa (*CIJ* no. 920; cf. Klein 1920, no. 155; Horbury and Noy 1992, no. 147: "Thanoum, son of Simon, grandson of Benjamin the centenarius of Parembole. Peace." The last word is written in Hebrew).

All four Gospels agree that Jesus gave Simon the nickname "Peter." In Matthew we not only have the nickname, we also have the well known play on words: "You are Peter and on this rock I shall build my church" (Matt 16:18). "Peter" (Πέτρος), of course, means "rock," which facilitates the play on words with πέτρα, the "rock" on which Jesus intended to build his community. In Aramaic the nickname is כפא, which in the Greek New Testament is transliterated Κηφᾶς, e.g., John 1:42b, "'You shall be called Cephas [Κηφᾶς],' which means rock [Πέτρος]" (for further discussion of linguistic and related issues, see *TDNT* 6:100–12; Lake 1921; Fitzmyer 1979, 121–32; Casey 1998, 84). The apostle Paul several times refers to Cephas, who is almost certainly Simon Peter (cf. 1 Cor 1:12 [and *1 Clem.* 47:3]; 3:22; 9:5; 15:5; Gal 1:18; 2:9, 11, 14).

Some have contended that כפא was not used as a proper name in the time of Jesus or before. Accordingly, it has been argued that Jesus did not give Simon the name "rock," but simply designated him as a rock. (The Aramaic word "rock" is found in pre-Christian sources, e.g., 11QtgJob 32:1; 33:9; 4QEnoch^{e} 4 iii 19.) This explanation is not convincing, for Paul calls the apostle כפא / Κηφᾶς ("Cephas") several times, as though it is a proper name (see the above references). In my view the issue has been settled by Joseph Fitzmyer (1979), who has called our attention to an Aramaic papyrus, in which כפא appears as a name. According to one of the papyri from the island of Elephantine, Egypt (*BMAP* no. 8, line 10, ca. 416 B.C.E.), one of the witnesses to the transfer of a slave from one owner to another is "'Aqab, son of Kepha'" (עקב בר כפא). The name 'Aqab may in fact be a shortened form of Jacob (i.e., יעקב). Because there are no known examples of men named

Peter prior to the nicknaming of Simon and because the Aramaic name Cephas is so rare (so far as our documentation goes), it is possible that Jesus' naming of Peter was unusual, if not unique.

Although it is true that no examples of the Greek name Peter have been found, dating to the middle of the first century C.E. or earlier, there is some evidence that this name was in use in the second half of the first century and in the second. Some have suggested that the name Peter (Πέτρος) is attested in Josephus: "Marsyas thereupon bade Peter, a freeman of Agrippa's mother Berenice . . ." (*Ant.* 18.6.3 §156). But most mss read Πρῶτον (i.e., *Protos*), not Πέτρον. The reading of the name Peter probably owes its origin to a Christian scribe. The Greek name does appear, in Hebrew transliteration, in rabbinic literature: פיטרס (*y. Mo'ed Qatan* 3.6, 82d: רבי יוסי בר פיטרס ["Rabbi Jose, son of Petros"]; cf. *Gen. Rab.* 62.2 [on Gen 25:8]; *Exod. Rab.* 52.3 [on Exod 39:33]). But this person Jose, son of Petros (or Peter), cannot be earlier than the second century. We also have a "Petron [פטרון], son of Joseph," in PYadin 46, and a "Petrine [פטרין], son of Istomachus," among the ostraca found at Masada (Mas no. 413). The papyrus dates to the Bar Kokhba era, the ostracon to the fall of Masada in 73 C.E. (cf. Ilan 2002, 303). See also Mas no. 668 "(belonging?) to the 'Stones'; son of 'Rocks'"(?) (Masada I, p. 66).

There is a striking point of comparison with Simon Peter and one of the many ossuary inscriptions that bear the name Simon: "Simon, builder of the temple" (Rahmani 1994a, no. 200; cf. Mas no. 561: "Simo [sic] the builder"). We immediately think of Matt 16:18, where Jesus tells Simon, whom he has nicknamed "Peter," "I will build my church." It is not suggested that either Jesus or the Matthean evangelist alluded to this person. Rather, it may well be that the occupational description, "builder of the temple," served a quasi-religious function. Simon and many others were builders of the temple of Jerusalem, a building project that commenced before Jesus was born and which finally concluded some thirty years after his death. Building the temple, therefore, was a constant throughout his lifetime. Perhaps mimicking this way of speaking, as reflected in the Simon ossuary inscription, Jesus declares that his Simon Peter will become the builder of Jesus' church, something parallel to and perhaps over against the temple.

The Matthean tradition also has Jesus address Simon Peter as "bar Jonah" (Βὰρ Ἰωνᾶ), or "son of Jonah" (Matt 16:17). Was Jonah the name of Simon's father, or is it one more nickname, i.e., Simon, the son of Jonah the prophet? According to John 1:42a, it is the name of

Simon's father: "So you are Simon, the son of John [Σίμων ὁ υἱὸς Ἰωάννου]?" John's Greek implies an underlying bar Yohanan, though Yonah could be an abbreviation of the fuller form of the name (*TDNT* 3:406–10). The names do seem interchangeable, at least in the mss in a few places in the OG (cf. 1 Chr 26:3; 1 Esdr 9:1, 23).

Ilan (2002, 143–44) identifies three other persons named Jonah, besides Simon Peter (or his father). One occurrence is found in the Mekilta deRabbi Ishmael; the other two occurrences are found inscribed on ossuaries, e.g., "Mariame, wife of Jonah [Ἰωνᾶ]" (Rahmani 1994a, no. 233). There are at least three examples of "Yohanan, son of Simon" (Milik 1956–1957, 242). We have a "Simon, son of Yohanan" (Ilan 2002, 221) in early rabbinic literature (cf. *Sifra* §160, *Zabim* 1.1 [on Lev 15:2]). The name and affiliation also occur on an ossuary from the Kidron Valley: שמעון בר יוחנן ("Simon, son of Yohanan"), though at points the reading is uncertain (Milik 1956–1957, 243).

James, the son of Zebedee (Ἰάκωβος ὁ τοῦ Ζεβεδαίου)

In Hebrew Zebedee (or Zebadiah), which is biblical (cf. 1 Chr 8:17; 26:2 OG: Ζαβαδιάς), is זבדיה (Ilan 2002, 89–90). It is found written on a pre-70 C.E. ostracon, found in Jerusalem. The name also occurs in the Babatha archive (PYadin 5) and dates to 110 C.E. It appears on two Masada ostraca as well, though with minor spelling variations (Mas nos. 399 [זבידא] and 468 [זבידו]). Spelling variations are seen in the OG as well (e.g., Ζαβαδιάς, Ζαβδειά, Ζαβδείας, Ζαβιβιά). We also find זבוד in Ezra 8:14 (OG: Ζαβούδ).

and John (Ἰωάννης), *the brother of James*

The name John (or "Yoannes") comes from the Hebrew יוחנן ("Yohanan") and is biblical (Jer 40:16). Ilan (2002, 134–43) catalogues some 129 individuals, historical as well as fictional, that bore this name. The name is prominent in the Hasmonean family, and many bear the name in the writings of Josephus. There is also the well-known John the Baptist, who appears in the New Testament and in Josephus (*Ant.* 18.5.2 §116). The name appears on several ossuaries (e.g., *CIJ* nos. 1257, 1393, 1394; Puech 1983, 503; Rahmani 1994a, nos. 198, 218, 435, 871), ostraca (e.g., Mas nos. 302–40, 395, 396, 397, 412, 417, 556, 558, 559; Mur 72, 74), and jars (e.g., Mas nos. 484, 485, 487). The name is even attested at Qumran (4Q477), which is unusual, given the rarity of personal names in this literature. The Greek form is also found inscribed on ossuaries (Milik 1956–1957, 267; Bagatti and Milik 1958, no. 18; Rahmani 1994a, nos. 50 and 89: "of John, of Jesus"); one ossuary bears the name in Latin (Rahmani 1994a, no. 202: "IOHANA").

whom he surnamed Boanerges (βοανηργές), *sons of thunder* (υἱοὶ βροντῆς)

James and John, sons of Zebedee were given the sobriquet "sons of thunder," at least, as the Markan evangelist translates his Semitic transliteration βοανηργές. Scholars are not sure what words actually lie behind this nickname. (Ancient scribes were not sure either, as attested by the variety of textual variants in the Greek mss.) Long ago Gustav Dalman suggested בני רגז (*beney regez*), "sons of agitation" (1902, 49; 1905, 112). More recently John Rook has suggested בני רעש (*beney re'esh*), "sons of the quaking (heavens)" (1981). But the suggestion that we take Mark's Greek translation at face value and suppose an underlying בני רעם (*beney re'em*), "sons of thunder" (so Buth 1997; Casey 1998, 197–98; Ilan 2002, 431), has the most to commend it. (It should be noted that the Semitic *'ayin* is sometimes transliterated with the Greek *gamma*, as in Gen 10:7; cf. Buth 1997, 266 n. 12; Ilan 2002, 18.)

Andrew ('Ανδρεάς)

The name is Greek (Andreas, though in English usually Andrew), probably meaning "manly" (from ἀνδρός, the genitive of ἀνήρ "man"); it appears inscribed on at least two Jewish ossuaries (cf. *CIJ* no. 1272 ['Ανδροῦς]; Puech 1983, 528 ['Ανδροῦς]). The second inscription was found on an ossuary in the Tomb of Jason. It reads: Σάολος ['Ιο]ύδου 'Ανδροῦς ("of Saul, of Judah, [son] of Andreas [or Andrew]"); Ilan 2002, 262–63).

Philip (Φίλιππος)

This name is also Greek, meaning "horse lover"; it appears in transliterated Hebrew as פלפס. Besides the apostle Philip, there is Philip the deacon (Acts 6:5). According to John 1:44, Philip was from Bethsaida (Ilan 2002, 310). See also John 6:5-8; 12:22.

The name has not yet turned up on an ossuary from Palestine of late antiquity. The name does appear on an epitaph from Leontopolis (Tell el-Yehoudieh), dating perhaps from 23 B.C.E. (cf. *CIJ* no. 1494: "Hilarion, daughter of Philip [Φιλίππου], untimely dead, friend of all, who caused pain to none, excellent girl, farewell. About six years old. In year 7, Epeiph 5"; Horbury and Noy 1992, no. 70), and on another from Rome (cf. *CIJ* no. 334: "Here lies Eutychis, daughter of Philip [Φιλίππου]. May her sleep be in peace"; Leon 1995, 314).

Bartholomew (Βαρθολομαῖος)

This name is Aramaic, *bar Talmai* ("son of Talmai"). He is not to be identified with Nathanael, the disciple whose name only appears in John's Gospel (cf. John 1:45-46). Commentators sometimes refer to the Hebrew name "Talmai" (תַּלְמַי), which occurs six times in the Hebrew Bible, three times in reference to a descendant of Anak (cf. Num 13:22; Josh 15:14; Judg 1:10) and three times in reference to the king of Geshur, who was related to David's family by marriage (cf. 2 Sam 3:3; 13:37; 1 Chr 3:2). In the Targum the name appears as תַּלְמַי. The name תלמי has been found written on an ostracon at Masada (*ca.* 73 C.E., cf. Mas no. 578).

The difficulty that we encounter is trying to explain the Greek form θολομαῖος (we assume, of course, that Βαρ = בַּר). In Numbers 13:22 the OG reads Θελαμιν, while in Joshua 15:14, Judges 1:10, and 2 Samuel 3:3 the OG reads Θολμι (although in Theodotion we find Θολμιν). But in 2 Samuel 13:37 and 1 Chronicles 3:2 we find Θολμαι. P. Billerbeck surveys a variety of possibilities that try to explain the underlying Semitic name without reference to the Biblical Talmai (St-B 1:536), e.g., *Tg. Ps.-J.* Genesis 49:5: "Simeon and Levi are *twin* brothers (תלאמין אחין)," or בר תלמיון in *Pesiq. R.* 22.6 and *Lev. Rab.* 6.3 (on Lev 5:1)—an identification accepted by Marcus Jastrow (Jastrow 1673)—or even a demon named בן תלמיון (*ben Talmeyon*) in *b. Me'ila* 51b. These suggestions are not convincing (and the rabbinic traditions may well be nothing more than slurs directed against the disciple himself, in which the Greek name has been retranslated into Hebrew).

The Greek form Θολεμαῖος occurs in Josephus in reference to two people, one of Herod's generals (cf. *J.W.* 1.16.5 §314 [with mss reading either Θολεμαῖος or Πτολεμαῖος]; *Ant.* 14.15.6 §431 [reading Πτολεμαῖος]) and a robber (cf. *Ant.* 20.1.1 §5; some mss read θολομαῖος or θοδομαῖος). The equivalence of Θολεμαῖος and Πτολεμαῖος, as well as the Rabbis' use of תלמי for both the biblical Talmai and the Greek name Ptolemy (e.g., *b. Meg.* 9a), leads Tal Ilan to understand the disciple Βαρθολομαῖος as "son of Θολομαῖος," or "son of Ptolemy" (Ilan 2002, 304–5). It is an interesting conjecture and it could be correct.

We are left, however, with a curious combination of the Aramaic *bar* and the Greek name Ptolemy. Perhaps the simplest and most plausible explanation after all is that Bartholomew's name was the Aramaic בר תלמי (*bar Talmai*, or "son of Talmai"), which in the Greek Gospels has been transliterated on the pattern observed in the OG of 2 Samuel 13:37 and 1 Chronicles 3:2 (i.e., Θολμαι), with the addition of the declinable ending ος and a vowel, as in Θελαμιν in Numbers 13:22, between *lambda* and *mu*. Thus the name Bartholomew is entirely Semitic and biblical, while the Greek form we find in the New Testament is a transliteration more or less guided by the OG.

Levi, the son of Alphaeus (Λευί)

In Mark 2:14 the tax collector is identified as Levi. But in the Matthean parallel (Matt 9:9) he is named Matthew. The Markan evangelist himself identifies this disciple as Matthew in Mark 3:18 (which is probably what prompted the Matthean evangelist to make the change in the earlier call story). Levi is of course the name of the famous patriarch (לוי), from whose line Israel's priesthood would spring. The Hebrew form of the name appears on an ossuary lid found in Bethphage (*CIJ* no. 1285) and the Greek form of the name appears on an ossuary found in Jerusalem (*CIJ* no. 1340). Another ossuary, from Ben Shemen, reads "Levi, son of Malosha, by himself" (Rahmani 1994a, no. 610), probably meaning that only the bones of Levi are to be placed in the ossuary. "Malosha" could be a nickname, meaning "the kneading trough." Ilan, however, reads "Meyasha" (2002, 183). The name Levi appears on several ostraca (e.g., Mur 74; Mas no. 577). We read about one Levi, a ruling priest, according to *POxy* 840 (line 10). The person in this instance may be fictional, but the underlying story may be in part historical. Other fictional Levis appear in pseudepigraphal writings (e.g., *Acts of Pilate*, *Pseudo-Matthew*, Slavonic additions to Josephus). It was a popular name in late antiquity; Ilan (2002, 182–83) catalogues twenty-nine in all. On the patronym Alphaeus, see below.

Matthew (Μαθθαῖος)

The Gospel form of the name is an abbreviation of Ματταθίας (cf. OG 1 Chr 15:21; 1 Macc 16:14; 2 Macc 14:19), which in turn transliterates מתתיה. The name is well represented; Ilan (2002, 191–96) catalogues more than sixty individuals. The name appears in Greek in other forms, including Ματθίας (1 Macc 2:1; 11:70), and in Hebrew in other forms, including מתיא (*m. Sheq.* 5:1; *m. Yeb.* 10:3; *'Abot* 4:15), מתי (Sukenik 1947, 358; Milik 1956–1957, 243, 245), מתתי (Rosenthal 1973, 73), and מתיה (*b. Hul.* 67a). The latter form appears in ossuary inscriptions (e.g., *CIJ* no. 1246, 1275; Bagatti and Milik 1958, 74 no. 3 "Matthew, son of Thaddaeus"). Greek forms are also found on ossuaries, including Ματταθίου (*CIJ* no. 1276) and Μαθία (Rahmani 1994a, no. 560). Several of the Greek and Hebrew forms are found in other inscriptions and written on ostraca and jars (such as at Murabba'at and Masada). On the relation of Matthew to Levi, son of Alphaeus, see above.

Thomas (Θωμᾶς)

The name of the apostle Thomas appears in all four Gospels and Acts. He figures prominently in the fourth Gospel. Because of his unbelief in the reports of Jesus' resurrection (John 20), he has become known as "doubting Thomas." In later traditions, especially those nurtured in gnostic circles, the reputation of Thomas is enhanced (as seen esp. in the *Gospel of Thomas*). The derivation and meaning of his name are debated. Three times in the fourth Gospel he is given the sobriquet "the twin" (John 11:16; 20:24; 21:2: Θωμᾶς ὁ λεγόμενος Δίδυμος). This has led scholars to think that underlying the nickname is either the Hebrew תאומים or Aramaic תיומא (cf. Gen 25:24: "there were twins in her womb" in the Masoretic Text or in the Targum). The twin meaning continues in later Christian tradition (e.g., *Clem. Hom.* 2.1). However, Ilan (2002, 416) thinks the name is derived from תומא, which in Aramaic means "simplicity," "garlic," or "fringe" (cf. Jastrow 1654). The form תמא (*Thoma*) is attested as a name (among Arabs and among Jews in Egypt), but it is not clear what meaning it had. Whatever the original meaning, Christians believed it meant "twin." The name is not found inscribed on ossuaries, but the Greek form Θωμᾶς is found in the Babatha archive, dating to 125 C.E. (PYadin 10 and 15). (The Greek name is inscribed on stone at least twice in sites in the Golan Heights, dating to the sixth century C.E.; cf. Gregg and Urman 1996, nos. 83 and 174.)

James son of Alphaeus (Ἰάκωβος ὁ τοῦ Ἁλφαίου)

Apart from his appearance in the apostolic list, we know nothing of this man. He is not to be identified with "James the Small" (Mark 15:40), nor with James the brother of Jesus (Mark 6:3; Gal 1:19; 1 Cor

15:6). The appearance of the odd patronym Alphaeus, which appeared with the mention of Levi in Mark 2:14, has led some to conclude that Levi and James were brothers. Perhaps, but what can be made of the name "Alphaeus"? This person has sometimes been identified with Clopas (Κλωπᾶς) of John 19:25 and Cleopas (Κλέοπας) of Luke 14:18. Phonetically the Hebrew name חלפי can account for all three Greek forms (viz. Ἁλφαῖος, Κλωπᾶς, Κλέοπας), though one may wonder why such diversity in the Gospels in the transliteration of the name of one individual. Accordingly, the identification is at best tentative. In Egyptian Greek papyri, the name occurs as Ἄλφιος, Ἀλφαῖος, and Ἄλφειος. In 1 Maccabees 11:70 it appears as Χαλφεί, and on two first-century C.E. Hebrew ostraca spelled in yet another form (cf. Mas no. 427 and Ilan 2002, 382: חלבו). In *t. B. Qam.* 9.31 it appears as חילפאי (and in later rabbinic literature as חילפי and חלפיי, while in Shem Tob's Hebrew Matthew, at Matthew 10:3, it appears as אלופיאי [*Aluphiai*], evidently cognate with אלף, perhaps with the sense of "prince" or "chief").

Thaddaeus (Θαδδαῖος)

Ilan (2002, 283–84) identifies some ten Jewish individuals who bore this name in late antiquity. The Greek form of the name, with minor spelling variations, appears in Jewish papyri in the second century (e.g., in the Babatha archive, cf. PYadin 14, line 20). Greek and Hebrew forms appear in ossuaries that pre-date 70 C.E. On an ossuary found in Jezreel Valley are inscribed the words Ἰούδας Θαδδαίου ("Judas, [son] of Thaddaeus"); Rahmani 1994a, no. 145). On the Mount of Olives another ossuary has come to light bearing the inscriptions Θαδδα and תדא. The first reads [Σαλα]μσι[ων Θα]δδα ("Salamsion [daughter of] Thaddaeus"; Bagatti and Milik 1958, 71–74 no. 2) and the second reads מתיה בן תדא ("Mattathiah, son of Thaddaeus"; Bagatti and Milik 1958, 74–76 no. 3). On an ossuary from Augusta Victoria (pre-70 C.E.) we find the name תדיון (*CIJ* no. 1265), which may be a variant form. The name also appears in later rabbinic literature spelled תדאי (cf. Jastrow 1647). The alternate spelling תודה in *b. Sanh.* 43a is deliberate, in order to accommodate an unfavorable play on words.

Two other ossuary inscriptions, from the Mount of Olives, have been reported (Vincent 1907; Klein 1920, 23 no. 36):

יהודה בן תודוס
יהודה בר תודוס

"Judah, son (*ben*) of Thaddaeus"
"Judah, son (*bar*) of Thaddaeus"

The sibilant ending in both inscriptions is interesting, suggesting influence from the Greek form Θαδδαῖος. And finally, Samuel Klein (1920, 102) suggests that the name Θεῦδας (cf. Josephus, *Ant.* 20.5.1 §97; Acts 5:36) also derives from תדאי and is a shortened form of Θαδδαῖος (cf. Θεύδοτος in *CIJ* no. 1573). Ilan (2002, 286) disagrees, classifying Θεῦδας as a shortened form of Θεόδωρος. Be that as it may, a Semitic equivalent of the name has been found on an ossuary on the Mount of Olives (i.e., תודוס; cf. Vincent 1907; *CIJ* no. 1255).

In some New Testament mss a curious variant is found; in place of Θαδδαῖος we read Λεββαῖος (cf. D W L Δ Θ Π). The explanation for this variant may well be found in the meaning of the underlying Semitic, for תדא (*tadda*') means "breast," while לב (*leb*) and לבב (*lebab*) mean "heart." The idea here is that the meaning of the name (i.e., breast or heart, which are closely related) gave rise to two distinct transliterations in Greek, reflecting the respective Semitic words. It is also possible that an early Christian wrote Λεββαῖος in order to introduce Levi into the apostolic list.

Simon the Cananaean (Σίμων ὁ Καναναῖος)

Because in the parallel passage Luke calls this disciple "Simon, the one called zealous" (Luke 6:15: Σίμω ὁ καλούμενος ζηλωτής), most scholars today understand Mark's and Matthew's transliteration (and Luke's translation) as reflecting the Aramaic קנאנא ("zealous"), and not כנעני ("Canaanite" or "trader"). The sobriquet seems to have been applied to a person in rabbinic literature: "Rabbi Nehonia, ben HaQanah [בֶּן הַקָּנָה], would pray a short prayer upon entering the study house and upon leaving" (*m. Ber.* 4:2; cf. *b. B. Bat.* 10b). We may also translate "Nehonia, 'son of zeal,'" though קנה usually means "jealous" or "hot" (cf. Jastrow 1390–91; Ilan 2002, 447; the Greek adjective ζῆλος also means "hot" or "boiling"). This Nehonia (or Nehunia) is said to have been a disciple of Rabban Yohanan ben Zakkai (second century C.E.). The sobriquet itself has not yet turned up inscribed on an ossuary. One should recall also the words said to have been spoken by Paul, in reference to himself: ". . . being zealous for God [ζηλωτὴς ὑπάρχων τοῦ θεοῦ] . . ." (Acts 22:3). However, the sobriquet may be attested at Masada, where on a jar we find the name יהוסף קני ("Joseph [the] Zealot," or "zealous Joseph"; Mas no. 474).

Judas Iscariot (in Mark Ἰούδας Ἰσκαριώθ, in Matthew Ἰούδας ὁ Ἰσκαριώτης, but Codex D reads Σκαριώθ)

The variants in the mss of the Greek New Testament witness the obscurity of the derivation of Judas Iscariot's name. The surname is sometimes explained as a transliteration for איש קריות ("man of Kerioth"), just as Ἰστώβ in the OG transliterates אִישׁ־טוֹב ("man [or men] of Tob" in 2 Samuel 10:6, 8 (cf. Josephus, *Ant.* 7.6.1 §121, who in reference to this passage reads Ἴστοβος). Kerioth may be the Καριώθ mentioned in LXX Jeremiah 31:24 (= 48:24 RSV), or the Kerioth in Joshua 15:25 (קְרִיּוֹת). Some New Testament mss apparently understand the epithet as a place name, reading ἀπὸ Καρυώτου ("from Karuot"; cf. א* Θ *fam.*[13] at John 6:71, and D at John 12:4; 13:2, 26; 14:22). Others have suggested that Iscariot is a transliteration of the Latin term *sicarius* or the Greek σικάριος ("assassin" or "dagger man"). This would have been an odd sobriquet, indeed, for one of the Twelve. Many other explanations have been offered. On balance, the place name "man of Kerioth" is the best option.

This disciple's given name, Judas, was popular in Jewish late antiquity (some 179 individuals are catalogued in Ilan 2002, 112–25), recalling the famous patriarch and, in more recent times, Judas, son of Mattathias (1 Macc 2:1), of the Hasmonean house. This well-known Judas also had his own sobriquet, Maqqaba' (from Aramaic מקבא or מקבת, meaning "hammer"; Hachlili 2000, 97) or Maccabeus (from Greek Μακκαβαῖος), after which this period of time has become known.

In Hebrew the name is *Yehudah* (יְהוּדָה), though there are other forms, such as Yudan (ידן), Yehud (יהוד), Yehudan (יהודן), and, in Aramaizing style, bar Yehudah (בר יהודה). Ossuary inscriptions include "Shalom, wife of Yehuda" (Rahmani 1994a, no. 24); "Yehudah, son of Yehohanan, son of Yitro (or Jethro)" (Rahmani 1994a, no. 57), and "Yehudah, son of Yeshu'a (or Jesus)" (Rahmani 1994a, no. 702). In the Greek the name is usually written Judas (Ἰούδας), though again there are variants, such as Ἰούδα (Goodenough 1953, 63; for facsimile, see Goodenough 1953c, no. 896), a common form in the OG (usually in reference to the nation, not to an individual). Greek ossuary inscriptions include "Jesus, (son) of Judas" (Bagatti and Milik 1958, no. 13; Rahmani 1994a, no. 113), "Judas, (son) of Thaddaeus" (Rahmani 1994a, no. 145), and "Mariame, wife of Judas" (Rahmani 1994a, no. 782). There is also a bilingual inscription: "Judas" (top), "Yehudah" (middle), and "Shappira" (bottom), with the first name in Greek and the second and third names in Hebrew (Rahmani 1994a, no. 35). The Hebrew name is found on several ostraca, jars, and papyri from Masada, Mishmar, and Jericho (Ilan 2002, 118).

Nathanael (Ναθαναήλ)

In Hebrew the name is נתנאל (cf. Num 1:8). This disciple of Jesus makes his appearance in John 1:45-49; 21:2. It has been suggested that Nathanael and Bartholomew are one and the same, and that the former is the given name and the latter his patronym (i.e., "son of Tolmai"). In the three synoptic Gospels Bartholomew is paired with Philip, and in the fourth Gospel Nathanael is paired with Philip. And finally, Bartholomew is only found in the Synoptics, never in the fourth Gospel; and Nathanael is only found in the fourth Gospel, never in the Synoptics. The identification is plausible, but it remains speculative.

There is a Jewish ambassador named Nathanael (cf. Josephus, *Ant.* 20.1.2 §14: Ναθανάηλος). There is a Rabbi Simeon ben Nathanael (or, vocalized more precisely, Netanel) in *m. Abot* 2:8. Both the Hebrew and the Greek forms of the name are attested on ossuaries (for Greek, see *CIJ* no. 1330; for Hebrew, see Rahmani 1994a, nos. 280 [though the inscription is omitted] and 796: "Mariah, daughter of Neta(na)el").

Review of the apostolic names and nicknames attests their commonness, for the most part. None of these names or nicknames stands out as peculiar or as distinctly Christian. All are Jewish, all were in circulation in first-century Palestine, and most were quite common. Even the nicknames themselves either find counterparts elsewhere or at least reflect the practices of this part of the Jewish world in this period of time. We may briefly review the names of other Gospel characters.

Mary (Μαρία or Μαριάμ)

There are several Marys in the New Testament, one of whom is the mother of Jesus (Mark 6:3: "Is not this the carpenter, the son of Mary [τῆς Μαρίας]?"; Matt 13:55: "Is not his mother called Mariam [Μαριάμ]?"). The name Mary comes from the biblical name מרים (Mariam—as in the sister of Moses; cf. Exod 15:20). Ilan (2002, 242–48) lists eighty persons with this name. In Hebrew papyri and inscriptions the biblical form appears, as well as the form מריה (Mariah), as seen in several ossuaries (cf. Bagatti and Milik 1958, nos. 7, 15, and 34; Rahmani 1994a, nos. 82, 152, 428, and 502; *CIJ* nos. 1249, 1281, and 1383, where the woman is identified as a proselyte). In Greek the name appears as Μαριάμνη (in the pseudepigraphal *Acta Philippi*), Μαριάμη (Bagatti and Milik 1958, no. 37; Rahmani 1994a, nos. 108, 233, 243, and 351; *CIJ* nos. 1192, 1341, 1352, 1387; Herod's wife, cf. Josephus, *J.W.* 1.12.3 §241), Μαριάμ (Rahmani 1994a, no. 64), and Μαρία (Rahmani 1994a, no. 405; *CIJ* nos. 1214, 1284) or Μαρίας (Rahmani 1994a, no. 425), as well as the curious forms Μαριεάμη (Rahmani 1994a, no. 559) and Μαριάδος (*CIJ* no. 1328). The name appears in the Babatha archive (e.g., PYadin 7, 26, 34, 42), at Murabba'at (e.g., Mur 10a, with the name spelled מרימא), and at Masada (e.g., Mas no. 785). With the exceptions Μαριάμνη and מרימא, all forms appear inscribed on ossuaries.

Martha (Μάρθα)

A woman named Martha, sister of Mary and brother of Lazarus, is mentioned in the Gospels of Luke and John (Luke 10:38-42; John 11:1). Martha is not a biblical name, but an Aramaic name that means "mistress." In Hebrew and Aramaic ossuary inscriptions the name appears usually as מרתא or מרתה (cf. Bagatti and Milik 1958, nos. 7 and 39; *CIJ* nos. 1219, 1261, 1263, and 1311; Rahmani 1994a, nos. 67, 220, 256, 287, 290, 354, and 468). In Greek we find Μάρθας (*CIJ* no. 1246), Μάρθα (Puech 1983, 527; Rahmani 1994a, no. 287), and possibly Μάρατ (possibly a misspelling [i.e., Μάρτα], or a variant of Μάρα; cf. Ilan 2002, 424).

Zechariah (Ζαχαρίας)

Zechariah the prophet is mentioned in Matthew 23:35, while in Luke 1:5 we are told that Zechariah (wife of Elizabeth) is the name of the father of John the Baptist. Zechariah (or Zachariah) is a biblical name (cf. Zech 1:1) and in Hebrew is usually spelled זכריה. In the OG it is spelled as we find it in the New Testament. The Hebrew form of the name is found on ostraca and jars from Masada (e.g., Mas nos. 418, 477) and on a few ossuaries: "Eleazar, son of Zechariah" (e.g., *CIJ* no. 1194; Rahmani 1994a, no. 456). The Greek form is also found on ossuaries (e.g., Bagatti and Milik 1958, nos. 30, 36, and 37). Ilan (2002, 90–91) classifies Ζακχαῖος (cf. 2 Macc 10:19; Luke 19:2), Σακχαῖος (cf. Josephus, *Vita* 46 §239), Ζωκήρ (Hegesippus, *Hypomnemata*), and זכאי,

which underlies Ζακχαῖος and Σακχαῖος (*m. 'Abot* 2:8; *t. Ber.* 2.16), as variant forms of the name. זכי, another biblical form (cf. Ezra 2:9), is related to זכאי.

Elizabeth (Ἐλισάβετ)

According to Luke, the mother of John the Baptist and wife of Zechariah the priest is Elizabeth (Luke 1:5). The name Elizabeth is a variant of the biblical name Elisheba (אלישבע), the wife of Aaron (cf. Exod 6:23), which in the OG is Ἐλισάβεθ. The Greek form Ἐλισάβη appears on an ossuary from Silwan, Jerusalem (cf. Spoer 1907; *CIJ* no. 1338).

Joses (Ἰωσῆς)

The name occurs three times in the New Testament, all three in Mark's Gospel (6:3; 15:40, 47) and in the genitive (Ἰωσῆτος). In Hebrew the shortened form is יוסי, the full form is Joseph (which will be discussed more fully in chapter 5).

Salome (Σαλώμη)

A woman named Salome appears in Mark 15:40 and 16:1. The name is derived from the Hebrew word for peace, שלום. In the Bible it appears as a man's name (cf. 2 Kgs 15:10), but in the New Testament period it was a very popular name for females. Both Hebrew and Greek forms, with some variants, appear often on ossuaries (Bagatti and Milik 1958, nos. 19, 31, and 38; *CIJ* nos. 1210, 1236 [Σαλαμάθ], 1237 [Σαλαμί], 1245, 1293 [bilingual]; 1294, 1296, 13,13, 1314, 1362, 1374; Rahmani 1994a, nos. 13, 66, 114 [Σαλώθ], 217, 226, 286, 430, 552 [Σαλώνα], 582, 682, 694, 700, 800), as well as on ostraca and jars from Masada (e.g., Mas nos. 404, 777, 891–94; cf. Ilan 2002, 249–53).

James "the Small" (Ἰάκωβος ὁ μικρός)

The meaning of Mark 15:40 is somewhat ambiguous: "Mary, the (mother? wife?) of James (or Jacob) the Small (or younger, i.e., James junior)." The nickname is dropped in the Matthean and Lukan parallels. This nickname occurs elsewhere. One thinks of the rabbinic authority "Samuel the Small [שמואל הקטן]," who was active in the first century C.E. (cf. *b. Ber.* 28b–29a; *b. Shab.* 33a; *b. Ta'an.* 25b; *b. Sota* 48b; *b. Sanh.* 11a). From a time slightly earlier we have "Honi the Small [חוני הקטן]" (*t. Rosh Hash.* 2.17), grandson of the famous Honi the

Circle-Drawer. Tomb inscriptions from Beth She'arim, Galilee, read: "Yehudah the Small [יהודה הקטן]" (Mazar 1973, no. 36), "Anina the Small [אנינא הקטן]" (Avigad 1976, no. 11), and "Domnika the tiny [ἡ μικρά]" (Schwabe and Lifshitz 1974, no. 198). By way of contrast, compare "Hillel the Elder [הלל הזקן]" (*m. Sheb.* 10:3), "Shammai the Elder [שמאי הזקן]" (*m. Suk.* 2:8), and "Rabban Gamaliel the Elder [רבן גמליאל הזקן]" (*m. Yeb.* 16:7).

Joanna, wife of Chuza (Ἰωάννα γυνὴ Χουζᾶ)

According to Luke 8:1-3, Joanna was one of a number of women who had been healed by Jesus and had provided for him and his disciples out of their means. Ilan (2002, 420–21) identifies twelve women who had this name. The Hebrew form is יחנה and is found on an ossuary (*CIJ* no. 1281) and in parchment and papyri from Muraba'at (Mur 9, 48). The form יהוחנה may also be feminine, also occurring on ossuaries (cf. Puech 1983, 522; Rahmani 1994a, nos. 270, 871).

Joanna's husband is one "Chuza, Herod's steward [ἐπιτρόπου]." The only attested occurrence of this name is in Luke 8:3. The name may come from a form of חזא or חזי, which means "to discern" or "see" (Jastrow 443; Ilan 2002, 441). If the letter כ (*kaph*) underlies the Greek X (*chi*) in this name, the Hebrew word כוזא ("pitcher" or "jug") may lie behind the name (Jastrow 618).

Susanna (Σουσάννα)

Like Joanna above, Susanna is said to be another woman of means who supported the ministry of Jesus (Luke 8:3). The name appears in one of the additions to Daniel (i.e., Susanna, the righteous woman falsely accused by two wicked judges of Israel, only to be vindicated by the youthful Daniel). The name comes from the biblical word שושנה ("lily"; Jastrow 1543–44). The shortened form שושן ("Susan") appears on an ossuary (cf. Ilan 2002, 426), and another example, from the Mount of Olives, will soon be published (cf. Ilan 2002, 451).

Jairus (Ἰάϊρος)

In the New Testament Jairus appears as a synagogue ruler, who with desperation seeks Jesus' help for his dying daughter (Mark 5:21-24, 35-43). The name is biblical ("Yair"; cf. Num 32:41 יָאִיר = OG: Ἰαΐρ). Ilan (2002, 111) identifies eight persons with this name. The name appears on several ossuaries (Rahmani 1994a, no. 560: "Mathia and Simon, brothers, sons of Yair ['Ιάιερε]; masters of the tomb" [note the irregular spelling]; *CIJ* nos. 1367, 1368, 1370; Bagatti and Milik 1958, 70 no. 1 'Ιάειρος [this spelling is attested in Josephus, *J.W.* 2.17.9 §447: "A few succeeded in escaping by stealth to Masada, among others Eleazar, son of Jairus"]). The name appears in Hebrew on an ostracon at Masada (Mas no. 437: בנ יאיר ["son of Yair"]) and may be the same person mentioned in Josephus.

Bartimaeus (Βαρτιμαῖος) the blind beggar (Mark 10:46)

The name is Aramaic, which the Markan evangelist translates for his Greek-speaking readers: ὁ υἱὸς Τιμαίου ("son of Timaeus"). No certain Semitic example has come to light (cf. Ilan 2002, 308).

Lazarus (Λάζαρος)

Lazarus is the name of the poor man in the parable in Luke 16:19-31 and of the dead man raised up by Jesus in John 11. Most think the name is a form of Eleazar, a biblical name (cf. Exod 6:23), which was very popular in late antiquity. Ilan (2002, 65–79) identifies 177 individuals (including some fictional characters) who had this name. The common Hebrew spelling is אלעזר, while the common Greek spelling is 'Ελεάζαρος (e.g., *Aristeas* 35, 50; Josephus, *J.W.* 2.17.9 §447; *Ant.* 1, proem 3 §11). אליעזר is found inscribed on an ossuary from Gezer (Macalister 1911; *CIJ* no 1181). The Greek form that we have in the New Testament has been found inscribed on an ossuary from the Mount of Olives (*CIJ* no. 1260). The form הלעזר has been found inscribed on an ossuary found in the Kidron Valley (*CIJ* no. 1288). A bilingual ossuary inscription has also been found (*CIJ* no. 1337; the Greek and Hebrew names have been written twice, with spelling variations; also see Bagatti and Milik 1958, no. 37; Rahmani 1994a, nos. 288, 342, 455, 456, 483, 576, 592, 783, 802). The name also appears on ostraca and jars at Masada (e.g., Mas nos. 390, 421, 469, 470, 476, 510, 511, 667, 697, 779).

Nicodemus (Νικόδημος)

A man named Nicodemus appears in the New Testament only in the Gospel of John (e.g., 3:1: "Now there was a man of the Pharisees, named Nicodemus, a ruler of the Jews"). The Greek name appears in Josephus (cf. *J.W.* 2.17.10 §451 Νικομήδους; *Ant.* 14.3.2 §37

Νικόδημος), while the Hebrew form נקדימון appears in rabbinic literature (cf. *y. Ketub.* 5.13, 30c: "Mariamne, daughter of Nicodemus"; *b. Gittin* 56a "Nicodemus, son of Gorion"; *Sifre Deut.* §305 [on Deut 31:14]: "I am the daughter of Nicodemus, son of Gorion"). The rabbinic passages may refer to the same individual (Ilan 2002, 298–99).

Herod (Ἡρῴδης)

The name Herod, whether in reference to the king of Chalcis or others of the well-known Herodian dynasty, several members of whom are mentioned in the New Testament and Josephus, is found on coins, statuary, weight-stones, public inscriptions, ostraca, and jars (Ilan 2002, 282–83). In Hebrew it is usually spelled הורדוס (*OGIS* nos. 414–15 [Herod the Great], 427 [Herod, king of Chalcis]) or הרדים (e.g., Mur 77 [ostracon]). For the Greek form of the name, see *OGIS* nos. 416–17 (Herod Antipatrus), as well as numerous references in the New Testament and in Josephus. (For inscriptions and ostraca bearing Herod's name and title, see pp. 48–50 above.)

Annas (ʿΑννας)

Annas (or Ananus) the high priest, whose five sons and son-in-law Caiaphas, served terms as high priest (cf. Josephus, *Ant.* 20.9.1 §198), is mentioned in the New Testament (cf. Luke 3:2: "the high-priesthood of Annas and Caiaphas"; John 18:13: "they led him to Annas; for he was the father-in-law of Caiaphas"; Acts 4:6: "Annas the high priest and Caiaphas and John and Alexander, and all who were of high-priestly family"). According to Josephus, the father of Annas is one Sethi (*Ant.* 18.2.1§26). This is probably the priestly family excoriated in rabbinic tradition (cf. *b. Pesahim* 57a; *m. Keritot* 1:7). (Son-in-law Caiphas is discussed below in chapter 5.)

There are several Hebrew and Greek forms of this common name Annas (some thirty-nine individuals; cf. Ilan 2002, 99–103). Its biblical form is חנן (cf. Jer 35:4). This form is found on an ossuary (cf. Rahmani 1994a, no. 430). חנין is also found (Rahmani 1994a, no. 570). "Anano" and "Anna" are the most common in Greek, though ʾΑνάνας is attested (Rahmani 1994a, no. 829). A bilingual חנין / ʾΑνίν has also been found (*CIJ* no. 1373). The priestly family name may even be attested among the ostraca of Masada (cf. Mas no. 461: "A[nani]as the high priest, ʿAqavia his son").

Barabbas (Βαραββᾶς)

One of the most notorious figures to make an appearance in the New Testament Gospels is Barabbas, whose release from Roman custody was gained the day Jesus of Nazareth was condemned to the cross (Mark 15:6-15). The name is Aramaic, made up of *bar* (בר) "son" and *abba* (אבא) "father." In Hebrew or Aramaic the name can be spelled אבה or אבי, as at Masada, on an ostracon (Mur 87; Mas no. 389) and on a jar (Mas no. 513). Greek forms include 'Ααβαί (Mur 94), and 'Ααβαεί (Mur 103). אבא appears on an ossuary (Rahmani 1994a, no. 344). An intriguing Aramaic inscription in a tomb found at Giv'at ha-Mivtar, Jerusalem, reads: "I, Abba [אבה], son of the priest Eleazar, son of Aaron the Great; I, Abba [אבה], the oppressed, the pursued, who was born at Jerusalem and went to exile into Babylonia and carried up for burial [Matta]i, son of Yehud; and I buried him in the cave that I purchased by the writ" (Rosenthal 1973, 72–73). The date and meaning of this inscription are unclear. Ilan (2002, 357), who dates the inscription prior to 70 C.E., thinks Abba had been tortured.

We may briefly mention a few other important figures in the early church, who do not appear in the Gospels.

Barsabbas (Βαρσαββᾶς)

There are two men in the New Testament called Barsabbas, one "Joseph, called Barsabbas, who was surnamed Justus" (Acts 1:23), and one "Judas, called Barsabbas" (Acts 15:22). The name is Aramaic, from בר סבא (*bar-seba'*, i.e., "son of the elder"; Ilan 2002, 395–96). The name is biblical (cf. 1 Chr 1:9). Josephus mentions a Samaritan of this name (*Ant.* 13.3.4 §75: Σαββαῖος). The name appears on at least two ossuaries (*CIJ* no. 1299: "Simon, son of Sabba (or the elder)"; Sukenik 1947, 357), and the form ברשבא appears on a papyrus deed at Murabba'at (Mur 25). Joseph, called Barsabbas, was also called Justus ('Ιοῦστος), which in Latin means "the Just One."

Barnabas (Βαρναβᾶς)

Readers of Acts are introduced to one "Joseph who was surnamed by the apostles Barnabas (which means, Son of Exhortation), a Levite, a native of Cyprus" (Acts 4:36). Apart from *bar* ("son"), the Semitic derivation of this name is not obvious. Although other suggestions have been made, the ναβας part of this sobriquet probably derives from נבא or נבוא, "prophet" or "prophecy." This Joseph, who would team up with

Saul of Tarsus in a missionary journey, had become known as the "Son of Prophecy" or "Prophetic Exhortation," which in Greek is υἱὸς παρακλήσεως. The sobriquet is adopted as a Christian name in the Byzantine period (cf. Gregg and Urman 1996, no. 135). Ilan (2002, 439) reports that the form ברנבו is recorded in Palmyra and that the form Ναβαῖος is recorded on a papyrus from Egypt.

Ananias (Ἁνανίας) *and Saphira* (Σαπφίρα)

Readers of Acts are appalled by the story of Ananias and his wife Saphira, who lie about a gift that they gave to the young Church and then are struck dead (Acts 5:1-10). Ananias is the Greek form of the Hebrew חנניה (Hananiah), a biblical name (cf. Jer 28:1). It is sometimes spelled חנינא, חנינה, and חננא. In Greek it appears as Ἁνανίας, Ἀνανίας, and Ἀνίνας. This name is well represented on ossuaries (see Rahmani 1994a, nos. 67, 132, 257, 354, 390, 469, 475, 488, 579, 829, 893; Avigad 1971, 194; Bagatti and Milik 1958, nos. 26 and 34), as well as in papyri and ostraca at Murabba'at and Masada (e.g., Mur 19, 22, 27, 30, 38, 89; Mas nos. 406, 461, 486, 488). Ilan (2002, 103–8) catalogues some eight-six individuals with this name.

The name Saphira is biblical (cf. Exod 1:15 שפרה [Shiphra]). In Greek it can also appear as Σαπῖρα, as on an ossuary from Augusta Victoria (*CIJ* no. 1272). שפירא appears on an epitaph (*CIJ* no. 1384), and in several other ossuary inscriptions (e.g., Bagatti and Milik 1958, no. 13; Rahmani 1994a, nos. 198, 455; Puech 1983, 521, 527 [different Greek form]; Fritz and Deines 1999, no. 16 שפירה), including a Silwan tomb inscription (*CIJ* no. 1393), and a bilingual ossuary reading שפירא / Σαφείρα (*CIJ* no. 1378). The name also appears on a papyrus deed from Murabba'at (Mur 29).

Gamaliel (Γαμαλιήλ)

Gamaliel is a biblical name (cf. Num 1:10, the son of Pedahzur, of the tribe of Manasseh). In Hebrew it is גמליאל. One Gamaliel appears in Acts, "a teacher of the law, held in honor by all the people," who counsels moderation in the treatment of the apostles (cf. Acts 5:34-37), and who, we are later told, was Paul's teacher (cf. Acts 22:3: "I am a Jew, born at Tarsus in Cilicia, but brought up in this city [Jerusalem] at the feet of Gamaliel, educated according to the strict manner of the law of our fathers, being zealous for God as you all are this day"). Josephus mentions the high priest Jesus, son of Γαμάλα (cf. *J.W.* 4.3.9 §159).

This honorable name is ubiquitous in rabbinic literature. In Greek the name is also spelled Γάμαλος (cf. Josephus, *Vita* 9 §33, one "Herod, son of Gamalos"). The shortened spelling גמלא appears on an ossuary (cf. *CIJ* no. 1353).

Saul (Σαῦλος)

Saul of Tarsus (Acts 7:58), who, after his conversion and call, is better known as the Apostle Paul, was given the biblical name שאול, the name of Israel's first king (cf. 1 Sam 9:2). The full Hebrew form of the name occurs on several ossuaries (e.g., Rahmani 1994a, nos. 226, 227, 228, 716, 730, and 820). The name also occurs without the *waw* on an ossuary (cf. Ilan 2002, 211) and on a jar from Masada (cf. Mas no. 508). The Greek forms Σάολος and Σάουλος also appear on ossuaries (e.g., Rahmani 1994a, nos. 122 [bilingual], 349, and 425; Puech 1983, 528). Perhaps the saddest inscription concerns a young woman named Shalom, who apparently died in childbirth: "Shalom, daughter of Saul, who failed to give birth. Peace, daughter!" (Rahmani 1994a, no. 226; the last part of the inscription probably deliberately plays on the meaning of Shalom's name).

Sergius Paulus (Σέργιος Παῦλος)

From Acts 13:9 on, Saul of Tarsus is called Paul (Παῦλος). This shift from Saul to Paul, at this point in the Acts narrative, may have been prompted by mention of the Roman Proconsul Sergius Paulus. This is a Latin name; and in fact there is an inscription in which the name *L. Sergius Paulus* occurs (cf. *CIL* no. 31545), possibly the man mentioned in Acts. The Greek form Παῦλος is found on at least two ossuaries (cf. Ilan 2002, 336).

Mark (Μᾶρκος)

The name is Latin (*Marcus*). Readers of Acts hear of one "Mary, the mother of John whose other name was Mark" (Acts 12:12). This Mark (sometimes called John Mark) joined Barnabas and Saul (or Paul) on their first missionary journey (Acts 12:25). He later occasioned a rift between the two missionaries (Acts 15:37-39). The New Testament Greek form of the name is found on an ossuary (cf. Ilan 2002, 334) and on a papyrus from Masada (cf. Mas no. 788). The form Μάρκεος is also inscribed on an ossuary from Ramat Eshkol (cf. Rahmani 1994a, no. 568).

Silas (Σίλας)

The name is from שילא (Sheila); it is not biblical, but was in circulation among Jews in late antiquity. The New Testament Greek form (cf. Acts 15:22) appears in Josephus (*J.W.* 2.19.2 §520 [Silas the Babylonian]; *Vita* 17 §89; *Ant.* 14.3.2 §40; 18.6.7 §204). The Hebrew form is found in reference to some rabbinic authorities (e.g., *t. Ber.* 2.10; *t. Hul.* 3.2). According to Ilan (2002, 414), שאילא is documented in Aramaic from Egypt in the Persian period, while the form סילא is documented among Hebrew seals from the first temple period. No ossuary inscriptions have yet come to light.

Chapter 5

Significant Ossuaries for Research in the Historical Jesus

We now turn to Jewish ossuaries, whose inscriptions and contents contribute in significant ways to our understanding of the world of Jesus and his first followers. The ossuaries are surveyed in the order of their discovery. (The so-called Christian ossuaries are not included; for discussion, see Wright 1946; Sukenik 1947; Kane 1971; 1978; Smith 1974; Gibson and Avni 1998).

Nicanor Ossuary Inscription – 1902

In 1902 a crypt consisting of four separate chambers was discovered on the Mount of Olives. In these chambers were seven ossuaries, on the end of one of which were inscribed three lines of Greek and one line of Hebrew/Aramaic (cf. Clermont-Ganneau 1903; Dickson 1903; Macalister 1905; Klein 1920, no. 9; *CIJ* no. 1256; Sukenik 1931a, 16–17; Goodenough 1953a, 130–31; Finegan 1969, 237–38; Kane 1978, 279–82):

ΟϹΤΑΤΩΝΤΟΥΝΕΙΚΑ
ΝΟΡΟϹΑΛΕΞΑΝΔΡΕΩϹ
ΠΟΙΗϹΑΝΤΟϹΤΑϹΘΥΡΑϹ
נקנר אלדסא

Or, with spacing, punctuation, and diacritical marks: ὀστᾶ τῶν τοῦ Νεικάνορος ᾿Αλεξανδρέως ποιήσαντος τὰς θύρας נקנר אלכסא ("Bones of the [sons] of Nicanor of Alexandria, who built the doors—Nicanor the Alexa[andrian]"). But it is also possible that the first two words are really one word (i.e., ὀστατῶν), an otherwise unattested word probably meaning "bone receptable." In this case the inscription reads: "Bone receptacle of Nicanor of Alexandria, who built the doors—Nicanor the Alexa(andrian)." (One should also note the final *kaph*, where one would expect a medial; medials where finals are expected, and vice versa, are not unusual in Hebrew and Aramaic inscriptions from this period.)

Since the discovery of this ossuary it has been speculated that this person Nicanor is none other than the person after whom the "Nicanor Gate" is named in rabbinic tradition. "There were seven gates in the temple court, three to the north, three to the south, and one to the east. . . . . to the east the Nicanor Gate . . ." (*b. Yoma* 19a). The same tractate later states that Nicanor fetched the gates from Alexandria of Egypt and that they were made of "Corinthian bronze" (*b. Yoma* 38a). This is precisely what Josephus says: "Of the gates nine were completely overlaid with gold and silver, as were also their door-posts and lintels; but one, that outside the sanctuary, was of Corinthian bronze, and far exceeded in value those plated with silver and gold" (*J.W.* 5.5.3 §201; cf. *m. Mid.* 2:3: "All the gates that were there had been changed with gold, save only the doors of the Nicanor Gate").

The agreement between the ossuary inscription and these literary traditions is so striking many scholars believe that the ossuary did indeed contain the remains of the man after whom the gate was named. At least one scholar, however, has challenged the identification (cf. Roussel 1924). But the rarity of the name (see Ilan 2002, 297, who can identify only three other real persons who bore this name) and the precision of the agreement in the essential details strongly argue for the identification. Commentators have wondered if the "Beautiful Gate" (ἡ ὡραία πύλη) mentioned in Acts (cf. 3:2, 10) is in fact the Nicanor Gate.

The ossuaries tell us of another builder of the Jerusalem temple, one Simon. We again have a bilingual inscription; this time involving Hebrew and Aramaic. The ossuary was found in 1968 at Giv'at Ha-Mivtar (ossuary no. 1). The deeply etched and legible inscription reads (Naveh 1970, 33–34; Tzaferis 1970, 28 no. 1; Rahmani 1994a, no. 200):

side סמונ בנה הכלה

end סמונ
בנא הכלה

Simon, builder of the temple
Simon,
builder of the temple

Although it has been suggested that "builder of the temple" be taken in a metaphorical sense (i.e., in that Simon was a priest or religious teacher; cf. the way Paul speaks of "building" the Church in Rom 15:20 and 1 Cor 3:10), it is probably better to take the words of the inscription literally. Simon, along with thousands of others, over a period of many years, was a "builder of the (Herodian) temple" (cf. John 2:20: "It has taken forty-six years to build this temple . . ."). (One will observe that the letter *nun*, the last letter in Simon's name, is medial in form, not the expected final form.)

At Dabbura in the Golan we have a bilingual inscription that acknowledges the contributions two men made to the building of the synagogue (Urman 1972; Gregg and Urman 1996, 126):

אלעזר בר אליעזר רבה עבד עמודיה דעל מן
כפתה ופצימיה. תהי לה ברכתה ΡΟΥϹΤΙΚΟϹ ЄΚΤΙϹЄΝ

Eleazar, son of Eliezer the Great, made the columns above the arches and beams. May he be blessed. Rusticus built (it).

There are other fragmentary Hebrew inscriptions, reading: "They made the house of . . . May he be blessed," and "Made the gate."

Finally, brief mention might be made of the discovery of a first century C.E. inscription on a temple stone found in the rubble in the vicinity and at the base of the southwest corner of the temple mount (cf. *NEAEHL* 2:740):

לביה התקיעה לה[כ . . .

To the place [lit. house] of trumpeting for the [or to] *k* [or *b*] . . .

It has been suggested that the inscription read: "To the place of trumpeting to declare" (לה[כריז]), or "to distinguish" (לה[בדיל]), based on Josephus (cf. *J.W.* 4.9.12 §582: "at the point where it was the custom for one of the priests to stand and to give notice, by sound of trumpet . . . of every seventh day, announcing to the people the respective hours for ceasing work and for resuming their labors") and *m. Suk.* 5:5 ("On the eve of the Sabbath they used to blow six more blasts [of the trumpet], three to cause the people to cease from work and three to distinguish [להבדיל] between the sacred and profane").

The Jesus Son of Joseph Ossuary – 1926(?)

In about 1926 Eleazar Lippa Sukenik found an ossuary, now identified as Jerusalem Tomb Ossuary 8, probably dating to the first century C.E., in the basement of the Department of Antiquities of Palestine (in Jerusalem). He published the discovery in 1931 (Sukenik 1931a, 19; Fitzmyer and Harrington 1978, 176–77, 233–34; Rahmani 1994a, no. 9). On the decorated side of this ossuary were the following inscriptions:

* ישו * ישוע בר יהוסף

* Yeshu * Yeshu'a, son of Yehoseph
or, Jesus, son of Joseph

We have the shortened form ישו (Yeshu, or Jesus) positioned in the center of the ossuary, between two rosettes (depicted above with asterisks). To the left of this shortened form is the fully spelled ישוע (Yeshu'a). Sukenik (1931a, 19 n. 1) suggested that Yeshu is a shortened form of Yeshu'a. This is probably correct. Rabbinic references to Jesus, where he is called Yeshu, support this suggestion (cf. *b. Sanh.* 43a, 103a [ישו הנוצרי], 107b; and probably *b. 'Abod. Zar.* 16b–17a, though the name Jesus is absent from most mss).

Although no serious scholar has suggested that this ossuary at one time contained the remains of Jesus of Nazareth, it is significant nonetheless. It provides first-century attestation of the shortened form Yeshu (the rabbinic references mentioned in the preceding note are from a later period), which in Greek was usually rendered Ἰησοῦς (the spelling variants are examined on p. 120). And of course, this ossuary attests the affiliation "Jesus, son of Joseph."

The Alexander Son of Simon Ossuary – 1941

Among the ossuaries found by Sukenik in the Kidron Valley in 1941, one bears what appear to be inscriptions referring to a certain Alexander the Cyrene, son of Simon. Although discovered in 1941 by E. L. Sukenik, who published a very brief announcement (in *BASOR* 88 [1942] 38), the inscriptions and a detailed description were not published for another twenty years (see Avigad 1962, 9–11 no. 9 + pl. 4; see also *NEAEHL* 2:753). We find on the front and back sides of ossuary no. 9 clumsy attempts to inscribe in Greek "Alexander (son) of Simon," while on the lid we find in Greek "(bones) of Alexander" and in Hebrew "Alexander (the) Cyrene." The inscriptions read:

front

ΑΛΕΞΑΝΔΡΟϹ — Alexander
ϹΙΜΩΝ — (son of) Simon

back

ϹΙΜΩΝ ΑΛΕ — Simon Ale
ΑΛΕΞΑΝΔΡΟϹ — Alexander
ϹΙΜΩΝΟϹ — (son) of Simon

lid

ΑΛΕΞΑΝΔΡΟΥ — of Alexander
אלכסנדרוס קרנית — Alexander QRNYT

The front and back inscriptions are flawed. On the front the inscriber left Simon in the nominative case (Σίμων), rather than in the genitive (Σίμωνος). On the back he makes the same mistake, realizes his error after inscribing the first three letters of Alexander, then starts over, getting it right in the second and third lines (for another example of an inscriber struggling with the name Alexander, see Rahmani 1994a, no. 179). On the lid the inscriber rightly puts Alexander in the genitive (as possessor of the contents, bones, etc. of the ossuary itself) and then inscribes the name in Hebrew.

It is the last word of the Hebrew epithet on the lid that is problematic. קרנית is thought by some to mean "Cyrenean" (or Cyreanite). J. T. Milik (in Bagatti and Milik 1958, 81) thinks קרנית is an inscriber's error and that קרניה ("[the] Cyrenean") was intended. Avigad (1962, 11) doubts this explanation, but he too thinks קרנית is related to Cyrene (the Hebrew New Testament renders "Cyrene" קוריני; e.g., Matt 27:32; Acts 2:10; 11:20; 13:1). On two ostraca from Masada הקרני appears, possibly in reference to a village in Judea. But it may also mean "the Cyrenean" or "Cyrene" (Mas nos. 26 and 424). On an ossuary lid from Bethphage, Milik reads בן קרנו (Milik 1971, 78). But given the similarity and frequent confusion of *waw* and *yod*, the inscription may read בן קרני ("son of [the] Cyreanite)."

In any event, we have in the Kidron Valley ossuary a very interesting constellation of names. Given the evidence (including the Theodotos Inscription reviewed above), we may actually have the ossuary of the Alexander, son of Simon, the man mentioned in Mark's Gospel: "they compelled a passer-by, Simon of Cyrene [τινα Σίμωνα Κυρηναῖον], who was coming in from the country, the father of Alexander [τὸν πατέρα 'Αλεξάνδρου] and Rufus, to carry his cross" (Mark 15:21; cf. Matt 27:32; Luke 23:26). Martin Hengel (1989, 67 n. 39) entertains the identification, while Pieter van der Horst (1991, 140–41) remarks that "there is at least a good chance that we have here the ossuary of the son of the man who carried Jesus' cross" (see also Kane 1978, 278–79).

Finally, it should be noted that both Matthew and Luke omit reference to Simon's sons Alexander and Rufus. Shem Tob's Hebrew Matthew at this point reflects either confusion or a different tradition; it reads: שמעון הכנעני ("Simeon the Canaanite"), probably under the influence of Matthew 10:4.

The Qorban Ossuary – 1956

In Mark 7:9-13 Jesus makes critical reference to the qorban tradition, whereby assets and property are consecrated, or "given" to God, and are therefore no longer available for profane, or secular use. In some cases, Pharisaic application of this tradition could have negative consequences. As Jesus puts it: ". . . you say, 'If a man tells his father or his mother, "What you would have gained from me is qorban"' (that is, given to God)—then you no longer permit him to do anything for his father or mother . . ." (vv. 11-12). In the past, commentators usually made reference to the mishnaic rules of qorban (esp. as spelled out in *Nedarim*; see, e.g., St-B 1:711–17 [on the parallel at Matt 15:5]).

However, four inscriptions have come to light that attest the custom, to which Jesus alluded, and clarify it helpfully. In 1893 Father Marie-Joseph Lagrange published two of these inscriptions. The first is found on a limestone block (2.4 m x 40 cm) that had been discovered in the excavation of Mount Zion, near "David's Gate" (Lagrange 1893, 220–21). The inscription is in Aramaic and it reads:

לאששא קרבן

for the fire, a gift

Lagrange plausibly surmises that this inscription has to do with someone's vow to provide for the fire for the altar, as seen, for example, in *m. Ned.* 1:3 and other passages where qorban vows are discussed and the provision of fire for the altar is one of the examples.

Lagrange cites a second inscription, this one found on an ossuary discovered on the Mount of Olives. It reads (1893, 221–22):

לאשתא קרבן
מרתה

for the fire, a gift
—Martha

The meaning here is probably the same as in the case of the first inscription (and both spellings אשׁשא and אשׁתא are from the same Aramaic word and mean "fire"). In this case the donor of the consecrated gift for the altar fire is a woman named Martha. Because her name and the inscription appear on an ossuary, it is possible that her gift was a bequest.

In the aftermath of the 1967 Six Day War, which resulted in east Jerusalem falling into Israeli hands, a series of excavations got under way that uncovered the ruins of a mansion (Rupprecht 1991), the so-called "Burnt House," and a variety of other interesting finds. Securing the Western Wall of the Temple Mount finally made it possible to excavate safely in this area as well. In the vicinity of the southwest corner of the Herodian wall that supports the Temple Mount the fragment of a stone vessel (perhaps one of its legs) was uncovered that bore the inscribed word קרבן (Mazar 1969; 1970, 55 + fig. 13).

The word *qorban* or "gift" (קרבן) is found written along with pictures of two birds (the word, in fact, seems to be superimposed over the birds). Mazar (1970, 55) wonders if use of this stone vessel had anything to do with Leviticus 12:8, the woman's offering after childbirth: "And if she cannot afford a lamb, then she shall take two turtledoves or two young pigeons, one for a burnt offering and the other for a sin offering; and the priest shall make atonement for her, and she shall be clean." Mazar also calls our attention to *m. Ma'aser Sheni* 4:10: "One who finds a vessel upon which is inscribed [the word] 'offering' [קרבן]."

It is the fourth inscription, found on an ossuary that was discovered in 1956, first published and discussed by Józef Tadeusz Milik (1956–1957, 235–39 + figs. 2 and 3), that has given us what is probably the parallel to Jesus' reference to qorban in Mark 7. The inscription, found on the lid of the ossuary, is in Aramaic and probably dates to the first century B.C.E. Joseph Fitzmyer (1959; cf. Fitzmyer and Harrington 1978, 168–69, 222–23) has transcribed and translated the inscription as follows:

כל די אנש מתהנה בחלתה דה
קרבן אלה מן דבגוה

Everything that a man will find to his profit in this ossuary (is) an offering to God from the one within it.

קרבן is translated "an offering," its normal meaning. Milik thought the inscription pronounced a curse on anyone who pilfered the contents of the ossuary, so he translated: "Quiconque réutilisera à son profit cet ossuaire-ci, malédiction de Dieu de la part de celui qui est dedans!" (cf. 1956–1957, 235), which in English may be rendered: "Whoever will re-use this ossuary to his profit, may there be a curse of God on behalf of him who is inside!" Milik acknowledges that קרבן is literally "offering" (and he inserts *offrande* in parentheses in his translation). But he understands this offering in an imprecatory sense, as we sometimes see in rabbinic use of the synonym קונם (*qonam*); e.g., *m. Ned.* 4:5. Fitzmyer rightly (1959, 96) finds this reasoning unconvincing.

Fitzmyer thinks it better to understand the inscription as a close parallel to Mark 7:11. "The new inscription does not alter the sense of the word in Matthew or Mark but provides a perfect contemporary parallel" (1959, 100). Fitzmyer is correct. The qorban inscription thus provides a valuable parallel to part of Jesus' teaching, which in this instance stands in tension with Pharisaic legal interpretation (i.e., *halakah*).

The Yehohanan Ossuary – 1968

The discovery in 1968 of an ossuary at Giv'at ha-Mivtar (ossuary no. 4), just north of the city limits of Jerusalem, containing the bones of a man crucified sometime in the 20s of the first century C.E., during the administration of Pontius Pilate, governor of Judea and Samaria, was one of the most dramatic single discoveries in biblical archaeology. In the right heel bone (or *calcaneum*) was found an iron spike (11.5 cm long—not 17–18 cm, as suggested by Haas 1970, 43) with wood fragments attached at both ends. Several studies of the osteological and inscriptional evidence have been published (Haas 1970; Naveh 1970; Tzaferis

1970, 20–27; Charlesworth 1972–1973; Yadin 1973; Møller-Christensen 1976; Kuhn 1979; Puech 1983, 505–7 no. 11; Tzaferis 1985; Zias and Sekeles 1985; Zias and Charlesworth 1992). To date, these are the only known remains of a person crucified in Roman Palestine. As such, this archaeological evidence makes an important contribution to our understanding of the literary evidence.

In recent studies Joe Zias, in collaboration with others, has concluded that most crucifixion victims in the Roman era were hung on crosses, with hands or arms tied or nailed to the crossbeam, and feet, usually heels, nailed to the vertical beam. Zias also concludes that in view of the evidence it is philologically appropriate to speak of being "hanged," with reference to crucifixion. This observation should shed light on the debate surrounding the words תלה and κρεμάννυμι in the Hebrew and Greek Testaments (e.g., Deut 21:23 in both the Hebrew and the LXX; cf. Luke 23:39; Acts 5:30; 10:39; Gal 3:13) and in the Dead Sea Scrolls (e.g., 4Q169 3–4 i 7–8: ". . . he used to hang men alive, [as it was done] in Israel in former times, for to anyone hanging alive on the tree . . ."; 4Q385a 5 i 3–4: ". . . to hang on the tree . . ."; 11QT 64:8–12 [= 4Q524 frag. 14, lines 2–4]: ". . . you are to hang him on a tree until dead. On the testimony of two or three witnesses he will be put to death, and they themselves shall hang him on the tree. If a man is convicted of a capital crime and flees to the nations, cursing his people and the children of Israel, you are to hang him, also, upon a tree until dead . . . anyone hung on a tree is accursed of God and men . . ."), which seem to be used in reference to crucifixion (see Zias and Sekeles 1985, 22–27; Zias and Charlesworth 1992, 282–85).

The inscription itself offers features of interest (Yadin 1973, 22; Rahmani 1994a, no. 218):

יהוחנן
יהוחנן
בן חגקול

Yehohanan
Yehohanan
son of HGQWL

Although Joseph Naveh thought all four words of the inscription were by the same hand (Naveh 1970, 35), it is almost certain that the top line was inscribed by one person and the second and third lines by another. Not only is the first occurrence of Yehohanan, in the upper right, not as deeply etched into the stone as the second and third lines, there are orthographical differences as well, as Yadin has rightly pointed out (1973, 18 and n. 5, though he exaggerates the differences when he says that "the shape of the letters differs greatly in each inscription"). The importance of these observations will be made clear when we turn to the James ossuary at the end of this chapter.

The chief difficulty in the study of the second inscription is the transcription and decipherment of חגקול. Various emendations have been suggested, but no one has succeeded in conjuring up a personal name that is convincing. Naveh (1970, 35) himself suggested a corrupt form of Ezekiel, which Rahmani (1994, 130) accepts. Yadin initially suggested a "corrupt transcription of a foreign name," which he himself subsequently found unconvincing (1973, 18). Yadin later suggested emending the third line to read בן העקול, meaning "son of the one (hanged) with his knees apart" (עיקל means "bowlegged"; cf. Jastrow 1074; *m. Bekhorot* 7:6). Accordingly, the first Yehohanan is the father, the second Yehohanan is the son, whose nickname grimly referred to the fate his father suffered.

Yadin's reconstruction, it must be admitted, is speculative. But it does gain some circumstantial support from an inscription found on an ossuary from the Kidron Valley (Rahmani 1994a, no. 62). The person's name is not inscribed; only his grim sobriquet הגדם ("the amputated [one]") (or, as Ilan 2002, 445 more expansively puts it: "the one whose hands and fingers are cut off"). Sobriquets based on deformities, disabilities, and injuries are not rare in this period of time. We hear of "'One-Eyed [עוירא],' son of Maris" (Rahmani 1994a, no. 822), "Maryam, wife of 'the Cow [העגל]'" (Rahmani 1994a, no. 821), "a certain Nabataeus from Adiabene, called from his misfortune by the name of Keagiras [Κεαγίρας = חגיר], signifying 'lame'" (Josephus, *J.W.* 5.11.5 §474), "Simon 'the Stammerer'" (Josephus, *Vita* 1.1 §3), "Matthias, called 'the Hump-Back'" (Josephus, *Vita* 1.1 §4), "Gaius 'the Dwarf [ננים]'" (Rahmani 1994a, no. 421), "Eleazar 'the Giant'" (Josephus, *Ant.* 18.4.5 §103), and a notorious ancestor, otherwise anonymous, simply called "the disgrace [καλλών / קלון]" (Klein 1920, nos. 6 and 7; *CIJ* nos. 1350–55; cf. Hachlili 2000, 94).

The importance of the discovery of the Yehohanan ossuary and its grim contents lies in the fact that we have at hand evidence from the early first century C.E. of the formal, or proper, burial of a crucifixion victim, a man crucified by the authority of Pontius Pilate, the very official who would not long after condemn Jesus to the same fate. Yehohanan's body was not simply thrown into an unmarked criminal's grave, or into a shallow pit and then covered over with lime. He was buried in a tomb and one year later, in keeping with Jewish practice, his bones were placed in an ossuary, on which his name had been inscribed, a box in which the bones of his son and those of another family member would later be placed. The implications of the Yehohanan ossuary do not support the hypothesis that as a victim of crucifixion Jesus was probably left on the cross or thrown into a shallow pit (cf. Crossan 1995, 188), where his corpse was mauled by animals. On the contrary, the remains of Yehohanan show that proper burial for Jewish crucifixion victims was permitted (at least during peacetime).

Neither Yehohanan nor Jesus of Nazareth was buried honorably. As executed criminals, they would have been denied the normal rites of public mourning, which normally perdured for seven days (cf. Josephus, *Ant.* 17.8.4 §200; *m. Sanh.* 6:6: "they used not to make [open] lamentation . . . for mourning has place in the heart alone"), and their bodies would have been barred from interment in their respective family crypts. Instead, their bodies would have been placed in a crypt reserved for executed criminals (cf. *m. Sanh.* 6:5: "They used not to bury him in the burying-place of his fathers, but two burying-places were kept in readiness by the court, one for them that were beheaded or strangled, and one for them that were stoned or burnt"). One year after death and interment, reburial was permitted. It was then that family members could gather the bones of the deceased, place them in an ossuary, and then place the ossuary in the family tomb (cf. *m. Sanh.* 6:6: "When the flesh had wasted away they gathered together the bones and buried them in their own place"; *Semahot* 13.7: "Neither a corpse nor the bones of a corpse may be transferred from a wretched place to an honored place, nor, needless to say, from an honored placed to a wretched place; but if to the family tomb, even from an honored place to a wretched place, it is permitted"; Zlotnick 1966, 84, 164).

Denying burial in one's family tomb has scriptural precedent and probably lies behind the laws and conventions of the first century. One thinks of the disobedient prophet, in the days of Rehoboam and Jeroboam, who was denied burial in his family's tomb. He is told by another prophet: "Because you have disobeyed the word of the LORD, and have not kept the commandment which the LORD your God commanded you . . . your body shall not come to the tomb of your fathers"

(1 Kgs 13:21-22). Josephus recounts the story, stating that the prophet's punishment was being "deprived of burial in the tombs of his fathers" (*Ant.* 8.9.1 §240).

Josephus remarks that the sins of the rebel Jeroboam were visited upon his family: "It came about, in accordance with the prophecy of God, that some of Jeroboam's kin met death in the city and were torn to pieces and devoured by dogs, while others were eaten by birds. Thus did the house of Jeroboam suffer fitting punishment for his impiety and lawlessness" (*Ant.* 8.11.4 §289). Josephus does not say so explicitly, but the point is not that that members of Jeroboam's family were torn and eaten by animals; it is that they were not properly buried.

A similar calamity overtakes Jehoram, king of Judah, who committed fratricide to consolidate his hold on power. Condemned by a prophet of the LORD, he fell ill and his "bowels came out because of his sickness and he died in great pain . . . he departed with no one's regret, and they buried him in the city of David, but not in the tombs of the kings" (2 Chr 21:19-20). Josephus elaborates with commentary: "The people treated even his dead body with indignity; as they reasoned, I supposed, that one who had died in this manner through the wrath of God was not worthy to obtain a form of burial befitting kings, they neither laid him to rest in the tombs of his fathers nor did they grant him any other honor, but buried him like a commoner" (*Ant.* 9.5.3 §104).

Honorable burial is denied King Joash, who had "forsaken the Lord" (2 Chr 24:24). He is buried in the City of David, but not in the tombs of the kings (2 Chr 24:25). Josephus adds that "he was indeed buried in Jerusalem, but not in the royal tombs of his forefathers, because of his impiety" (*Ant.* 9.8.4 §172).

Perhaps the most grisly account of non-burial involves Jezebel, the wicked queen and wife of Ahab. Because of their sins, which included idolatry and murder, the prophet Elijah foretold that dogs will eat Jezebel and that the relatives of Ahab who die in the city will be eaten by dogs and those who die in the field the birds will eat (1 Kgs 21:23-24). Sure enough, the queen meets a violent and disgraceful end. At Jehu's command, she is thrown from the battlements and trampled under foot. After eating and drinking, the new king commands that "this cursed woman" be buried, "for she is a king's daughter" (2 Kgs 9:34). But when they went to bury her, "they found no more of her than the skull and the feet and the palms of her hands" (2 Kgs 9:35). The prophecy of Elijah was recalled, though with some embellishment: "In the property of Jezreel the dogs shall eat the flesh of Jezebel; and the corpse of Jezebel shall be as dung on the face of the field in the property of Jezreel, so they cannot say 'This is Jezebel'" (2 Kgs 9:36-37). Because of the murder of Naboth, in order to take possession of his vineyard in Jezreel, Jezebel has herself become fertilizer for this field (and that is the implication of having been eaten by dogs, as foretold by the prophet—eaten then defecated). But even more significant is the final statement that people "cannot say 'This is Jezebel.'" That is, she has not been buried; she has no tomb; there is no marker. She has been annihilated in death, as well as in life.

The discovery of the remains of the crucified Yehohanan is consistent with this custom. One year after his death, his family was permitted to gather his bones and place them in an ossuary and place the ossuary in the family vault, where some years later the bones of his son could be added to the bones of the father. Although there is no ossuary or vault in the case of Jesus of Nazareth, we nevertheless find important coherence with this custom also. According to the Synoptic and Johannine Gospels, the body of Jesus (and presumably the bodies of the other two men crucified with Jesus) was placed in a crypt belonging to a member of the court (or, at least a crypt, to which members of the court had access). The story of Jesus' burial at the hands of Joseph of Arimathea (Matt 27:57-61; Mark 15:42-47; Luke 23:50-56; John 19:38-42) exhibits many traces of legendary and apologetic development (such as Joseph being a sympathizer, even a disciple of Jesus; the tomb being new, never used; Nicodemus, another Sanhedrin member, taking part; great quantities of spices and perfumes), but it is in essential agreement with the laws and customs of Jewish Palestine in this period. Jesus' mourning family and friends fully expected to gather his bones one year later and place them in the family tomb (see Wright 2003, 707-8).

House of David Ossuary – 1971

In 1971 Amos Kloner excavated a burial cave at Giv'at Ha-Mivtar, in which were found sixteen ossuaries. The inscription on ossuary M, in burial niche no. 6, reads (Kloner 1972; *NEAEHL* 2:755 + plate; Rahmani 1994a, no. 430; Flusser 1997, 180–86):

של בי דוד

belonging to the house of David

Although it is disputed, דוד is probably best vocalized as "David," and not *dod* ("uncle") or some other form. The Aramaic בי should be understood as the equivalent of the Hebrew בית ("house"). Thus understood, the inscription may be translated "belonging to the house of David," that is, the bones and other contents of the ossuary belong to a descendant of David. As such, this inscription seems to corroborate literary evidence that in the time of Jesus there were Jews who believed that they were indeed descendants of Israel's famous king (e.g., Menahem son of Judah, if we rightly understand the implications of Josephus, *J.W.* 2.17.8–9 §433–48 [Menahem entered Jerusalem "like a veritable king"; one of his followers was named "Absalom"]; *y. Ber.* 2.4; and Eusebius, who reports that various Roman emperors persecuted Davidic descendants; cf. *Hist. Eccl.* 3.12–13: "Vespasian . . . ordered a search to be made for all who were of the family of David"; 3.19–20: "Domitian gave orders for the execution of those of the family of David . . . he asked them if they were of the house of David and they admitted it"; 3.32.3–4: Certain heretics "accused Simon the son of Clopas of being descended from David . . . when Trajan was emperor"; *m. Ta'anit* 4.5: "The wood-offering of the priests and the people was brought nine times . . . on the 20th of Tammuz by the family of David of the tribe of Judah"; cf. Jeremias 1969, 226, 277, 288–89; Jeremias defends the Davidic descent of Menahem, as well as various rabbis, including Hillel).

The "Caiaphas" Ossuary – 1990

In November 1990, while working in Jerusalem's Peace Forest (North Talpiyot), which is 1.5 km south of the Old City, a crew inadvertently uncovered a crypt with four loculi, in which twelve ossuaries were discovered. Happily, most of the ossuaries were found intact, unmolested by grave robbers. Coins and the style of writing seen in the inscriptions have dated these ossuaries to the first century C.E. On one of the ornate ossuaries (ossuary no. 6, measuring 74 cm long, 29 cm wide, and 38 cm high; now on display in the Israel National Museum in Jerusalem), two very interesting inscriptions were found. The inscriptions have been transcribed as follows (cf. Reich 1991 + plates and facsimiles; 1992b + figs. 5 and 6):

side of ossuary:

יהוסף בר
קיפא

Yehoseph bar
Qyph'

end of ossuary:

יהוסף בר קפא

Yehoseph bar Qph'

This ossuary contained the bones of a sixty year old man (and those of two infants, a toddler, a young boy, and a woman) and is thought by some (including the authorities of the aforementioned museum) to be the ossuary of Caiaphas the High Priest, to whom Josephus refers as Joseph Caiaphas (cf. *Ant.* 18.2.2 §35: 'Ιώσηπος ὁ Καϊάφας and 18.4.3 §95: τὸν ἀρχιερέα 'Ιώσηπον τὸν Καϊάφαν ἐπικαλούμενον) and the Gospels and Acts call more simply Caiaphas (Καϊάφας; cf. Matt 26:3, 57; Luke 3:2; John 11:49; 18:13, 14, 24, 28; Acts 4:6). Those who think the ossuary belonged to Caiaphas vocalize the inscribed name as *Qayapha* (or *Qayyapha*), the Hebrew or Aramaic equivalent of the Greek Caiaphas (for more discussion, see Riesner 1991; Greenhut 1992a; 1992b; Reich 1992a; Evans 2000a; for general discussion of Caiaphas and family, see Roth 1971; for report of excavation of what may have been the house of Caiaphas, see Rupprecht 1991).

The High Priest Caiaphas apparently is not mentioned in rabbinic literature, though the family name may appear. In a discussion concerning the ashes of the red heifer, the Mishnah asks, "Who prepared them (since the time of Ezra)? Simeon the Just and Yohanan the High Priest prepared two each, and Elyo'enai the son of ha-Qayaf and Hanamel the Egyptian and Ishmael the son of Piabi prepared one each" (*m. Par.* 3:5). This Elyo'enai the son of ha-Qayaf (הקיף) may have been a son of Joseph Caiaphas (see Schlatter 1959, 733; Stern 1966). Some mss, however, read *ha-Qoph* or *ha-Quph* (הקוף), thus making the identification uncertain. According to the Tosefta, Rabbi Joshua said: "I hereby give testimony concerning the family of the house of 'Aluba'i of Bet Sheba'im and concerning the family of the house of Qayapha [קיפא] of Bet Meqoshesh, that they are children of co-wives, and from them High Priests have been chosen, and they offered up sacrifices on the Temple altar" (*t. Yeb.* 1.10). The identification of this "house of Qayapha" with the Caiaphas family is probable. However, we learn nothing from this tradition beyond the simple fact that this family was a high priestly family that offered sacrifices on the Temple altar.

A slightly different version of the Tosefta tradition appears in Babli: "I testify to you concerning two great families—the house of Zebo'im of Ben 'Akmai and the house of Ben Quphai [קופאי] of Ben Meqoshesh, that they were sons of rivals and yet some of them were High Priests who ministered upon the altar" (*b. Yeb.* 15b). This tradition adds nothing to what we already know, but the spelling variation in the name Quphai attests to the possibilities of variation, which in turn may have a bearing on the question of the spelling and identification of the name found in the famous ossuary. Finally, the Caiaphas family name may also be mentioned in Yerushalmi, where in *Ma'aserot* 8.7 (52a) we hear of one "Menahem, son of Maxima, the brother of Jonathan Caiapha [יונתן קיפא]." Apart from the name itself, there is nothing here that suggests that this Jonathan was related to the high priestly family of Caiaphas.

A second ossuary in the tomb (ossuary no. 3) bears the name קפא. In a third ossuary (ossuary no. 8), containing the bones of a woman and bearing the name מרים ברת שמעון ("Miriam, daughter of Simon"), a coin minted during the reign of Agrippa I (42/43 C.E., with inscription ΒΑϹΙΛΕωϹ [ΑΓΡΙΠΠΑ], "King [Agrippa]") was found in the mouth of the skull, probably reflecting the pagan custom of payment to the Greek god Charon for safe passage across the River Styx (Hachlili and Killebrew 1983a, 148–49; Greenhut 1992b, 70), a custom documented as early as the fifth century B.C.E., and perhaps implying belief in an afterlife (so Bivian 1991). Knowledge among Jewish priestly aristocrats of Greek afterlife mythology is attested by Josephus (*J.W.* 2.8.11 §155–56), by at least one epitaph (*IG* no. 1648; *NewDocs* 4:221–29 no. 114; Horbury and Noy 1992, no. 141: "O pitiless Charon"), and by later rabbinic tradition (*b. Mo'ed Qatan* 28b, in a lament for the departed: "tumbling aboard the ferry and having to borrow his fare"). Depictions of boats on Jewish ossuaries or crypt walls may also allude to the belief of the deceased ferried across the water to the land of the dead (as in Mazar 1973, pl. XX [= Beth She'arim, Hall P, catacomb no. 1]; see also Goodenough 1953a, 97–98 [= Goodenough 1953c, nos. 67 and 77], for examples in Palestine; and Goodenough 1953b, 43 [= Goodenough 1953c, no. 836], for an example in Rome). Saul Lieberman (1965, 512–13) thinks that the "numerous boats on the Jewish graves in Palestine most probably represent the ferry to the other world, i.e. either the divine bark of the ancient Orientals, or Charon's ferry of the Greeks." Benjamin Mazar (1973, 129), however, thinks boat drawings depict only transport of the coffin or ossuary from overseas to the Holy

Land. But Lieberman's explanation is more plausible; after all, overland modes of transport are not depicted in burial settings.

Whatever we are to think of the boat drawings, the practice of placing a coin in the mouth of the deceased cannot be said to be common in Jewish late antiquity. Coins were found in two skulls in tombs in Jericho from our period (in one case a coin from Herod Archelaus, 4 B.C.E.–6 C.E., and in the other case a coin, bearing the image of a ship, from Agrippa I, 41–44 C.E.; Hachlili 1980, 238). But the fact that it was only two out of hundreds strongly suggests that the practice was not common among Jews (rightly Hachlili and Killebrew 1983a; Rahmani 1986, 1993). To return to the Talpiyot crypt, someone evidently placed a coin in the mouth of Simon's daughter Miriam, but we do not know if that had been her wish. It may well have been the superstitious impulse of a friend or servant. Whatever the intention, the coin nevertheless greatly assists in the dating of the ossuaries found in this crypt.

Several scholars and archaeologists (e.g., Greenhut 1992a; 1992b; 1994; Reich 1991; 1992a; 1992b; 1994; Domeris and Long 1994; Flusser 1992; 1997, 195–206) have concluded that the Joseph bar Qyph' ossuary belonged to the former high priest, "Joseph called Qayapha" (as Josephus refers to him). Indeed, some regard the identification as a foregone conclusion, as seen, for example, in the confidence expressed by Dominic Crossan and Jonathan Reed (2001, 242): "There should be no doubt that the chamber was the resting place of the family of the high priest Caiaphas named in the gospels for his role in the crucifixion, and it's very likely that the elderly man's bones were those of Caiaphas himself." In fact, there is substantial doubt.

Some scholars, including Emile Puech (1993a; 1993b) and William Horbury (1994), have expressed reservations. There are three principal reasons for doubting the high priestly identification. The first lies in the fact that the crypt in which the ossuary was found is not on the level of ostentation that one would have expected to find in the case of a former high priest and son-in-law of Annas, the most influential high priest of the first century. In contrast to the ornate, almost palatial crypt of Annas (see description above) is the "Caiaphas" crypt, which is relatively plain (Puech 1993a, 45–46).

Moreover, it seems strange that the ossuary containing the remains of such an important person, who served for nearly nineteen years as high priest, would display such poorly incised inscriptions. The inscribing was not professional, but may have been done by the relative who placed the bones in the box. Indeed, the inscribing may have been done with one or both of the two rusty nails found in the crypt. Further, it seems strange that relatives of such an exalted figure would have placed his bones in an ossuary along with the bones of several other persons, including young children.

The second and far more serious reason for doubting the Caiaphas identification lies in the spelling of the name. It is not at all clear that the second letter in קיפא is a *yod*; it may well be a *waw*, i.e., קופא. In fact, it probably is a *waw*, which more easily explains its absence in קפא in the second inscription on the ossuary and on the other ossuary. For when used as a vowel, the *waw* often drops out (as, e.g., in אלוהים / אלהים, in biblical and post-biblical literature). However, a Caiaphas vocalization requires a consonantal *yod*, i.e., *Qayapha*. The *yod* is not optional and therefore should not drop out. If *Qayapha* was intended, then it is hard to explain the absence of the *yod*. However, if the letter is a *waw* (and the *yod* and *waw* are notoriously difficult to distinguish in the Hebrew script of this period), then the two spellings קופא and קפא are not difficult to explain (so Horbury 1994, 41: *yod* rather than *waw* "seems less likely"; 46: an "ambiguous vowel letter is more probably *waw* than *yodh*"). The incised names should be vocalized as either *Qopha* or *Qupha* (Puech 1993a, 46). That is to say, the inscription refers to one "Joseph, son of Qopha" or "Joseph, son of Qupha" (and even if we read *yod*, the vocalization could be *Qeypha*). There is in fact a person mentioned in Eusebius (*Hist. Eccl.* 4.7.7), whose name is Βαρκώφ, which in Aramaic would be בר קוף ("son of Qoph"). And, of course, the Qoph vocalization agrees with the oldest mishnaic reading (i.e., *m. Para* 3:5), in the oldest manuscripts.

Thirdly, Josephus does not actually call the high priest "Joseph, son of Caiaphas"; he refers to him as "Joseph Caiaphas" and "Joseph called [ἐπικαλούμενον] Caiaphas." So even if we accept the unlikely vocalization *Yehoseph bar Qayapha*, we really do not have a match with the high priest's name as given in Josephus. Although the high priestly identification is not conclusively ruled out, the difficulties are such that it is probably wise to leave the question open. Horbury (1994, 46) thinks that given the coherence with the rabbinic tradition, the name on the ossuary may well have been a priest or related to a priestly family. Puech (1993a; 1993b, 193–95), however, does not think so.

Before ending this discussion, mention should perhaps be made of inscriptional evidence that unambiguously relates to two high priests, and perhaps to two more. The first concerns Theophilus, son of Annas (or Ananus) and brother-in-law of Caiaphas, whose name appears on the ossuary of Yehohanah, granddaughter of the high priest. The ossuary made its appearance in the antiquities market in 1983 and almost certainly was looted from a crypt either in Jerusalem or in nearby Hizma. The inscription is found on the decorated side of the ossuary, within the middle arch of three arches. It reads (Barag and Flusser 1986, 39; Rahmani 1994a, no. 871):

יהוחנה
יהוחנה ברת יהוחנן
בר תפלוס הכהן הגדל

Yehohanah
Yehohanah, daughter of Yehohanan,
son of Theophilus the high priest

Theophilus was appointed to the office of high priest in 37 C.E. by Vitellius, who ordered Pontius Pilate to return to Rome, after the Samaritan incident in late 36 C.E. According to Josephus, Vitellius "deposed Jonathan [immediate successor to Caiaphas] from his office as high priest and conferred it on Jonathan's brother Theophilus" (*Ant.* 18.5.3 §123).

The name Theophilus in the ossuary inscription (תפלוס) is a transliteration of the Greek name Θεόφιλος. Among Jews the name is relatively rare. The name appears in the *Letter of Aristeas* (49), but this character is fictional. The name appears in the Lukan evangelist's prefaces to the Gospel of Luke (1:3) and the book of Acts (1:1), but this individual (who is a real person, not a symbol or metaphor) is probably not Jewish. The feminine form of the name appears in Greek (Θε[ο]φίλα) and Hebrew (תפלה) on another ossuary (Sukenik 1932a, 25–26; *CIJ* no. 1241).

On an ostracon found at Masada (Mas no. 461) were inked the words:

ח[נני]ה כהנא רבא עקביא בריה

A[nani]as the high priest, 'Aqavia his son

The inscription may refer to Ananias, son of Nedebaeus, who served as high priest from 47–59 C.E. According to Josephus, "Herod, king of Chalcis, now removed Joseph, the son of Camei, from the high priesthood and assigned the office to Ananias, the son of Nedebaeus, as successor" (*Ant.* 20.5.2 §103). This may be the man mentioned in the New Testament, who orders Paul be struck (Acts 23:2-5). In the aftermath of the violence between Samaritans and Galileans and various accusations, Ananias is placed in chains and sent to Rome (*Ant.* 20.6.2 §131). The outcome of this trial is not clear. It is possible that the "Eleazar, son of Ananias the high priest," who persuaded officials to discontinue sacrifices for Rome and the Roman Emperor (*J.W.* 2.17.2 §409–10), is the son of Ananias, son of Nedebaeus.

The appearance of his name on an ostracon at Masada does not mean that the former high priest was numbered among the rebels during the war, or that he had been at Masada, or that he owned the jar on which his name has been found. It is speculated that his son 'Aqavia simply appealed to the prestige of his father, who had served as high priest, perhaps guaranteeing the purity of the contents of the jar.

We may have the name of a third high priest attested. On a circular stone weight found in the ruins of the "Burnt House" (70 C.E.) in the old city of Jerusalem (not too far from the southwest corner of the Temple Mount) we find inscribed:

[ד]בר
קתרס

[of] the son of
Qatros

The name may also be found inked on an ostracon from Masada (Mas no. 405). It reads: בת קתרא ("daughter of Qatra").

The son of Qatros on the stone weight from Jerusalem and (somewhat less probably) the daughter of Qatra on the ostracon from Masada may have been members of one of the principal high priestly families that held sway in the last century or so of the Second Temple period. Later rabbis would remember these families in a critical light: "Violent men of the priesthood came and took away (the tithes) by force . . . Concerning these and people like them . . . Abba Saul ben Bitnit and Abba Yose ben Yohanan of Jerusalem say: 'Woe is me because of the House of Boethos. Woe is me because of their clubs. Woe is me because of the house of Qadros [קדרוס]. Woe is me because of their pen. Woe is me because of the house of Hanan (i.e., Annas). Woe is me because of their whispering. Woe is me because of the house of Ishmael ben Phiabi'" (*t. Menah.* 13.19, 21). This activity of violence and theft is also described by Josephus: "But Ananias [probably the son of Hanan, or Annas] had servants who were utter rascals and who, combining operations with the most reckless men, would go to the threshing floors and take by force the tithes of the priests; nor did they refrain from beating those who refused to give. The high priests were guilty of the same practices as his slaves, and no one could stop them" (*Ant.* 20.9.2 §206). This Qatros may be the Cantheras (Κανθήρας) mentioned by Josephus (*Ant.* 20.1.3 §16; see Brody 1990). Attempts to identify Cantheras with Caiaphas are not persuasive.

And finally, we may also have the name of Boethos, whose name appeared above in the passage cited from the Tosefta. On an ossuary found on the western slope of Mount Scopus, Jerusalem, we find inscribed (Sukenik 1934b, 67; Rahmani 1994a, no. 41):

בוטון
שמעון בוטון

Boethos
Shim'on, of (the family of) Boethos

Sukenik (1934b) links this inscription and ossuary to the family of Simon, son of Boethos (Σίμων . . . υἱὸς Βοηθοῦ) of Alexandria, whom Herod appointed to the high priesthood, in order to marry his daughter (Josephus, *Ant.* 15.9.3 §320–22). The Qatros, or Canteras, mentioned above, may have been his son. The form בוטון (*Boton*), Sukenik suggests, represents the genitive plural (Βοηθῶν) of Βοηθός. Accordingly, the inscription literally means "Simon, of the Boethians." Sukenik's suggestions are plausible and may well be correct, even if they remain unproven. Goodenough (1953a, 115; 1953c, figs. 107 and 108) comments on the peculiarity of the artwork on this ossuary, but says nothing about the inscription itself.

We may have inscriptional evidence of yet another member of this family. On an ossuary we have "Yoezer, son of Simon" (*CIJ* no. 1354) and on ostraca from Masada we have "Yoezer" (Mas no. 383) and "Simeon ben Yoezer" (Mas no. 466; Yadin 1966, 96). The affiliation of Yoezer and Simeon is significant in light of what Josephus relates: "Jozar [= Yoezer], also a Pharisee, came of a priestly family; the youngest, Simon, was descended from high priests" (*Vita* 39 §197). This "Jozar" may be the same person as Joazar, son of Boethos (cf. Josephus, *Ant.* 17.6.4 §164; 18.1.1 §3), who himself served as high priest briefly in 4 B.C.E.

In the rabbinic passage cited above, it is said of the family of Boethos: "Woe is me because of their clubs." The tradition is probably recalling the violence some of the ruling priests practiced against their lower-ranking brethren in the final years of the second temple. Josephus refers to this violence, though in reference to the high priest Ananias in the passage cited above (i.e., *Ant.* 20.9.2 §206).

The Talpiot district of Jerusalem, where the so-called Caiaphas crypt was discovered, has yielded up many tombs and ossuaries (see Fishwick 1963; Kloner 1996).

The James Ossuary – 2002

The discovery of the ossuary, on which are inscribed the words, "James, son of Joseph, brother of Jesus," was mentioned above in the Introduction (see also Shanks 2003a; 2003b; Silberman 2003; Evans 2003, 39–40). We may now turn to the study of this ossuary, though no position here is taken with respect to the antiquity or authenticity of the inscription that has generated so much controversy.

The ossuary is some 50 cm long, at the base, widening to 56 cm at the top, some 30 cm wide at one end and about 26 cm wide at the other, and about 30 cm high. (Thus the ossuary is not perfectly rectangular in form.) The inscription, which is made up of five words, is 19 cm long. The lid is flat and rests on a ledge inside the rim. One corner of the lid is chipped away. Badly weathered, the ossuary reveals faint traces of rosettes on one side. It is also reported that the ossuary contained several small bone fragments.

The inscription reads as follows:

יעקוב בר יוסף אחוי דישוע

Jacob, son of Joseph, brother of Yeshu'a
or James, son of Joseph, brother of Jesus

There are no spaces between the words; the letters are quite legible, and are deeply etched into the limestone. Andre Lemaire (2002, 28, 33) has concluded that the style of writing points to the last two decades prior to the destruction of Jerusalem and that in all probability the inscription is authentic and is in reference to early Christianity's James the brother of Jesus.

James the brother of Jesus is mentioned a few times in the New Testament. He and his brothers and sisters are mentioned when Jesus is rebuffed in Nazareth: "Is not this the carpenter, the son of Mary and brother of James [ἀδελφὸς Ἰακώβου] and Joses and Judas and Simon, and are not his sisters here with us?" (Mark 6:3; cf. Matt 13:55). No indication is given in the Gospels that James was a disciple of Jesus. But that changes after Easter, for James emerges as the leader of the Jerusalem church (cf. Acts 12:17: "Tell this to James and to the brethren"; 15:13; 21:18). According to Paul, the risen Jesus appeared to James (cf. 1 Cor 15:7: "Then he appeared to James, then to all the apostles") and was regarded as a "pillar" in the early church (cf. Gal 1:19: "James the Lord's brother" [Ἰάκωβον τὸν ἀδελφὸν τοῦ κυρίου]; 2:9 : "James and Cephas and John, who were reputed to be pillars"; 2:12: "certain men came from James"). The letter of Jude identifies the author as "Jude, a servant of Jesus Christ and brother of James [ἀδελφὸς δὲ Ἰακώβου]" (v. 1; cf. Mark 6:3: "brother of James . . . and Judas"). And, of course, the New Testament contains a letter whose author is identified as "James, a servant of God and of the Lord Jesus Christ" (v. 1).

According to Hegesippus, James "was called the 'Just' by every one from the Lord's time till our own, for there were many Jameses" (*apud* Eusebius, *Hist. Eccl.* 2.23.4). Eusebius goes on to say (*Hist. Eccl.* 2.23.4–8) that James was "holy from the womb," that he apparently observed the Nazirite requirements, that he frequented the temple, praying for the people, and that he was referred to as the "gate of Jesus," perhaps alluding to Psalm 118:19-20 ("this is the gate of the Lord"). When James refuses to discontinue his proclamation of Jesus as Messiah he is flung from the pinnacle of the temple (cf. Matt 4:5), stoned and clubbed to death, and buried nearby (*Hist. Eccl.* 2.23.11–18: "they buried him on the spot by the temple, and his gravestone remains by the temple"). Josephus apparently also refers to the death of James:

> Ananus thought that he had a favorable opportunity because Festus was dead and Albinus was still on the way. And so he convened the judges of the Sanhedrin and brought before them a man named James, the brother of Jesus [τὸν ἀδελφὸν Ἰησοῦ . . . Ἰάκωβος ὄνομα αὐτῷ] who was called the Christ [cf. *Ant.* 18.3.3 §63–64], and certain others. He accused them of having transgressed the law and delivered them up to be stoned. Those of the inhabitants of the city who were considered the most fair-minded and who were strict in observance of the law were offended at this. . . . King Agrippa, because of Ananus' action, deposed him from the high priesthood,

> which he had held for three months, and replaced him with Jesus the son of Damnaeus. (*Ant.* 20.9.1 §200–3)

If the James mentioned here is the brother of Jesus (and so we assume that the passage as we have it is authentic), then James died in 62 C.E., not long after Festus the Roman procurator died. If so, then we may further assume that the bones of James would have been gathered and placed in an ossuary in 63 C.E.

James is mentioned in other early Christian writers, including Clement of Alexandria, who says: "After the ascension of the Savior, Peter, James, and John did not claim preeminence because the Savior had specially honored them, but chose James the Just as bishop of Jerusalem" (*Hypotyposes* 6); and at greater length:

> James the Just, John, and Peter were entrusted by the Lord after his resurrection with the higher knowledge. They imparted it to the other apostles, and the other apostles to the seventy, one of whom was Barnabas. There were two Jameses, one of the Just, who was thrown down from the pinnacle and beaten to death with a fuller's club, the other the James who was beheaded. (*Hypotyposes* 7)

The sobriquet "the Just" (ὁ δίκαιος) is interesting. We also have a high priest "Simon the Just." Of him Josephus says: "On the death of the high priest Onias, he was succeeded by his son Simon, who was surnamed the Just [ὁ δίκαιος] because of both his piety toward God and his benevolence to his countrymen" (*Ant.* 12.2.5 §43; cf. Sir 50:1). The sobriquet also parallels the title given the Teacher of Righteous mentioned in the Dead Sea Scrolls (the Greek and Hebrew words translated "just" and "righteous" are the same). These parallels support a Judaic, if not authentic background for the honorific title applied to James.

The life, teaching, and martyrdom of James are featured in a variety of sources. For example, we have the *Protevangelium of James*, which fills in the gaps of Jesus' family, and the *Ascents of James*, which interprets the significance of James' ascent up the steps of the temple. (The interesting figure James of Kefar Sekaniah, who is described in rabbinic literature as a disciple of Jesus [cf. *t. Hullin* 2.22; *b. 'Abod. Zar.* 17a], is probably not to be identified with James the brother of Jesus.)

Because of his relationship to Jesus, James is a favorite in Gnostic circles, lending his name to the *Apocryphon of James* (NHC I, 2), the *First Apocalypse of James* (NHC V, 3), and the *Second Apocalypse of James* (NHC V, 4). In the *Gospel of Thomas*, which gives the apostle

Thomas pride of place (cf. Prologue, §1, §13), we find an interesting saying about James:

> The disciples say to Jesus: "We know that you will go away from us. Who is it that shall be Rabbi over us?" Jesus says to them: "In the place that you have come, you shall go to James the Just, for whose sake heaven and earth came to be." (§12)

The declaration that it was for the sake of James that "heaven and earth came to be" has a rabbinic ring to it. In reference to Hanina ben Dosa, a first-century sage known for piety and powerful prayers, we are told: "Each day a heavenly voice issued forth from Mount Horeb and said: 'The whole universe is sustained on account of my son, Hanina'" (*b. Ta'anit* 24b).

What we have in these traditions, and only a sampling has been provided (for fuller presentations of the primary materials, see Bauckham 1999a; 1999b; Chilton and Evans 1999; Painter 1999; Chilton and Neusner 2001), is significant evidence of the importance of James, the brother of Jesus, in the first decades of the Jesus movement. The recently discovered James ossuary, if indeed it was the ossuary of James, the brother of Jesus, could potentially provide additional information about this important figure.

There are three major issues involved in the study of the ossuary. The first issue is linguistic. Is this Aramaic inscription genuine Aramaic, and, if it is, is it Aramaic in use in the first century? These questions touch on the larger issue of the inscription's authenticity. The second issue concerns the three names that appear in the inscription. Is there any way to identify them? The third issue concerns the significance of the ossuary. If the inscription reflects genuine first-century Aramaic, and if the James of the inscription is the James of the early Church, what is gained?

Paleographical and Linguistic Issues

Shortly after the announcement of the existence of the ossuary and the publication of photographs, some scholars and writers expressed skepticism with regard to the authenticity of the inscription on morphological and paleographical grounds. It was noticed that the *dalet* (i.e., the letter d, here meaning "of") prefixed to Yeshu'a is oddly formed, almost having the appearance of a misformed *'ayin*. Others thought they could detect slight differences in style among the words themselves. Accordingly, some scholars have expressed suspicions that the last two words, אחוי ("[his] brother") and דישוע ("of Yeshu'a"), were written by a second hand, perhaps at a date much later than the first century. In other words, the ossuary is probably genuine, reaching back to the first century, and the first three Aramaic words, "James, son of Joseph," are probably also genuine. It is the last two Aramaic words, "brother of Jesus," that were added at a later time. Perhaps. But the linguistic and paleographical evidence for this suspicion is feeble (cf. Fitzmyer 2002). First of all, recognized paleographers who know the morphology of Hebrew and Aramaic better than anyone see nothing amiss in the James ossuary inscription. These people include Ada Yardeni, André Lemaire, Frank Cross, the dean of Hebrew and Aramaic paleography (cf. Cross 1961), and others. They see nothing that suggests that the form of the letters in the inscription does not date from the first century or that the last two words of the inscription were composed by a second hand (for study of ossuary paleography, see Cross 1961; Rosenthaler 1975; Barkay 1989).

The most problematic letter, in terms of morphology, is the letter *dalet*, as has been mentioned. In the James ossuary inscription the vertical stroke of this letter moves to the left as it moves downward, the horizontal part stroke moves somewhat upward as it goes from right to left, and there is an exaggerated kern rising above the horizontal stroke. However, we find a similar form in the first *dalet* in the "house of David" ossuary inscription (cf. Rahmani 1994a, no. 430) and almost identical forms of *dalet* in the "Judith, daughter of Nadab" ossuary inscription (Rahmani 1994a, no. 572). There are simply no grounds for disputing either the authenticity or identification of the letter *dalet* in the James ossuary inscription.

Secondly, the inscription has been found to be linguistically sound. Some journalists, even a few scholars, early on claimed that the Aramaic was flawed, that the last two words אחוי דישוע (*ahui deYeshu'a*) were somehow redundant, as though they meant "brother of of Jesus." This objection, however, is completely without foundation, for the construction אחוי ("[his] brother" or "brother [of]"), followed by a noun or proper name prefixed with a *dalet*, is well attested in Aramaic. One need look no further than the Targum for examples. In Genesis 14:13 "brother of Eshcol and of Aner" in Hebrew is אחי אשכל ואחי ענר, but in Aramaic it is אחוי דאשכל ואחוי דענר (cf. *Tg. Neof.*), precisely the form we have in the James ossuary (see also *Tg. Neof.* Gen 10:21; 28:5; 43:29).

The אחוי form is also attested in an inscription from the Umm el-'Amed synagogue: שמעון אחוי ("Simeon, his brother"; Fitzmyer and Harrington 1978, 268–69, 298). More importantly, the form is attested in *1QapGen* 21:34: לות בר אחוי ("Lot, son of his [Abram's] brother"; Fitzmyer and Harrington 1978, 122).

Perhaps the closest and most important parallel is found inscribed on another ossuary, dating from either the first century B.C.E. or the first century C.E. and found on Mount Scopus. The inscription reads (Rahmani 1994a, no. 570 + plate 80):

שימי בר עשיה אחוי [ד]חנין

Shimi, son of Asaiah, brother of Hanin

The *dalet* prefix must be partially restored; the horizontal stroke is effaced, but the vertical stroke is plainly visible. The name Hanin is quite legible, as well as the preceding אחוי ("[his] brother"). The *dalet* is therefore probable, for no other letter will serve the context. שימי is a contraction of שמאי ("Shemaia"). Both forms of the name were used by rabbinic authorities (for Shemaia, cf. *b. Pesah.* 7a; *b. Yeb.* 71a; for Shimi, cf. *b. Ber.* 10a, 31a; *b. Shab.* 109b). The name עשיה ("Asaiah") appears in the Bible (cf. 2 Kgs 22:12, 14; 1 Chr 4:36; 6:30; 9:5; 15:6, 11; 2 Chr 34:20). The name חנין ("Hanin"), a contraction of חנינא ("Hanina" or "Hananiah") and perhaps also a form of חנן ("Hanan"), is very common in the late second temple period, well attested in rabbinic literature and—in the uncontracted form—in ossuary inscriptions (cf. Ilan 2002, 99–102 [thirty-nine individuals named Hanan], 103–8 [eighty-six individuals named Hananiah]).

It has been plausibly suggested that the addition of the words "brother of Jesus" or "brother of Hanin" to the respective inscriptions implies that the brother is better known than the occupant of the ossuary. If the occupant of the James ossuary is none other than James, brother of Jesus, this is certainly the case. Who was Shimi's brother Hanin? Because the name is so common, it is not possible to identify this person. Identification with the high priestly dynasty of Hanin would certainly satisfy the hypothesis, but this identification is doubtful. Hanin, the great patriarch (Annas ["Anna"] in the New Testament; cf. Luke 3:2; John 18:13, 24; Acts 4:6), sharply criticized in rabbinic literature (cf. *b. Pesah.* 57a: "Woe is me because of the house of Hanin!"), was the son of Sethi (or perhaps Seth), according to Josephus (cf. *Ant.*

18.2.1 §26: "Quirinius . . . installed Ananus, the son of Sethi [῎Ανανον τὸν Σεθί] as high priest"), not the son of Asaiah. He cannot therefore be the brother of Shimi. We also have a well-known Rabbi Hanin (cf. *b. Ber.* 32b; *b. Shab.* 32a; *b. Yoma* 41b), but there are other rabbis named Hanin (and Hanina, the uncontracted form of the name). None of these rabbinic authorities is further identified as a "son of Asaiah." Therefore, unless another inscription or source comes to light, in which this Hanin, son of Asaiah, is identified, we shall never know who he was or why the inscriber of Shimi's ossuary thought he was an important person.

The skepticism with which the discovery of the James ossuary was met is reminiscent of the skepticism expressed with regard to the Uzziah inscription, when it came to light more than seventy years ago. William F. Albright (1932, 8) had this to say:

> Owing to the circumstances of its discovery a number of scholars have expressed doubts regarding its authenticity. The writer is generally inclined to be hypersceptical concerning the genuineness of inscriptions not found in excavations, but in this case he believes that there is as little reason for suspicion as there is in the case of the Mesha Stone and the Elephantine Papyri, both of which were at first declared to be forgeries, ancient or modern, by scholars of some reputation. When the Mesha Stone was discovered its script and language were both unique; now we have many inscriptions with the same forms of characters, and belonging to the same century, while the suspected linguistic details have been paralleled in large part by old Canaanite documents from Byblos and elsewhere. The mass of material illustrating the script, language, and other data of the Elephantine Papyri is increasing yearly, and thousands of confirmatory facts may easily be adduced.

The relevance of Albright's comments for the current debate surrounding the James ossuary requires no elaboration.

The Names

All three names of the James ossuary (Jacob, Joseph, and Jesus) were common in the late second temple period and are well represented among ossuary and crypt inscriptions.

James (or Jacob)

Ilan (2002, 171–74) identifies forty-five individuals who bore the name Jacob. In the James ossuary Jacob is spelled with the *waw*: יעקוב (as in Jer 30:18 יַעֲקוֹב). It appears in this form in at least three other ossuaries: "Jacob," "Aha and Jacob, his son," and "Jacob" (Rahmani 1994a, nos. 104, 396, and 678, respectively). Jacob also appears on two ossuaries without the *waw* (i.e., יעקב, as in Gen 25:26 *et passim* יַעֲקֹב): "Martha, daughter of Joseph, son of Jacob, wife of Joseph, from Hin" and "Jacob Birebbi," or "Jacob, son of the great" (Rahmani 1994a, nos. 290 and 865, respectively). In Greek inscriptions Jacob appears, spelled variously Ἰακώ (*CIJ* no. 956; Schwabe and Lifshitz 1974, nos. 83, 126, and 130), Ἰακώβ (Schwabe and Lifshitz 1974, no. 75), Ἰακώβω (*CIJ* no. 1482), Ἰάκωβος (Schwabe and Lifshitz 1974, no. 125), Ἰάκκωβος (Schwabe and Lifshitz 1974, no. 6), Ἰακώς (Schwabe and Lifshitz 1974, no. 203), Ἰάκουβος (*CIJ* nos. 1467 and 1505), and Ἴκουβος (Schwabe and Lifshitz 1974, nos. 94 and 96). In the LXX it regularly appears as Ἰακώβ, while in the New Testament it appears as Ἰακώβ or Ἰάκωβος. The latter form is an accommodation to Greek inflection.

Joseph

Ilan (2002, 150–68, 449) identifies 232 individuals who bore the name Joseph. In the James ossuary Joseph is spelled יוסף (*Yoseph*), which is the standard spelling of the name in the Hebrew Bible (e.g., Gen 30:24: יוֹסֵף). There is one other example of this spelling in an ossuary inscription: "Pinhas, son of Joseph" (Rahmani 1994a, no. 573). The most common spelling is יהוסף (*Yehoseph*), which only occurs once in the Hebrew Bible (cf. Ps 81:6 [Eng. 81:5]: יְהוֹסֵף). There are numerous examples of this spelling in ossuary inscriptions: "Our father, Simeon the elder, Joseph his son," "Master Joseph, son of Benaia, son of Judah," "Joseph, son of Haggai," and many others (Rahmani 1994a, nos. 12, 327, and 603). Other Semitic forms include יהוסיף, יהסף, יוסי, and יוסה. Greek forms include Ἰωσέ, Ἰοσέ, Ἰοσῆ (Schwabe and Lifshitz 1974, nos. 19, 41, 43, 48, 93, 124, and 221), Ἰωσήφ (Schwabe and Lifshitz 1974, nos. 23, 26, 32, 33, 44, and 178), Ἰωσῆφος (*CIJ* no. 1485; Horbury and Noy 1992, no. 132), Ἰωασάφ (Schwabe and Lifshitz 1974, no. 45), Ἰώσεφος (Horbury and Noy 1992, no. 12), Ἰώσηπος (*CIJ* no. 1427), and Ἰωσῆς (Horbury and Noy 1992, no. 143). The most common biblical Greek form is Ἰωσήφ, though Ἰώσηπος is attested a few times in the Apocrypha.

Jesus

Ilan (2002, 126–33, 449) identifies 104 individuals who bore the name Jesus or its older form Joshua. There is a similar range of diversity in the forms of the name Jesus, as we have seen in the names Jacob and Joseph. In the James ossuary it is spelled ישוע (*Yeshu'a*). This form is late biblical and is vocalized יֵשׁוּעַ, occurring several times in Ezra, Nehemiah, and Chronicles. The older, fuller form is יְהוֹשֻׁעַ (*Yehoshu'a*), or Joshua. In post-biblical Hebrew ישוע was sometimes abbreviated יֵשׁוּ (*Yeshu*). ישוע, the form found in the James ossuary, is attested in at least another four or five ossuaries: "Jesus, son of Dostas," "Jesus," "Judah, son of Jesus," and "Jesus, son of Joseph" (Rahmani 1994a, nos. 121, 140, 702, and 704; the Joshua form is attested in no. 63). In one example, the longer form ישוע and its abbreviation ישו occur together: "Yeshu . . . Yeshu'a, son of Joseph" (Rahmani 1994a, no. 9). In rabbinic literature the abbreviated form is used in reference to Jesus (cf. *b. Sanh.* 43a, 103a "Yeshu ha-Nosri," or "Jesus the Nazarene"; see Herford 1903, 56–57, 83–86). Greek forms of the name Jesus include Ἰησοῦς (the most common form in the LXX and New Testament, as well as in the Greek ossuary inscriptions; cf. *CIJ* nos. 1476 and 1511; Schwabe and Lifshitz 1974, no. 51; Rahmani 1994a, nos. 56, 113, 114, and 751), Ἰήσιος (Rahmani 1994a, no. 89), Ἰεσοῦς (Klein 1920, no. 46), Ἰέσουος (Schwabe and Lifshitz 1974, nos. 138, 139, and 140), and Ἴσουος (Lifshitz 1967, 58).

These names are common in Jewish late antiquity. What encourages us to entertain the possibility that the Jacob (or James) of the James ossuary is none other than the brother of Jesus are two factors: (1) the proper affiliation of three names, and (2) the unsual reference to the brother. The first point narrows the odds considerably. Because we do not know the population of Israel in the middle of the first century C.E., or even the population of the city of Jerusalem (cf. Broshi 1975, 1978; Byatt 1973; Wilkinson 1974; Strange 1982), and because we do not know exactly how many men were named Jacob, Joseph, and Jesus in the middle of the first century, we can only guess how many families had a father named Joseph, who had two sons named Jacob and Jesus. But it is the second point, the reference to the brother, that narrows the odds significantly, perhaps decisively. It is reasonably conjectured that the addition of "brother of so-and-so" implies that the brother is well known, probably better known than either the father or the deceased himself. This would certainly be the case if the James ossuary was in fact the ossuary of James, the brother of Jesus. Although we cannot conclude that the James ossuary has been identified with certainty, we should be able to speak of probability.

Significance of the James Ossuary and Inscription

If the James ossuary was indeed the ossuary of James, the brother of Jesus, what is gained? It seems to me we gain at least four things, all four of which contribute significantly to understanding better the world in which James lived and the early Christian movement grew.

(1) James and family probably spoke Aramaic, which scholars have long recognized as Jesus' first language. The James ossuary lends an important measure of support to this hypothesis. Of course, one could object and say that all we know is that the inscriber of the ossuary spoke Aramaic; not necessarily James. But given the personal, family-oriented reality of ossilegium, it is wiser to assume that the language used in the inscription is the language of the family and, therefore, of the deceased.

(2) James, originally of Galilee, continued to live in or near Jerusalem. We are left with this impression in the New Testament (particularly the book of Acts and Paul's letter to the churches of Galatia). After all, if James' family and home were still in Galilee, then we should not have expected his ossuary to be found in Jerusalem. Its discovery in Jerusalem shows that in all probability his home had become Jerusalem. Therefore, when his bones were gathered and placed in an ossuary, the ossuary remained in Jerusalem, in the family tomb.

(3) The James ossuary may also suggest that James probably died in or near Jerusalem, as early church traditions maintain. If the ossuary was discovered in a burial vault near the Temple Mount, perhaps in the Kidron Valley, as has been conjectured, this may offer a measure of support to the tradition that James was closely associated with the temple, even if at odds with the powerful priestly family of Annas (a.k.a. Hanin). Of course, this suggestion is at best tenuous, but the discovery of the ossuary of James in the general vicinity of the Temple Mount does lend a small measure of support to Christian tradition and to the brief report of James' death found in Josephus.

(4) And finally, secondary burial, according to Jewish burial custom, implies that James, though a follower of Jesus and part of a movement that was beginning to drift away from its Jewish heritage, continued to live as a Jew, and so was buried as a Jew. The Christianity of James, we

may infer, was not understood as something separate from or opposed to Jewish faith. This observation is completely in step with a critical reading of the traditions about James found in the New Testament, especially in the unvarnished account we have in Paul, in his letter to the churches of Galatia. There we are told that even a major figure like Peter was cowed by the arrival in Antioch of "men from James," with the result that the apostle no longer ate with Gentiles (Gal 2:11-14). It is clear from the context that Peter withdrew from Gentiles because the men from James were Torah-observant and evidently expected Peter and other Jewish believers (such as Barnabas) to be Torah-observant also.

If the James ossuary is indeed the ossuary of James, the brother of Jesus, we are in possession of a truly significant artifact that confirms and clarifies several important aspects of the life and impact of James, an important leader in the early Christian movement, who has by and large been overlooked and whose contribution has been minimized. The discovery of the James ossuary, if nothing else, may have the happy result of raising the level of interest in this significant person.

Conclusion

Study of Jewish ossuaries and burial practices is rewarding. Apart from texts themselves, ossuaries and tomb inscriptions are arguably the most important surviving artifacts from Jewish late antiquity. Remains of buildings, especially synagogues, are very helpful, to be sure. But the artwork and inscriptions of sepulture tell us a great deal about the world of the living. We are better acquainted with names (occasionally identifiable names), family relations, occupations, titles, customs, and beliefs. The contents of sepulture provide us with the usual artifactual data (from pottery, coins, and the like), but they also provide us important anthropological and social data (from the human remains and how they were treated). We have more accurate ideas of the health, longevity, and mortality of the Jewish people of late antiquity

Some of the ossuaries and inscriptions directly contribute to issues surrounding the historical Jesus. One ossuary refers to qorban in a way that clarifies Jesus' debate in Mark 7. Another ossuary contained the remains of a man who had been crucified during the administration of Pontius Pilate, the very Roman governor who sentenced Jesus to death on the cross. The relevance this find has for the question of what happened to the body of Jesus is obvious, even if not all agree with respect to the answer. Still another ossuary may well refer to the man from Cyrene, who carried Jesus' cross. Possibly, though not probably, we have an ossuary that may have contained the remains of Caiaphas, the high priest who interrogated Jesus and delivered him to the Roman governor. We may not have uncovered the tomb of Caiaphas, but we may have located the tomb of the family of his father-in-law Annas. And, of course, we may even have the ossuary that at one time contained the skeletal remains of James, the brother of Jesus. If the inscription on this ossuary is authentic, and if it refers to this James, then we have important clarification and corroboration of New Testament and early Christian traditions about this important figure in the early church.

Jewish burial practices, including ossilegium, clarify at important points Jesus' teaching and ministry. His reference to white-washed tombs, his curious injunction to "let the dead bury their own dead," and other references to tombs and the dead are significantly nuanced in the light of the study of Jewish sepulture in late antiquity. The entire drama surrounding the burial of Jesus—taking note of where his body was placed, returning Sunday morning for further ministrations—is clarified by study of Jewish burial practices and beliefs.

The practice of ossilegium among the Jewish people is itself an intriguing field of study. In what way, if any, it contributed to or reflected belief in the resurrection of the dead (perhaps reflective of Ezekiel 37) is an important question. How, if at all, this practice may have been understood differently in the Herodian period is a related question and will no doubt continue to be the subject of debate.

The study of Jewish sepulture in late antiquity enables us to take a significant step back and into the world of Jesus and his first followers. As in the case of archaeology in general, little is proven, but much is learned. The value of this study lies not in apologetics, but in what light it sheds on customs, beliefs, historical events, and meaning in texts.

It is hoped that this little book will prove useful to the nonexpert who wants to know more about a subject that strikes many as arcane, if not morbid. It is hoped that this little book will also prove useful to the scholar, who perhaps needs to be persuaded of the study of Jewish material culture, if we are to understand biblical literature as fully as our limited sources permit.

Abbreviations

Modern

ABD	D. N. Freedman et al., eds., *The Anchor Bible Dictionary* (6 vols., New York: Doubleday, 1992)
ABRL	Anchor Bible Reference Library
ABW	*Archaeology in the Biblical World*
ADAJ	*Annual of the Department of Antiquities of Jordan*
AGJU	Arbeiten zur Geschichte des antiken Judentums and des Urchristentums
AJA	*American Journal of Archaeology*
AJP	*American Journal of Philology*
ANRW	*Aufstieg und Niedergang der römischen Welt*
BA	*Biblical Archaeologist*
BAR	*Biblical Archaeology Review*
BASOR	*Bulletin of the Schools of Oriental Research*
BBR	*Bulletin for Biblical Research*
BeO	*Bibbia e Oriente*
BibOr	Biblica et orientalia
BibSem	The Biblical Seminar
BJ	*Bonner Jahrbücher*
BK	*Bibel und Kirche*
BMAP	E. G. Kraeling, ed., *Brooklyn Museum Aramaic Papyri: New Documents of the Fifth Century* B.C. *from the Jewish Colony at Elephantine* (London: Geoffrey Cumberlege; New Haven: Yale University Press, 1953)
CBQ	*Catholic Biblical Quarterly*

CClCr	*Civiltà classica e cristiana*
CIG	A. Boeckhuis, ed., *Corpus Inscriptionum Graecarum* (4 vols., Berlin: G. Reimer, 1828–1877)
CIJ	J. B. Frey, ed., *Corpus Inscriptionum Judaicarum* (2 vols., Rome: Pontifical Institute of Christian Archaeology, 1936–1952)
CIL	Th. Mommsen et al., eds., *Corpus Inscriptionum Latinarum* (Berlin: G. Reimer, 1862–)
CJZC	G. Lüderitz, ed., *Corpus jüdischer Zeugnisse aus der Cyrenaika* (Beihefte zum Tübinger Atlas des vorderen Orients: Reihe B–Geisteswissenschaften 53; Wiesbaden: L. Reichert, 1983)
CPJ	V. A. Tcherikover and A. Fuks, eds., *Corpus Papyrorum Judaicarum* (2 vols., Cambridge: Harvard University Press, 1957–1960)
CRB	Cahiers de la *Revue biblique*
DJD	Discoveries in the Judaean Desert
DMOA	Documenta et monumenta orientis antiqui
DNTB	C. A. Evans and S. E. Porter, eds., *Dictionary of New Testament Background* (Downers Grove: InterVarsity Press, 2000)
DTBMT	*Documents from the Time of the Bible, the Mishna and the Talmud* (Jerusalem: Israel Museum, 1973)
EBib	Etudes bibliques
EG	G. Kaibel, ed., *Epigrammata Graeca* (Berlin: G. Reimer, 1878)
EI	*Eretz-Israel* (Hebrew)
EncJud	C. Roth, ed., *Encyclopaedia Judaica* (17 vols., Jerusalem: Keter, 1972)
ExpTim	*Expository Times*
HOS	Handbook of Oriental Studies
HTR	*Harvard Theological Review*
IAA	Israel Antiquities Authority
IEJ	*Israel Exploration Journal*
IG	*Inscriptiones Graecae* (Deutsche Akademie der Wissenschaften zu Berlin; Berlin: G. Reimer, 1873–)
ILS	H. Dessau, ed., *Inscriptiones Latinae selectae* (3 vols. in 5 parts; Berlin: Weidmann, 1892–1916)
IMJ	*The Israel Museum Journal*
JA	*Journal Asiatique*

JAOS	*Journal of the American Oriental Society*
Jastrow	M. Jastrow, *A Dictionary of the Targumim, the Talmud Babli and Yerushalmi, and the Midrashic Literature* (2 vols., London: Putnam, 1895–1903)
JBL	*Journal of Biblical Literature*
JCCAR	*Journal of the Central Conference of American Rabbis*
JerCath	*Jerusalem Cathedra*
JJS	*Journal of Jewish Studies*
JPOS	*Journal of the Palestine Oriental Society*
JQR	*Jewish Quarterly Review*
JRS	*Journal of Roman Studies*
JSS	*Journal of Semitic Studies*
JTS	*Journal of Theological Studies*
JTSA	*Journal of Theology for Southern Africa*
Krauss	S. Krauss, *Griechische und lateinische Lehnwörter im Talmud, Midrasch und Targum* (2 vols., Berlin: S. Calvary, 1898–1899; repr. Hildesheim: Olms, 1987)
LA	*Liber Annuus: Studii Biblici Franciscani*
LSJ	H. G. Liddell, R. Scott, H. S. Jones, *A Greek-English Lexicon* (9th ed., Oxford: Clarendon, 1996)
Mas	Y. Yadin, J. Naveh, and Y. Meshorer, *Masada I: The Yigael Yadin Excavations 1963–1965 Final Reports. The Aramaic and Hebrew Ostraca and Jar Inscriptions / The Coins of Masada* (Jerusalem: Israel Exploration Society, 1989) nos. 1–701; H. M. Cotton and J. Geiger, *Masada II: The Yigael Yadin Excavations 1963–1965 Final Reports. The Latin and Greek Documents* (Jerusalem: Israel Exploration Society, 1989) nos. 721–951
MdB	*Le monde de la Bible*
MGWJ	*Monatsschrift für Geschichte und Wissenschaft des Judentums*
Mur	J. T. Milik and P. Benoit, eds., *Les Grottes de Murabba'at* (DJD 2; Oxford: Clarendon, 1961)
NEAEHL	E. Stern, ed., *The New Encyclopedia of Archaeological Excavations in the Holy Land* (4 vols., Jerusalem: The Israel Exploration Society, 1993)
NEASB	*Near East Archaeological Society Bulletin*
NewDocs	G. R. Horsley et al., eds., *New Documents Illustrating Early Christianity* (9 vols., North Ryde: Macquarie University; Grand Rapids: Eerdmans, 1981–)

NovTSup	Novum Testamentum, Supplements
NTS	*New Testament Studies*
NTTS	New Testament Tools and Studies
OGIS	Dittenberger, W., ed. *Orientis Graeci Inscriptiones Selectae: Supplementum Sylloges Inscriptionum Graecarum* (2 vols., Leipzig: S. Hirzel, 1903–1905; repr, Hildesheim: Olms, 1986)
PEF	*Palestine Exploration Fund*
PEFQ	*Palestine Exploration Fund Quarterly*
PEQ	*Palestine Exploration Quarterly*
PYadin 1–4, 6–10, 36, 42–47, 49–51, 53–58, 60–63	A. Yardeni, ed., *Textbook of Aramaic, Hebrew, and Nabataean Documentary Texts from the Judaean Desert and Related Material*, vol. 1 (Jerusalem: Hebrew University, 2000)
PYadin 5, 11–35	N. Lewis, ed., *The Documents from the Bar Kokhba Period in the Cave of Letters: Greek Papyri* (Jerusalem: Israel Exploration Society, 1989)
QDAP	*Quarterly of the Department of Antiquities in Palestine*
RAr	*Revue archéologique*
RB	*Revue biblique*
REG	*Revue des études grecques*
REJ	*Revue des études juives*
RenIL	*Rendiconti dell'Istituto Lombardo*
RGM	B. Galsterer and H. Galsterer, eds., *Wissenschaftliche Kataloge des römisch-germanischen Museums Köln* (Köln: Greven & Bechtold, 1975)
RivAC	*Rivista di Archeologia Cristiana*
RH	*Revue historique*
RSN	*Religious Studies News*
SBF	Studium Biblicum Franciscanum: Collectio Maior
SBL	Society of Biblical Literature
SBLSBS	Society of Biblical Literature Sources for Biblical Studies
SCI	*Scripta Classica Israelica*
SEG	*Supplementum Epigraphicum Graecum* (Leiden and Amsterdam: J. C. Gieben, 1923–)
SNTSMS	Society for New Testament Studies Monograph Series

ST	*Studia Theologica*
St-B	(H. L. Strack and) P. Billerbeck, *Kommentar zum Neuen Testament aus Talmud und Midrasch* (6 vols., Munich: C. H. Beck, 1922–1928)
TDNT	G. Kittel, ed., *Theological Dictionary of the New Testament* (10 vols., Grand Rapids: Eerdmans, 1964–1976)
TSAJ	Texte und Studien zum antiken Judentum
USF	University of South Florida
YJS	Yale Judaica Series
ZDPV	*Zeitschrift des deutschen Palästina-Vereins*

Biblical Texts and Versions

ASV	American Standard Version
LXX	Septuagint
MT	Masoretic Text
NHC	Nag Hammadi Codices
OG	Old Greek
Q	Qumran
RSV	Revised Standard Version

Ancient

1QapGen	Genesis Apocryphon, from Qumran, cave 1
1QH	Hymn Scroll, from Qumran, cave 1
1QS	Rule Scroll, from Qumran, cave 1
1QSb	*Rule of the Blessings* (appendix b to 1QS)
11QT	Temple Scroll, from Qumran, cave 11
4QtgJob	Job Targum, from Qumran, cave 4
11QtgJob	Job Targum, from Qumran, cave 11
'Abod. Zar.	*Avodah Zarah*
Ag. Ap.	Josephus, *Against Apion*
Ant.	Josephus, *Jewish Antiquities*
b.	*Talmud Babli*, or the *Babylonian Talmud*
B. Bat.	*Bava Batra*
B. Qam.	*Bava Qamma*
Bar.	*Baruch*
Ber.	*Berakhot*
CD	Cairo Genizah copy of the *Damascus Document*

Clem.	Clement
Clem. Hom.	*Clementine Homilies*
fam.	family (in reference to Greek NT mss.)
Hor.	*Horayot*
Hul.	*Hullin*
Jub.	*Jubilees*
J.W.	Josephus, *Jewish War*
Ketub.	*Ketubot*
Kil.	*Kil'ayim*
Legat.	Philo, *Legatio ad Gaium*
m.	*Mishnah*
Midd.	*Middot*
Meg.	*Megillah*
Ned.	*Nedarim*
POxy	*Papyri Oxyrhynchus*
Pss. Sol.	*Psalms of Solomon*
Prob.	Philo, *Quod omnis probus liber sit*
Pesah.	*Pesahim*
Pesiq. R.	*Pesiqta Rabbati*
Pesiq. Rab Kah.	*Pesiqta of Rab Kahana*
Qoh.	*Qohelet* (or Eccelsiasticus)
Rab.	*Rabbah* (+ biblical book)
Rosh Hash.	*Rosh HaShanah*
Sanh.	*Sanhedrin*
Shab.	*Shabbat*
Sheb.	*Shebu'ot*
Sheq.	*Sheqalim*
Suk.	*Sukkah*
t.	*Tosefta*
Ta'an.	*Ta'anit*
y.	*Yerushalmi*, or the *Palestinian Talmud*
Tg. Neof.	*Targum Neofiti*
T. Levi	*Testament of Levi*
Tg. Ps.-J.	*Targum Pseudo-Jonathan*
Yeb.	*Yebamot*

Bibliography

Albright 1932 — Albright, W. F. "The Discovery of an Aramaic Inscription Relating to King Uzziah," *BASOR* 44 (1932) 8–10.

Alföldy 1999 — Alföldy, G. "Pontius Pilatus und das Tiberieum von Caesarea Maritima," *SCI* 18 (1999) 85–108.

Allegretti 1982 — Allegretti, S. "Una tomba del primo periodo romano sul Monte Oliveto," *LA* 32 (1982) 335–54.

Avigad 1950–1951 — Avigad, N. "The Rock-Carved Façades of the Jerusalem Necropolis," *IEJ* 1 (1950–1951) 96–106.

Avigad 1962 — Avigad, N. "A Depository of Inscribed Ossuaries in the Kidron Valley," *IEJ* 12 (1962) 1–2 + plates 1–4.

Avigad 1967 — Avigad, N. "Aramaic Inscriptions in the Tomb of Jason," *IEJ* 17 (1967) 101–11.

Avigad 1971 — Avigad, N. "The Burial Vault of a Nazirite Family on Mount Scopus," *IEJ* 21 (1971) 185–200.

Avigad 1976 — Avigad, N. *Beth She'arim: The Excavations 1953–1958*. Vol. 3: *Catacombs 12–23* (New Brunswick: Rutgers University Press, 1976).

Avi-Yonah 1962 — Avi-Yonah, M. "A List of Priestly Courses from Caesarea," *IEJ* 12 (1962) 137–39 + pl.

Avi-Yonah 1964 Avi-Yonah, M. "The Caesarea Inscription of the Twenty-Four Priestly Courses," in E. J. Vardaman and J. L. Garrett, eds., *The Teacher's Yoke: Studies in Memory of Henry Trantham* (Waco, Tex.: Baylor University Press, 1964) 46–57.

Avni 1993 Avni, G. "Christian Secondary Use of Jewish Burial Caves in Jerusalem in the Light of New Excavations at the Aceldama Tombs," in F. Manns and E. Alliata, eds., *Early Christianity in Context: Monuments and Documents* (SBF 38; Jerusalem: Franciscan Printing Press, 1993) 265–76.

Avni and Greenhut 1996 Avni, G., Z. Greenhut, et al. *The Akeldama Tombs: Three Burial Caves in the Kidron Valley, Jerusalem* (IAA Reports 1; Jerusalem: Israel Antiquities Authority, 1996).

Avni, Greenhut, Ilan 1994 Avni, G., Z. Greenhut, and T. Ilan. "Three New Burial Caves of the Second Temple Period in Aceldama (Kidron Valley)," in H. Geva, ed., *Ancient Jerusalem Revealed* (Jerusalem: Israel Exploration Society, 1994) 206–18 [= Hebrew article in *Qadmoniot* 25 (1992) 100–10].

Bagatti 1967 Bagatti, B. *Gli scavi di Nazaret*. Vol. 1: *Dalle origin al secolo XII* (Jerusalem: Francescani, 1967).

Bagatti and Milik 1958 Bagatti, B. and J. T. Milik. *Gli Scavi del 'Dominus Flevit'* (Jerusalem: Francescani, 1958).

Barag and Flusser 1986 Barag, D. and D. Flusser. "The Ossuary of Yehohanah Granddaughter of the High Priest Theophilus," *IEJ* 36 (1986) 39–44.

Barkay 1983 Barkay, R. *Samaritan Sarcophagi of the Roman Period in Erets Israel* (Jerusalem: Hebrew University, 1983).

Barkay 1989 Barkay, G. "Another Palaeo-Hebrew Ossuary Inscription," *IEJ* 39 (1989) 201–3.

Batey 1984 — Batey, R. A. "Jesus and the Theatre," *NTS* 30 (1984) 563–74.

Bauckham 1998 — Bauckham, R.J. "Life, Death, and the Afterlife in Second Temple Judaism," in R. N. Longenecker, ed., *Life in the Face of Death; The Resurrection Message of the New Testament* (Grand Rapids; Eerdmans, 1998) 80–95.

Bauckham 1999a — Bauckham, R. J. "For What Offense was James Put to Death?" in B. D. Chilton and C. A. Evans, eds., *James the Just and Christian Origins* (NovTSup 98; Leiden: Brill, 1999) 199–232.

Bauckham 1999b — Bauckham, R. J. *James* (New Testament Readings; London: Routledge, 1999).

Baumgarten 1982 — Baumgarten, J. M. "Exclusions from the Temple: Proselytes and Agrippa I," *JJS* 33 (1982) 215–25.

Bees 1921 — Bees, N. A. "Epigraphik," *Byzantinish-neugriechische Jarhrbücher* 2 (1921) 259.

Bennett 1965 — Bennett, C. M. "Tombs of the Roman Period," in K. M. Kenyon, ed., *Excavations at Jericho*. Vol. 2: *The Tombs Excavated in 1955–58* (London: The British School of Archaeology, 1965) 516–45.

Benoit 1967 — Benoit, P. "L'Inscription grecque du tombeau de Jason," *IEJ* 17 (1967) 112–13.

Betz 1982 — Betz, A. "Zur Pontius Pilatus-Inschrift von Caesarea-Maritima," in W. Alzinger et al., eds., *Pro Arte Antiqua. Festschrift für Hedwig Kenner* (2 vols., Österreichisches Archäologisches Institut in Wien, Sonderschriften 18; Vienna and Berlin: A. F. Koska, 1982) 1:33–35 + plate XIV.

Bickerman 1946–1947 — Bickerman, E. J. "The Warning Inscriptions of Herod's Temple," *JQR* 37 (1946–1947) 387– 405.

Birkeland 1949 — Birkeland, H. "The Belief in the Resurrection of the Dead in the Old Testament," *ST* 3 (1949) 60–78.

Bivian 1991	Bivian, D. "A Sadducee Who Believed in an Afterlife?" *Jerusalem Perspective* 4/4–5 (1991) 7.
Boadt 1993	Boadt, L. "Recent Archaeological Finds in Jerusalem Related to the Early Church," *The Catholic World 236* (Jan–Feb 1993) 40–45.
Boffo 1994	Boffo, L. *Iscrizioni greche e latine per lo studio della Bibbia* (Brescia: Paideia Editrice, 1994).
Bolt 1998	Bolt, P. G. "Life, Death, and the Afterlife in the Greco-Roman World," in R.N. Longnecker ed., *Life in the Face of Death; the Resurrection Message of the New Testament* (Grand Rapids; Eerdmans, 1998) 51–79.
Braude 1969	Braude, W. G. "The Land as Purgatory," *JCCAR* (1969) 80–84.
Brody 1990	Brody, R. "Caiaphas and Cantheras," in D. R. Schwartz, *Agrippa I: The Last King of Judaea* (TSAJ 23; Tübingen: Mohr [Siebeck], 1990) 190–95.
Broshi 1975	Broshi, M. "La population de l'ancienne Jérusalem," *RB* 82 (1975) 5–14.
Broshi 1978	Broshi, M. "Estimating the Population of Ancient Jerusalem," *BAR* 4/2 (June 1978) 10–15.
Broshi and Eshel 2003	Broshi, M. and H. Eshel. "Whose Bones?" *BAR* 29/1 (2003) 26–33, 71.
Brown 1931	Brown, F. E. "Violation of Sepulture in Palestine," *AJP* 52 (1931) 1–29.
Brown 1994	Brown, R. E. *The Death of the Messiah: From Gethsemane to the Grave. A Commentary on the Passion Narratives in the Four Gospels* (2 vols., ABRL; New York: Doubleday, 1994).
Brussa Gerra 1966	Brusa Gerra, C. "Le Iscrizióni," in G. Dell' Amore, ed., *Scavi di Caesarea Maritima* (Rome: Bretschneider, 1966) 217–28.
Buth 1997	Buth, R. "Mark 3.17 Βονερέγεμ and Popular Etymology," in S. E. Porter and C.

A. Evans, eds., *New Testament Text and Language: A Sheffield Reader* (BibSem 44; Sheffield: Sheffield Academic Press, 1997) 263–66.

Byatt 1973 — Byatt, A. "Josephus and Population Numbers in First Century Palestine," *PEFQ Statement* 105 (1973) 51–60.

Calloway 1963 — Calloway, J. A. "Burials in Palestine: From the Stone Age to Abraham," *BA* 26 (1963) 74–91.

Casey 1998 — Casey, M. *Aramaic Sources of Mark's Gospel* (SNTSMS 102; Cambridge: Cambridge University Press, 1998).

Chancey 2002 — Chancey, M. A. *The Myth of a Gentile Galilee* (SNTSMS 118; Cambridge: Cambridge University Press, 2002).

Chancey and Meyers 2001 — Chancey, M. A. and E. M. Meyers. "How Jewish Was Sepphoris in Jesus' Time?" *BAR* 26/4 (2000) 18–33, 61.

Charles 1913 — Charles, R. H. *Eschatology: The Doctrine of a Future Life in Israel, Judaism, and Christianity* (2nd ed., London: A. & C. Black, 1913).

Charlesworth 1972–1973 — Charlesworth, J. H. "Jesus and Jehohanan: An Archaeological Note on Crucifixion," *ExpTim* 84 (1972–73) 147–50.

Chilton and Evans 1999 — Chilton, B. D. and C. A. Evans, eds. *James the Just and Christian Origins* (NovTSup 98; Leiden: Brill, 1999).

Chilton and Neusner 2001 — Chilton, B. D. and J. Neusner, eds. *The Brother of Jesus: James the Just and His Mission* (Louisville: Westminster John Knox, 2001).

Chilton and Yamauchi 2000 — Chilton, B. D. and E. M. Yamauchi, "Synagogues," *DNTB* 1145–53.

Clermont-Ganneau 1872 — Clermont-Ganneau, C. S. "Une stèle du temple de Jérusalem," *RAr* 28 (1872) 214–34, 290–96 + plate X.

Clermont-Ganneau 1873 — Clermont-Ganneau, C. S. "Nouveaux ossuaires juifs avec inscriptions grecques et hébraïques," *RAr* 25 [2nd series] (1873) 398–414.

Clermont-Ganneau 1878 Clermont-Ganneau, C. S. "Ossuaire juif de Joseph, fils de Jean," *RAr* 36 [2nd series] (1878) 305–11.

Clermont-Ganneau 1899 Clermont-Ganneau, C. S. *Archaeological Researches in Palestine*, vol. 1 (London: Palestine Exploration Fund, 1899).

Clermont-Ganneau 1903 Clermont-Ganneau, C. S. "The 'Gate of Nicanor' in the Temple of Jerusalem," *PEFQ Statement* (1903) 93, 125–31.

Clermont-Ganneau 1920 Clermont-Ganneau, C. S. "Découverte à Jérusalem d'une synagogue de l'époque hérodienne," *Syria* 1 (1920) 190–97 + pl.

Cohen 1981–1982 Cohen, S. J. D. "Epigraphical Rabbis," *JQR* 72 (1981–1982) 1–17.

Conder 1876 Conder, C. R. "Rock-cut Tombs," *PEF* (1876) 17–20.

Cook 1987 Cook, B. F. *Greek Inscriptions* (London: British Museum; Berkeley: University of California Press, 1987).

Cook 1932 Cook, S. A. "A Nazareth Inscription on the Violation of Tombs," *PEFQ Statement* (1932) 85–87.

Cotton and Geiger 1989 Cotton, H. M. and J. Geiger. "Wine for Herod," *Cathedra* 53 (1989) 3–12 (Hebrew).

Cross 1961 Cross, F. M. "The Development of Jewish Scripts," in G. E. Wright, ed., *The Bible and the Ancient Near East: Essays in Honor of William Foxwell Albright* (Garden City, NY: Doubleday; London: Routledge & Kegan Paul, 1961) 133–202.

Cross 1983 Cross, F. M. "A Note on a Burial Inscription from Mount Scopus," *IEJ* 33 (1983) 245–46.

Crossan 1991 Crossan, J. D. *The Historical Jesus: The Life of a Mediterranean Jewish Peasant* (San Francisco: HarperCollins, 1991).

Crossan 1995 Crossan, J. D. *Who Killed Jesus? Exposing the*

Roots of Anti-Semitism in the Gospel Story of the Death of Jesus (San Francisco: HarperCollins, 1995).

Crossan and Reed 2001 — Crossan, J. D. and J. L. Reed. *Excavating Jesus: Beneath the Stones, Behind the Texts* (San Francisco: HarperCollins, 2001).

Cumont 1930 — Cumont, F. "Un rescrit impérial sur la violation de sépulture," *RH* 163 (1930) 241–66.

Cumont 1933 — Cumont, F. "Les ossuaires juifs et le Διάταγμα Καίσαρος," *Syria* 14 (1933) 223–24.

Dajani 1966 — Dajani, R. W. "Nablus—A Roman Cemetery Discovered," *ADAJ* 11 (1966) 103.

Dalman 1902 — Dalman, G. H. *The Words of Jesus* (Edinburgh: T. & T. Clark, 1902).

Dalman 1905 — Dalman, G. H. *Grammatik des jüdisch-palästinischen Aramäisch nach den Idiomen des palästinischen Talmud, des Onkelostargum und Prophetentargum, und der jerusalemischen Targume* (2d ed., Leipzig: J. C. Hinrichs, 1905).

Dalman 1914 — Dalman, G. H. "Inschriften aus Palästina," *ZDPV* 37 (1914) 135–50.

Dalman 1922 — Dalman, G. H. "Die Ausgrabungen von Raymond Weill in der Davidstadt," *ZDPV* 45 (1922) 22–30.

Damati 1972 — Damati, E. "Askar," *IEJ* 22 (1972) 174.

Deissmann 1927 — Deissmann, A. *Light from the Ancient East* (London: Hodder & Stoughton; New York: George H. Doran, 1927; repr. Peabody: Hendrickson, 1995).

Derenbourg 1872 — Derenbourg, J. "Une stèle du temple d'Hérod," *JA* 20 (1872) 178–95.

Dickson 1903 — Dickson, G. "The Tomb of Nicanor of Alexandria," *PEFQ Statement* (1903) 326–32.

Dinkler 1974 — Dinkler, E. "Schalom—Eirene—Pax: Jüdische Sepulkralinschriften und ihr

	Verhältnis zum frühen Christentum," *RivAC* 50 (1974) 121–44.
Dittenberger 1903–1905	Dittenberger, W., ed. *Orientis Graeci Inscriptiones Selectae: Supplementum Sylloges Inscriptionum Graecarum* (2 vols., Leipzig: S. Hirzel, 1903–1905; repr, Hildesheim: Olms, 1986).
Domeris and Long 1994	Domeris, W. R. and S. M. Long. "The Recently Excavated Tomb of Joseph Bar Caipha and the Biblical Caiaphas," *JTSA* 89 (1994) 50–58.
Evans 1999	Evans, C. A. "Jesus and James: Martyrs of the Temple," in B. D. Chilton and C. A. Evans, eds., *James the Just and Christian Origins* (NovTSup 98; Leiden: Brill, 1999) 233–49.
Evans 2000a	Evans, C. A. "Caiaphas Ossuary," *DNTB* 179–80.
Evans 2000b	Evans, C. A. "Pilate Inscription," *DNTB* 803–4.
Evans 2003	Evans, C. A. "Jesus and the Ossuaries," *BBR* 13 (2003) 21–46.
Fedak 1990	Fedak, J. *Monumental Tombs of the Hellenistic Age: A Study of Selected Tombs from the Pre-Classical to the Early Imperial Era* (Toronto: University of Toronto Press, 1990).
Feldman and Roth 2002	Feldman, S. and N. E. Roth, "The Short List: The New Testament Figures Known to History," *BAR* 28/6 (2002) 34–37.
Figueras 1983	Figueras, P. *Decorated Jewish Ossuaries* (DMOA 20; Leiden: Brill, 1983).
Figueras 1984–1985	Figueras, P. "Jewish Ossuaries and Secondary Burial: Their Significance for Early Christianity," *Immanuel* 19 (1984–85) 41–57.
Fine 2000	Fine, S. "A Note on Ossuary Burial and the Resurrection of the Dead in First-Century Jerusalem," *JJS* 51 (2000) 69–76.
Finegan 1969	Finegan, J. *The Archaeology of the New*

Testament (Princeton: Princeton University Press, 1969).

Fishwick 1963 — Fishwick, D. "The Talpioth Ossuaries Again," *NTS* 10 (1963) 49–61.

Fitzmyer 1959 — Fitzmyer, J. A. "The Aramaic Qorbân Inscription from Jebel Hallet et-Tûrî and Mk 7:11/Mt 15:5," *JBL* 78 (1959) 60–65; repr. in J. A. Fitzmyer, *Essays on the Semitic Background of the New Testament* (London: Geoffrey Chapman, 1971; repr. SBLSBS 5; Missoula: Scholars Press, 1974) 93–100.

Fitzmyer 1963 — Fitzmyer, J. A. "The Name Simon," *HTR* 56 (1963) 1–5; repr. in J. A. Fitzmyer, *Essays on the Semitic Background of the New Testament* (London: Geoffrey Chapman, 1971; repr. SBLSBS 5; Missoula: Scholars Press, 1974) 105–10.

Fitzmyer 1979 — Fitzmyer, J. A. "Aramaic Kepha' and Peter's Name in the New Testament," in E. Best and R. M. Wilson, eds., *Text and Interpretation: Studies in the New Testament Presented to Matthew Black* (Cambridge: Cambridge University Press, 1979) 121–32; repr. in J. A. Fitzmyer, *To Advance the Gospel: New Testament Studies* (New York: Crossroad, 1981) 112–24.

Fitzmyer 2002 — Fitzmyer, J. A. "Whose Name Is This?" *America* 187/16 (18 Nov. 2002) 9–13.

Fitzmyer and Harrington 1978 — Fitzmyer, J. A. and D. J. Harrington. *A Manual of Palestinian Aramaic Texts (Second Century B.C.—Second Century A.D.)* (BibOr 34; Rome: Pontifical Biblical Institute Press, 1978).

Flusser 1986 — Flusser, D. "'The House of David' on an Ossuary," *IMJ* 5 (1986) 37–40.

Flusser 1992 — Flusser, D. "Caiaphas in the New Testament," *'Atiqot* 21 (1992) 81–87.

Flusser 1997 — Flusser, D. *Jesus* (rev. ed., with R. S. Notley; Jerusalem: Magnes Press, 1997).

Foakes Jackson and Lake 1932 — Foakes Jackson, F. J. and K. Lake. *The Beginnings of Christianity*, vol. 4 (London: Macmillan, 1932).

Fritz and Deines 1999 — Fritz, V. and R. Deines. "Catalogue of the Jewish Ossuaries in the German Protestant Institute of Archaeology," *IEJ* 49 (1999) 222–41.

Frova 1961 — Frova, A. "L'iscrizione di Ponzio Pilato a Cesarea," *RenIL* 95 (1961) 419–34.

Gafni 1981 — Gafni, I. "Reinterment in the Land of Israel: Notes on the Origin and Development of a Custom," in L. I. Levine, ed., *Jerusalem Cathedra: Studies in the History, Archaeology, Geography, and Ethnography of the Land of Israel*, vol. 1 (Jerusalem: Yad Izhak Ben-Zvi Institute; Detroit, Mich.: Wayne State University Press, 1981) 96–104.

Gatti 1981 — Gatti, C. "A proposito di una rilettura dell' epigrafe di Ponzio Pilato," *Aevum* 55 (1981) 13–21.

Geraty 1975 — Geraty, L. T. "A Thrice Repeated Ossuary Inscription from French Hill, Jerusalem," *BASOR* 219 (1975) 73–78.

Gibson and Avni 1998 — Gibson, S. and G. Avni. "The 'Jewish-Christian' Tomb from the Mount of Offence (Batn al-Hawa') in Jerusalem Reconsidered," *RB* 105 (1998) 161–75.

Goitein 1970 — Goitein, S. D. "Nicknames as Family Names," *JAOS* 90 (1970) 517–24.

Goldstein, Arensburg, Nathan 1981 — Goldstein, M. S., B. Arensburg, and H. Nathan. "Skeletal Remains of Jews from the Hellenistic and Roman Periods in Israel," *Bulletins et mémoires de la société d'anthropologie de Paris* 8: series 13 (1981) 11–24.

Goodenough 1953a — Goodenough, E. R. *Jewish Symbols in the Greco-Roman Period*. Vol. 1: *The Archaeological Evidence from Palestine* (Bollingen

Series 37; New York: Pantheon Books, 1953).

Goodenough 1953b — Goodenough, E. R. *Jewish Symbols in the Greco-Roman Period*. Vol. 2: *The Archaeological Evidence from the Diaspora* (Bollingen Series 37; New York: Pantheon Books, 1953).

Goodenough 1953c — Goodenough, E. R. *Jewish Symbols in the Greco-Roman Period*. Vol. 3: *Illustrations* (Bollingen Series 37; New York: Pantheon Books, 1953).

Gordon 1983 — Gordon, A. E. *Illustrated Introduction to Latin Epigraphy* (Berkeley: University of California Press, 1983).

Grabbe 1988 — Grabbe, L. L. "Synagogues in Pre-70 Palestine: A Reassessment," *JTS* 39 (1988) 401–10.

Graetz 1881 — Graetz, H. "Die jüdischen Steinsarkophage in Palästina," *MGWJ* 30 (1881) 529–39.

Gray 1914 — Gray, G. B. "Inscriptions on Jewish Ossuaries," *PEFQ Statement* (1914) 40–42.

Greenhut 1992a — Greenhut, Z. "Burial Cave of the Caiaphas Family," *BAR* 18/5 (1992) 29–36, 76.

Greenhut 1992b — Greenhut, Z. "The 'Caiaphas' Tomb in North Talpiyot, Jerusalem," *'Atiqot* 21 (1992) 63–71.

Greenhut 1994 — Greenhut, Z. "The Caiaphas Tomb in North Talpiyot, Jerusalem," in H. Geva, ed., *Ancient Jerusalem Revealed* (Jerusalem: Israel Exploration Society, 1994) 219–22.

Gregg and Urman 1996 — Gregg, R. C. and D. Urman. *Jews, Pagans, and Christians in the Golan Heights: Greek and Other Inscriptions of the Roman and Byzantine Eras* (USF Studies in the History of Judaism 140; Atlanta: Scholars Press, 1996).

Grossberg 1996 — Grossberg, A. "Behold the Temple: Is It Depicted on a Priestly Ossuary?" *BAR* 22/3 (1996) 46–51, 66.

Haas 1970	Haas, N. "Anthropological Observations on the Skeletal Remains from Giv'at ha-Mivtar," *IEJ* 20 (1970) 38–59.
Hachlili 1978	Hachlili, R. "A Jerusalem Family in Jericho," *BASOR* 230 (1978) 45–56.
Hachlili 1979	Hachlili, R. "The Goliath Family in Jericho: Funerary Inscriptions from a First Century A.D. Jewish Monumental Tomb," *BASOR* 235 (1979) 31–66.
Hachlili 1980	Hachlili, R. "A Second Temple Period Jewish Necropolis in Jericho," *BA* 43 (1980) 235–40.
Hachlili 1997	Hachlili, R. "A Jericho Ossuary and a Jerusalem Workshop," *IEJ* 47 (1997) 238–47.
Hachlili 2000	Hachlili, R. "Hebrew Names, Personal Names, Family Names and Nicknames of Jews in the Second Temple Period," in J. W. van Henten and A. Brenner, eds., *Families and Family Relations as Represented in Early Judaisms and Early Christianities: Texts and Fictions* (Studies in Theology and Religion 2; Leiden: Deo, 2000) 83–115.
Hachlili and Killebrew 1983a	Hachlili, R. and A. Killebrew. "Was the Coin-on-Eye Custom a Jewish Burial Practice in the Second Temple Period?" *BA* 46 (1983) 147–53.
Hachlili and Killebrew 1983b	Hachlili, R. and A. Killebrew. "Jewish Funerary Customs during the Second Temple Period, in the Light of the Excavations at the Jericho Necropolis," *PEQ* 115 (1983) 109–39.
Hachlili and Killebrew 1983c	Hachlili, R. and A. Killebrew. "The Saga of the Goliath Family," *BAR* 9/1 (1983) 44–53.
Hachlili and Smith 1979	Hachlili, R. and P. Smith. "The Geneology [sic] of the Goliath Family," *BASOR* 235 (1979) 67–70.
Hengel 1989	Hengel, M. *The 'Hellenization' of Judaea in the First Century after Christ* (London: SCM

Press; Philadelphia: Trinity Press International, 1989).

Herford 1903 — Herford, R. T. *Christianity in Talmud and Midrash* (London: Williams & Norgate, 1903; repr. New York: Ktav, 1975).

Hohlfelder 1982 — Hohlfelder, R. L. "Caesarea Beneath the Sea," *BAR* 8/3 (1982) 42–47, 56.

Hohlfelder 1983 — Hohlfelder, R. L. et al., "Sebastos, Herod's Harbor at Caesarea Maritima," *BA* 46 (1983) 133–43.

Hölscher 1925 — Hölscher, G. "Zur jüdischen Namenkunde," in K. Budde, ed., *Vom Alten Testament: Karl Marti zum siebzigsten Geburtstage gewidmet* (BZAW 41; Giessen: Töpelmann, 1925) 148–57.

Horbury 1994 — Horbury, W. "The 'Caiaphas' Ossuaries and Joseph Caiaphas," *PEQ* 126 (1994) 32–48.

Horbury and Noy 1992 — Horbury, W. and D. Noy. *Jewish Inscriptions of Graeco-Roman Egypt* (Cambridge: Cambridge University Press, 1992).

Hornstein 1900 — Hornstein, C. A. "Newly Discovered Tomb on Mount Scopus," *PEFQ Statement* (1900) 75–76.

Horsley and Hanson 1988 — Horsley, R. A. and J. S. Hanson, *Bandits, Prophets, and Messiahs: Popular Movements at the Time of Jesus* (San Francisco: Harper & Row, 1988).

Ilan 1987–1988 — Ilan, T. "The Greek Names of the Hasmoneans," *JQR* 78 (1987–1988) 1–20.

Ilan 1991–1992 — Ilan, T. "New Ossuary Inscriptions from Jerusalem," *SCI* 11 (1991–1992) 149–59.

Ilan 2001 — Ilan, T. "An Inscribed Ossuary from a Private Collection," *IEJ* 51 (2001) 92–95.

Ilan 2002 — Ilan, T. *Lexicon of Jewish Names in Late Antiquity* (TSAJ 91; Tübingen: Mohr Siebeck, 2002).

Iliffe 1936 — Iliffe, J. H. "The θάνατος Inscription from Herod's Temple: Fragment of a Second Copy," *QDAP* 6 (1936) 1–3 + plates I–II.

Jeremias 1958 — Jeremias, J. *Heiligengräber in Jesu Umwelt*

(Göttingen: Vandenhoeck & Ruprecht, 1958).

Jeremias 1969 — Jeremias, J. *Jerusalem in the Time of Jesus: An Investigation into Economic and Social Conditions during the New Testament Period* (London: SCM Press; Philadelphia: Fortress, 1969).

Jones 1960 — Jones, A. H. M. "Procurators and Prefects in the Early Principate," in *Studies in Roman Government and Law* (Oxford: Blackwell, 1960) 117–25.

Jotham-Rothschild 1952 — Jotham-Rothschild, J. "The Tombs of the Sanhedria," *PEQ* 84 (1952) 23–38.

Kahane 1952 — Kahane, P. "Pottery Types from the Jewish Ossuary-Tombs around Jerusalem," *IEJ* 2 (1952) 125–39, 176–82; 3 (1953) 48–54.

Kane 1971 — Kane, J. P. "By No Means 'The Earliest Records of Christianity'—With an Emended Reading of the Talpioth Inscription ΙΗΣΟΥΣ ΙΟΥ," *PEQ* 103 (1971) 103–8.

Kane 1978 — Kane, J. P. "The Ossuary Inscriptions of Jerusalem," *JSS* 23 (1978) 268–82.

Kant 1987 — Kant, L. H. "Jewish Inscriptions in Greek and Latin," *ANRW* II.20.2 (1987) 671–713.

Kee 1990 — Kee, H. C. "The Transformation of the Synagogue after 70 C.E.: Its Import for Early Christianity," *NTS* 36 (1990) 481–500.

Kee 1994 — Kee, H. C. "The Changing Meaning of Synagogue: A Response to Richard Oster," *NTS* 40 (1994) 281–83.

Kee 1995 — Kee, H. C. "Defining the First-Century CE Synagogue: Problems and Progress," *NTS* 41 (1995) 481–500.

Keppie 1991 — Keppie, L. J. F. *Understanding Roman Inscriptions* (Baltimore: Johns Hopkins University Press, 1991).

Klein 1920 — Klein, S. *Jüdisch-Palästinisches Corpus*

Inscriptionum (Ossuar-, Grab- und Synagogeninschriften) (Vienna and Berlin: Löwit, 1920).

Kloner 1972 — Kloner, A. "A Burial Cave of the Second Temple Period at Giv'at Ha-Mivtar, Jerusalem," *Qadmoniot* 19–20 (1972) 108–9 (Hebrew).

Kloner 1980 — Kloner, A. "A Tomb of the Second Temple Period at French Hill, Jerusalem," *IEJ* 30 (1980) 99–108.

Kloner 1994 — Kloner, A. "An Ossuary from Jerusalem Ornamented with Monumental Façades," in H. Geva, ed., *Ancient Jerusalem Revealed* (Jerusalem: Israel Exploration Society, 1994) 235–38.

Kloner 1996 — Kloner, A. "A Tomb with Inscribed Ossuaries in East Talpiyot, Jerusalem," *'Atiqot* 29 (1996) 15–22.

Kloppenborg Verbin 2000 — Kloppenborg Verbin, J. S. "Dating Theodotos (*CIJ* 1404)," *JJS* 51 (2000) 243–80.

Kraemer 2000 — Kraemer, D. *The Meaning of Death in Rabbinic Judaism* (London: Routledge, 2000).

Kuhn 1979 — Kuhn, H.-W. "Der Gekreuzigte von Giv'at ha-Mivtar: Bilanz einer Entdeckung," in C. Andresen and G. Klein, eds., *Theologia Crucis–Signum Crucis* (Erich Dinkler Festschrift; Tübingen: Mohr, 1979) 303–34.

Kurtz and Boardman 1971 — Kurtz, D. C. and J. Boardman, *Greek Burial Customs* (Aspects of Greek and Roman Life; Ithaca, NY: Cornell University Press, 1971).

Lagrange 1893 — Lagrange, M.-J. "Epigraphie sémitique," *RB* 2 (1893) 220–22.

Lake 1921 — Lake, K. "Simon, Cephas, Peter," *HTR* 14 (1921) 95–97.

Lattimore 1942 — Lattimore, R. A. *Themes in Greek and Latin Epitaphs* (Illinois Studies in Language and Literature 28/1–2; Urbana: University of Illinois Press, 1942).

Lemaire 2002 — Lemaire, A. "Burial Box of James the

Brother of Jesus," *BAR* 28/6 (2002) 24–33, 70.

Lémonon 1981 — Lémonon, J.-P. *Pilate et le gouvernement de la Judée: Textes et monuments* (EBib; Paris: Gabalda, 1981).

Leon 1995 — Leon, H. J. *The Jews of Ancient Rome* (The Morris Loeb series; Philadelphia: Jewish Publication Society of America, 1960; rev., with Introduction by C. Osiek; Peabody: Hendrickson, 1995).

Levine 1996 — Levine, L. I. "The Nature and Origin of the Palestinian Synagogue Reconsidered," *JBL* 115 (1996) 425–48.

Lidzbarski 1913 — Lidzbarski, M. "An Inscribed Jewish Ossuary," *PEFQ Statement* (1913) 84–85.

Lieberman 1965 — Lieberman, S. "Some Aspects of After Life in Early Rabbinic Literature," in S. Lieberman et al., eds., *Harry Austryn Wolfson: Jubilee Volume on the Occasion of His Seventy-Fifth Birthday*, vol. 2 (Jerusalem: American Academy for Jewish Research, 1965) 495–532.

Lietzmann 1921 — Lietzmann, H. "Notizen," *ZNW* 20 (1921) 171–73.

Lifshitz 1963a — Lifshitz, B. "Inscriptions latines de Césarée," *Latomus* 22 (1963) 783–84 + plates LXIII–LXIV.

Lifshitz 1963b — Lifshitz, B. "Notes d'épigraphie grecque," *RB* 70 (1963) 255–65.

Lifshitz 1967 — Lifshitz, B. *Donateurs et fondateurs dans les synagogues juives: répertoire des dédicaces grecques relatives à la construction et à la réfection des synagogues* (CRB 7; Paris: Gabalda, 1967).

Llewelyn and Kearsley 1994 — Llewelyn, S. R., and R. A. Kearsley. *New Documents Illustrating Early Chirstianity*, 1994.

Macalister 1905 — Macalister, R. A. S. "Further Observations on the Ossuary of Nicanor of Alexandria," *PEFQ Statement* (1905) 253–57.

Macalister 1908 — Macalister, R. A. S. "A Tomb with Aramaic Inscriptions near Silwan," *PEFQ Statement* (1908) 341–42.

Magen 1993 — Magen, Y. "The 'Samaritan' Sarcophagi," in F. Manns and E. Alliata, eds., *Early Christianity in Context: Monuments and Documents* (SBF 38; Jerusalem: Franciscan Printing Press, 1993) 149–66.

Maisler 1931 — Maisler, B. "A Hebrew Ossuary Inscription," *PEFQ Statement* (1931) 171–72.

Manns and Alliata 1993 — Manns, F. and E. Alliata, eds. *Early Christianity in Context: Monuments and Documents* (SBF 38; Jerusalem: Franciscan Printing Press, 1993).

Marmorstein 1927 — Marmorstein, A. "About the Inscription of Judah ben Ishmael," *PEFQ Statement* (1927) 101–2.

Mazar 1969 — Mazar, B. "The Excavations in the Old City of Jerusalem," in *EI* 9 (1969) 168–70 + p. 45 no. 5 (Hebrew).

Mazar 1970 — Mazar, B. "The Excavations South and West of the Temple Mount in Jerusalem: The Herodian Period," *BA* 33 (1970) 47–60.

Mazar 1973 — Mazar, B. *Beth She'arim: Report on the Excavations During 1936–1940.* Vol. 1: *Catacombs 1–4* (New Brunswick: Rutgers University Press, 1973).

McCane 1990 — McCane, B. R. "'Let the Dead Bury Their Own Dead': Secondary Burial and Matt 8:21–22," *HTR* 83 (1990) 31–43.

McCane 1999 — McCane, B. R. "'Where no one had yet been laid': The Shame of Jesus' Burial," in B. D. Chilton and C. A. Evans, eds., *Authenticating the Activities of Jesus* (NTTS 28/2; Leiden: Brill, 1999) 431–52.

McCane 2000 — McCane, B. R. "Burial Practices, Jewish," *DNTB* 173–75.

McCane 2003 — McCane, B. R. *Roll Back the Stone: Death*

and Burial in the World of Jesus (Harrisburg, Penn.: Trinity Press International, 2003),

McGing 1991 McGing, B. C. "Pontius Pilate and the Sources," *CBQ* 53 (1991) 416–38.

Meshorer 1967 Meshorer, Y. *Jewish Coins of the Second Temple Period* (Tel Aviv: Am Hassefer, 1967).

Metzger 1980 Metzger, B. M. "The Nazareth Inscription Once Again," in *New Testament Studies: Philological, Versional, and Patristic* (NTTS 10; Leiden: Brill) 75–92.

Meyers 1970 Meyers, E. M. "Secondary Burials in Palestine," *BA* 33 (1970) 2–29.

Meyers 1971 Meyers, E. M. *Jewish Ossuaries: Reburial and Rebirth* (BibOr 24; Rome: Pontifical Biblical Institute Press, 1971).

Meyers 1971–1972 Meyers, E. M. "The Theological Implications of an Ancient Jewish Burial Custom," *JQR* 62 (1971–1972) 95–119.

Meyers 1988 Meyers, E. M. "Early Judaism and Christianity in the Light of Archaeology," *BA* 51 (1988) 69–79.

Meyers 1992a Meyers, E. M. "The Challenge of Hellenism for Early Judaism and Christianity," *BA* 55 (1992) 84–91.

Meyers 1992b Meyers, E. M. "Synagogue," *ABD* 6:251–60.

Meyers 1993 Meyers, E. M. "Aspects of Roman Sepphoris in the Light of Recent Archaeology," in F. Manns and E. Alliata, eds., *Early Christianity in Context: Monuments and Documents* (SBF 38; Jerusalem: Franciscan Printing Press, 1993) 29–36.

Meyers and Meyers 1981 Meyers, E. M. and C. L. Meyers. "Finders of a Real Lost Ark: American Archaeologists Find Remains of Ancient Synagogue Ark in Galilee," *BAR* 7/6 (1981) 24–39.

Meyers, Netzer, Meyers 1986 Meyers, E. M., E. Netzer, and C. L. Meyers. "Sepphoris: 'Ornament of All Galilee,'" *BA* 49 (1986) 4–19.

Meyers and Strange 1981 Meyers E. M. and J. F. Strange. *Archaeology,* the Rabbis and Early Christianity* (London: SCM Press, 1981).

Meyshan 1959 — Meyshan, J. "The Symbols on the Coinage of Herod the Great and their Meanings," *PEQ* 91 (1959) 109–21.

Milik 1956–1957 — Milik, J. T. "Trois tombeaux juifs récemment découverts au Sud–Est de Jérusalem," *LA* 7 (1956–1957) 232–67.

Milik 1971 — Milik, J. T. "Le couvercle de Bethpagé," in *Hommages à André Dupont-Sommer* (Paris: Adrien-Maisonneuve, 1971) 75–96.

Miller 1992 — Miller, S. S. "Sepphoris, the Well Remembered City," *BA* 55 (1992) 74–83.

Møller-Christensen 1976 — Møller-Christensen, V. "Skeletal Remains from Giv'at ha-Mivtar," *IEJ* 26 (1976) 35–38.

Naveh 1970 — Naveh, J. "The Ossuary Inscriptions from Giv'at ha-Mivtar, Jerusalem," *IEJ* 20 (1970) 33–37.

Naveh 1990 — Naveh, J. "Nameless People," *IEJ* 40 (1990) 108–23.

Oren and Rappaport 1984 — Oren, E. D. and U. Rappaport. "The Necropolis of Maresha-Beth Govrin," *IEJ* 34 (1984) 114–53.

Ory 1927 — Ory, J. "An Inscription Newly Found in the Synagogue of Kerazeh," *PEFQ Statement* (1927) 51–52.

Oster 1993 — Oster, R. E. "Supposed Anachronism in Luke–Acts' Use of συναγωγή: A Rejoinder to H. C. Kee," *NTS* 39 (1993) 178–208.

Painter 1999 — Painter, J. *Just James: The Brother of Jesus in History and Tradition* (Studies on Personalities of the New Testament; Minneapolis: Fortress, 1999; 1st ed., Columbia: University of South Carolina Press, 1997).

Peleg 2002 — Peleg, Y. "Gender and Ossuaries: Ideology and Meaning," *BASOR* 325 (2002) 65–73.

Prandi — Prandi, L. "Una nuova ipotesi sull'iscrizione di Ponzio Pilato," *CClCr* 2 (1981) 25–35.

Puech 1982 — Puech, E. "Ossuaires inscrits d'une tombe du Mont des Oliviers," *LA* 32 (1982) 355–72.

Puech 1983 — Puech, E. "Inscriptions funéraires Palestiniennes: Tombeau de Jason et ossuaires," *RB* 90 (1983) 481–583.

Puech 1993a — Puech, E. "A-t-on redécouvert le tombeau du grand-prêtre Caïphe?" *MdB* 80 (1993) 42–47.

Puech 1993b — Puech, E. *La croyance des Esséniens en la vie future*, vol. 1 (EBib 21; Paris: Gabald, 1993).

Raban and Linder 1978 — Raban, A. and E. Linder. "Caesarea, the Herodian Harbour," in *The International Journal of Nautical Archaeology and Underwater Exploration* 7 (1978) 238–43.

Rahmani 1958 — Rahmani, L. Y. "A Jewish Tomb on Shahin Hill, Jerusalem," *IEJ* 8 (1958) 101–5.

Rahmani 1961 — Rahmani, L. Y. "Jewish Rock-cut Tombs in Jerusalem," *'Atiqot* 3 (1961) 93–120.

Rahmani 1967 — Rahmani, L. Y. "Jason's Tomb," *IEJ* 17 (1967) 61–100.

Rahmani 1968 — Rahmani, L. Y. "Jerusalem's Tomb Monuments on Jewish Ossuaries," *IEJ* 18 (1968) 220–25.

Rahmani 1980 — Rahmani, L. Y. "A Jewish Rock-cut Tomb on Mt. Scopus," *'Atiqot* 14 (1980) 49–54.

Rahmani 1986 — Rahmani, L. Y. "'Whose Likeness and Inscription is This?' (Mark 12:16)," BA 49 (1986) 60–61.

Rahmani 1993 — Rahmani, L. Y. "A Note on Charon's Obol," *'Atiqot* 22 (1993) 149–50.

Rahmani 1994a — Rahmani, L. Y. A *Catalogue of Jewish Ossuaries in the Collections of the State of Israel* (Jerusalem: The Israel Antiquities Authority, 1994).

Rahmani 1994b — Rahmani, L. Y. "Ossuaries and Ossilegium (Bone-Gathering) in the Late Second Temple Period," in H. Geva, ed., *Ancient*

Jerusalem Revealed (Jerusalem: Israel Exploration Society, 1994) 191–205.

Rahmani 1994c — Rahmani, L. Y. "Representations of the Menorah on Ossuaries," in H. Geva, ed., *Ancient Jerusalem Revealed* (Jerusalem: Israel Exploration Society, 1994) 239–43.

Rahmani 1994d — Rahmani, L. Y. "Sarcophagi of the Late Second Temple Period in Secondary Use," in H. Geva, ed., *Ancient Jerusalem Revealed* (Jerusalem: Israel Exploration Society, 1994) 231–34.

Regev 2001 — Regev, E. "The Individualistic Meaning of Jewish Ossuaries: A Socio-Anthropological Perspective on Burial Practice," *PEQ* 133 (2001) 39–49.

Reich 1991 — Reich, R. "Ossuary Inscriptions from the Caiaphas Tomb," *Jerusalem Perspective* 4/4–5 (1991) 13–21.

Reich 1992a — Reich, R. "Caiaphas' Name Inscribed on Bone Boxes," *BAR* 18/5 (1992) 38–44, 76.

Reich 1992b — Reich, R. "Ossuary Inscriptions from the 'Caiaphas' Tomb," *'Atiqot* 21 (1992) 72–77.

Reich 1994 — Reich, R. "Ossuary Inscriptions of the Caiaphas Family from Jerusalem," in H. Geva, ed., *Ancient Jerusalem Revealed* (Jerusalem: Israel Exploration Society, 1994) 223–25.

Reinach 1920 — Reinach, Th. "L'inscription de Théodotos," *REJ* 71 (1920) 46–56.

Renov 1955–56 — Renov, I. "The Seat of Moses," *IEJ* 5 (1955) 262–67.

Riesner 1991 — Riesner, R. "Wurde des Familiengrab des Hohenpriesters Kajaphas entdeckt?" *BK* 46 (1991) 82–84.

Riesner 1995 — Riesner, R. "Synagogues in Jerusalem," in R. Baukham, ed., *The Book of Acts in its First-Century Setting*. Vol. 4: *Palestinian Setting* (Grand Rapids: Eerdmans, 1995) 179–211.

Rinaldi 1962 — Rinaldi, G. "Cesarea di Palestina," *BeO* 4 (1962) 100–3 + plates V–VI.

Ringel 1975 — J. Ringel, *Césarée de Palestine: Étude historique et archéologique* (Paris: Ophrys, 1975).

Ritmeyer and Ritmeyer 1994 — Ritmeyer, L. and K. "Akeldama: Potter's Field or High Priest's Tomb?" *BAR* 20/6 (1994) 22–35, 76, 78.

Rook 1981 — Rook, J. T. "'Boanerges, Sons of Thunder' (Mark 3:17)," *JBL* 100 (1981) 94–95.

Rosenthal 1973 — Rosenthal, E. S. "The Giv'at ha-Mivtar Inscription," *IEJ* 23 (1973) 72–81.

Rosenthaler 1975 — Rosenthaler, M. "A Paleo-Hebrew Ossuary Inscription," *IEJ* 25 (1975) 138–39.

Roth 1971 — Roth, L. "Caiaphas, Joseph," *EncJud* 5:19–20.

Roussel 1924 — Roussel, P. "Nikanor d'Alexandrie et la porte du temple de Jérusalem," *REG* 37 (1924) 79–82.

Rupprecht 1991 — Rupprecht, A. "The House of Annas-Caiaphas," *ABW* 1 (1991) 4–17.

Sandys 1927 — Sandys, J. E. *Latin Epigraphy: An Introduction to the Study of Latin Inscriptions* (2d ed., rev. by S. G. Campbell; Cambridge: Cambridge University Press, 1927).

Savignac — Savignac, M. R. "Nouveaux ossuaires juifs avec inscriptions," *RB* 38 (1929) 229–36.

Schlatter 1959 — Schlatter, A. *Der Evangelist Matthäus: Seine Sprache, sein Ziel, seine Selbständigkeit* (5th ed., Stuttgart: Calwer, 1959).

Schürer 1973–1987 — Schürer, E. *The History of the Jewish People in the Age of Jesus Christ* (3 vols.; rev. by G. Vermes, F. Millar, and M. Black; Edinburgh: T & T Clark, 1973–1987).

Schwabe and Lifshitz 1974 — Schwabe, M. and B. Lifshitz. *Beth She'arim*. Vol. 2: *The Greek Inscriptions* (New Brunswick: Rutgers University Press, 1974).

Schwartz 1992 — Schwartz, D. R. "Pontius Pilate," *ABD* 5:395–401.

Segal 1989 — Segal, P. "The Penalty of the Warning Inscription from the Temple of Jerusalem," *IEJ* 39 (1989) 79–84.

Sellers 1945 — Sellers, O. R. "Israelite Belief in Immortality," *BA* 8 (1945) 1–16.

Sevenster 1968 — Sevenster, J. N. *Do You Know Greek? How Much Greek Could the First Jewish Christian Have Known?* (NovTSup 19; Leiden: Brill, 1968).

Shanks 2003a — Shanks, H. "Between Authenticity and Forgery," *RSN*: SBL Edition 4/2 (2003) 6–8.

Shanks 2003b — Shanks, H. "Cracks in James Bone Box Repaired," *BAR* 29/1 (2003) 20–25.

Shore 1997 — Shore, P. *Rest Lightly: An Anthology of Latin and Greek Tomb Inscriptions* (Wauconda, Ill.: Bolchazy-Carducci, 1997).

Silberman 1991 — Silberman, N. A. "Ossuary: A Box for Bones," *BAR* 17/3 (1991) 73–74.

Silberman 2003 — Silberman, N. A. "On Relics, Forgeries, and Biblical Archaeology," *RSN*: SBL Edition 4/2 (2003) 1–5.

Smith 1973 — Smith, R. H. "An Early Roman Sarcophagus of Palestine and Its School," *PEQ* 105 (1973) 71–82.

Smith 1974 — Smith, R. H. "The Cross Marks on Jewish Ossuaries," *PEQ* 106 (1974) 53–66.

Solin 1970 — Solin, H. "Analecta Epigraphica," *Arctos* 6 (1970) 101–12.

Spoer 1907 — Spoer, H. H. "Some Hebrew and Phoenician Inscriptions," *JAOS* 28 (1907) 355–59.

Spoer 1914 — Spoer, H. H. "An Inscribed Jewish Ossuary," *PEFQ Statement* (1914) 200–1.

di Stefano Manzella 1997 — di Stefano Manzella, I. "Pontius Pilatus nell'iscrizione di Cesarea di Palestina," in di Stefano Manzella, ed., *Le iscrizioni dei cristiani in Vaticano: Materiali e contributi scientifici per una mostra epigrafica* (Inscriptiones sanctae sedis 2; Vatican City:

Edizioni Quasar, 1997) 209–15 + plate 3.1.2.

Stern 1966 — Stern, M. "Herod's Policies and Jewish Society at the End of the Second Temple Period," *Tarbiz* 35 (1966) 235–53 (Hebrew).

Strange 1975 — Strange, J. F. "Late Hellenistic and Herodian Ossuary Tombs at French Hill, Jerusalem," *BASOR* 219 (1975) 39–67.

Strange 1982 — Strange, J. F. "New Developments in Greco-Roman Archaeology in Palestine," *BA* 45 (1982) 85–88.

Strange 1992 — Strange, J. F. "Some Implications of Archaeology for New Testament Studies," in J. H. Charlesworth and W. P. Weaver, eds., *What Has Archaeology To Do with Faith?* (Faith and Scholarship Colloquies; Philadelphia: Trinity Press International, 1992) 23–59.

Strange 1995 — Strange, J. F. "The Art and Archaeology of Ancient Judaism," in J. Neusner, ed., *Judaism in Late Antiquity*. Part 1: *The Literary and Archaeological Sources* (HOS 16; Leiden: Brill, 1995) 64–114.

Strange and Shanks 1982 — Strange, J. F. and H. Shanks. "Has the House Where Jesus Stayed in Capernaum Been Found?" *BAR* 8/6 (1982) 26–37.

Strange and Shanks 1983 — Strange, J. F. and H. Shanks. "Synagogue Where Jesus Preached Found at Capernaum," *BAR* 9/6 (1983) 24–31.

Strathmann 1967 — Strathmann, H. "Λιβερτῖνοι," *TDNT* 4:265–66.

Strubbe 1994 — Strubbe, J. H. M. "Curses against Violation of the Grave in Jewish Epitaphs from Asia Minor," in J. W. van Henten and P. W. van der Horst, eds., *Studies in Early Jewish Epigraphy* (AGJU 21; Leiden: Brill, 1994) 70–128.

Sukenik 1928 — Sukenik, E. L. "A Jewish Hypogeum near Jerusalem," *JPOS* 8 (1928) 113–21.

Sukenik 1929 — Sukenik, E. L. "Additional Note on 'A Jewish Hypogeum near Jerusalem,'" *JPOS* 9 (1929) 45–49.

Sukenik 1931a — Sukenik, E. L. *Jüdische Gräber Jerusalems um Christi Geburt* (Jerusalem: Azriel, 1931).

Sukenik 1931b — Sukenik, E. L. "Funerary Tablet of Uzziah, King of Judah," *PEFQ Statement* (1931) 217–21.

Sukenik 1932a — Sukenik, E. L. "Two Jewish Hypogea," *JPOS* 12 (1932) 22–31.

Sukenik 1932b — Sukenik, E. L. "The Funerary Tablet of Uzziah," *PEFQ Statement* (1932) 106–7.

Sukenik 1934a — Sukenik, E. L. *Ancient Synagogues in Palestine and Greece* (The Schweich Lectures on Biblical Archaeology, 1930; London: British Academy, 1934).

Sukenik 1934b — Sukenik, E. L. "A Jewish Tomb Cave on the Slope of Mount Scopus," *Qovetz* 3 (1934) 62–73 (Hebrew).

Sukenik 1937 — Sukenik, E. L. "A Jewish Tomb in the Kedron Valley," *PEFQ* Statement (1937) 126–30.

Sukenik 1947 — Sukenik, E. L. "The Earliest Records of Christianity," *AJA* 51 (1947) 351–65.

Sussman 1994 — Sussman, V. "A Jewish Burial Cave on Mount Scopus," in H. Geva, ed., *Ancient Jerusalem Revealed* (Jerusalem: Israel Exploration Society, 1994) 226–30.

Toynbee 1971 — Toynbee, J. M. C. *Death and Burial in the Roman World* (Aspects of Greek and Roman Life; Ithaca, NY: Cornell University Press, 1971).

Tromp 1969 — Tromp, N. J. *Primitive Conceptions of Death and the Nether World in the Old Testament* (BibOr 21; Rome: Pontifical Biblical Institute, 1969).

Tzaferis 1970 — Tzaferis, V. "Jewish Tombs at and near Giv'at ha-Mivtar," *IEJ* 20 (1970) 18–32.

Tzaferis 1985 — Tzaferis, V. "Crucifixion: The Archaeological Evidence," *BAR* 11/1 (1985) 44–53.

Urman 1972 — Urman, D. "Jewish Inscriptions from Dabbura in the Golan," *IEJ* 22 (1972) 16–23.

van der Horst 1991 — van der Horst, P. W. *Ancient Jewish Epitaphs: An Introductory Survey of a Millennium of Jewish Funerary Epigraphy* (300 BCE–700 CE) (Kampen: Kok Pharos, 1991).

Vann 1983 — Vann, L. "Herod's Harbor Construction Recovered Underwater," *BAR* 9/3 (1983) 10–14.

Vardaman 1962 — Vardaman, E. J. "A New Inscription which Mentions Pilate as 'Prefect,'" *JBL* 81 (1962) 70–71.

Vardaman 1964 — Vardaman, E. J. "Introduction to the Caesarea Inscription of the Twenty-Four Priestly Courses," in E. J. Vardaman and J. L. Garrett, eds., *The Teacher's Yoke: Studies in Memory of Henry Trantham* (Waco, Tex.: Baylor University Press, 1964) 42–45.

Vincent 1902 — Vincent, L.-H. "Nouveaux ossuaires juifs," *RB* 11 (1902) 103–7.

Vincent 1907 — Vincent, L.-H. "Ossuaires juifs," *RB* 16 (1907) 410–14.

Vincent 1921 — Vincent, L.-H. "Découverte de la 'Synagogue des Affranchis' à Jérusalem," *RB* 30 (1921) 247–77.

Volkmann 1968 — Volkmann, H. "Die Pilatusinschrift von Caesarea Maritima," *Gymnasium* 75 (1968) 124–35 + plates XIII–XV.

Weber 1971 — Weber, E. "Zur Inschrift des Pontius Pilatus," *BJ* 171 (1971) 194–200.

Weill 1919 — Weill, R. "La Cité de David: Compte rendu des fouilles exécutées à Jérusalem sur le site de la ville primitive. Campaigne de 1913–1914," *REJ* 69 (1919) 3–85 + pls.

Weill 1920a — Weill, R. "La Cité de David: Compte rendu des fouilles exécutées à Jérusalem sur le site

	de la ville primitive. Campaigne de 1913–1914," *REJ* 70 (1920) 1–36.
Weill 1920b	Weill, R. "La Cité de David: Compte rendu des fouilles exécutées à Jérusalem sur le site de la ville primitive. Campaigne de 1913–1914," *REJ* 70 (1920) 149–79.
Weill 1920c	Weill, R. "La Cité de David: Compte rendu des fouilles exécutées à Jérusalem sur le site de la ville primitive. Campaigne de 1913–1914," *REJ* 71 (1920) 1–45.
Wilkinson 1974	Wilkinson, J. "Ancient Jerusalem, Its Water Supply and Population," *PEFQ Statement* 106 (1974) 33–51.
Wirgin 1964	Wirgin, W. "The Menorah as Symbol of Afterlife," *IEJ* 14 (1964) 102–4.
Wise, Abegg, Cook 1996	Wise M. O., M. G. Abegg, Jr., and E. Cook. *The Dead Sea Scrolls: A New Translation* (San Francisco: HarperCollins, 1996).
Wright 1946	Wright, G. E. "New Information Regarding the Supposed 'Christian' Ossuaries," *BA* 9 (1946) 43.
Wright 2003	Wright, N. T. *The Resurrection of the Son of God* (Christian Origins and the Question of God 3; Minneapolis: Fortress, 2003).
Yadin 1966	Yadin, Y. *Masada: Herod's Fortress and the Zealots' Last Stand* (New York: Random House, 1966).
Yadin 1973	Yadin, Y. "Epigraphy and Crucifixion," *IEJ* 23 (1973) 18–22 + plate.
Yamauchi 1985	Yamauchi, E. M. "Obelisks and Pyramids," *NEASB 24* (1985) 111–15.
Yamauchi 1990	Yamauchi, E. M. *Persia and the Bible* (Grand Rapids: Baker, 1990).
Yamauchi 1992	Yamauchi, E. M. "The Archaeology of Biblical Africa: Cyrene in Libya," *ABW 2* (1992) 6–18.
Yamauchi 1998	Yamauchi, E. M. "Life, Death, and the Afterlife in the Ancient Near East," in R. N. Longenecker, ed., *Life in the Face of Death: The Resurrection Message of the New*

Testament (Grand Rapids: Eerdmans, 1998) 21–50.

Yamauchi 2000 — Yamauchi, E. M. "Attitudes Toward the Aged in Antiquity," *NEASB* 45 (2000) 1–9.

Yellin 1929 — Yellin, D. "On the Newly Discovered Ossuary Inscriptions," *JPOS* 9 (1929) 41–44.

Zeitlin 1947–48 — Zeitlin, S. "The Warning Inscription of the Temple," *JQR* 38 (1947–48) 111–16.

Zias 1990 — Zias, J. "Anthropological Observations," in S. Wachsmann et al., *The Excavations of an Ancient Boat in the Sea of Galilee (Lake Kinneret)* ('Atiqot English Series 19; Jerusalem: Israel Antiquities Authority, 1990) 125.

Zias 1992 — Zias, J. "Human Skeletal Remains from the 'Caiaphas' Tomb," *'Atiqot* 21 (1992) 78–80.

Zias 1996 — Zias, J. "Anthropological Analysis of Human Skeletal Remains," in G. Avni and Z. Greenhut et al., *The Akeldama Tombs: Three Burial Caves in the Kidron Valley, Jerusalem* (IAA Reports 1; Jerusalem: Israel Antiquities Authority, 1996) 117–21.

Zias and Charlesworth 1992 — Zias, J. and J. H. Charlesworth. "Crucifixion: Archaeology, Jesus, and the Dead Sea Scrolls," in J. H. Charlesworth, ed., *Jesus and the Dead Sea Scrolls* (ABRL; New York: Doubleday, 1992) 273–89 + plates following p. 184.

Zias and Sekeles 1985 — Zias, J. and E. Sekeles. "The Crucified Man from Giv'at ha-Mivtar: A Reappraisal," *IEJ* 35 (1985) 22–27.

Zlotnick 1966 — Zlotnick, D. *The Tractate "Mourning"* (YJS 17; New Haven: Yale University Press, 1966).

de Zulueta 1932 — Zulueta, F. de. "Violation of Sepulture in Palestine at the Beginning of the Christian Era," *JRS* 22 (1932) 184–97.

Index of Biblical Literature

Old Testament

Apocrypha

New Testament

Index of Modern Writers